AF526601

FROM MIND TO SUPER-MIND

FROM MIND TO SUPER-MIND

A Commentary on *The Bhagavad Gita*

ROHIT MEHTA

MOTILAL BANARSIDASS PUBLISHERS
PRIVATE LIMITED • DELHI

Reprint : Delhi, 1995, 1997, 2000, ***2006***
Second Revised Edition: Pondicherry, 1972
First Published: Ahmedabad, 1966

© ROHIT MEHTA
All Rights Reserved

ISBN 81-208-0964-5 (Cloth)
ISBN 81-208-0965-3 (Paper)

MOTILAL BANARSIDASS
41 U.A. Bungalow Road, Jawahar Nagar, Delhi 110 007
8 Mahalaxmi Chamber, 22 Bhulabhai Desai Road, Mumbai 400 026
236, 9th Main III Block, Jayanagar, Bangalore 560 011
203 Royapettah High Road, Mylapore, Chennai 600 004
Sanas Plaza, 1302 Baji Rao Road, Pune 411 002
8 Camac Street, Kolkata 700 017
Ashok Rajpath, Patna 800 004
Chowk, Varanasi 221 001

Printed in India
BY JAINENDRA PRAKASH JAIN AT SHRI JAINENDRA PRESS,
A-45 NARAINA, PHASE-I, NEW DELHI 110 028
AND PUBLISHED BY NARENDRA PRAKASH JAIN FOR
MOTILAL BANARSIDASS PUBLISHERS PRIVATE LIMITED,
BUNGALOW ROAD, DELHI 110 007

INTRODUCTION

THE GREAT SCRIPTURES of the world are beyond the limitations of time and space: they are Eternal and Universal. The *Bhagavad Gita* belongs to this category of scriptures and, as such, it is not a Book merely for the Hindus; its message has a universal application. It is as fresh today at it was when given to Arjuna many centuries ago. In fact, modern man is in need of the message of the *Bhagavad Gita* if he is to find freedom from the tensions and anxieties brought into his life by the scientific and technological developments of today.

What indeed is the problem of the modern man? The new advances in science and technology have brought about an utter confusion of values in the life of men and women living in the present-day civilization. There is increasing stress on quantitative rather than qualitative values. His inner life is poor, and he is striving to free himself from the thraldom of this poverty by acquiring more and more of the material things that science and technology have made available. Man is seeking a physical solution to a problem which is fundamentally psychological. He thinks that science, being so powerful, can solve all problems. But he forgets that while science can solve the problem of speed, it can give no guidance as to the direction that one must follow. He has lost sight of the fact that while science can give comfort, it cannot give happiness; for happiness consists not in the possession of things, but in freeing the mind of all its inhibitions so that it is rendered pure and innocent. While the modern age has known the conquest over matter, it has yet to learn the secrets of conquering the mind—and without the latter the former is not only meaningless but positively dangerous. Man may have gained in knowledge, but he lacks wisdom. Unless he can transform knowledge into wisdom, his future and the future of the entire race is dark and dismal. In other words, man needs today, above everything else, a Right Philosophy of Life.

It is this right philosophy of life which the *Bhagavad Gita* provides through its priceless message. It points to a way of life which will help the modern man to find a solution to the baffling problems of existence. The *Bhagavad Gita* not only enunciates the Gospel of Right Action, it also unmistakably points to the fact that Right Action is possible only if there is Right Perception. And Right Perception in terms of the *Gita* is that condition of the human mind in which it is capable of total and undistracted attention, freed from confusion of thought, and not caught in the play of the opposites. The teaching of the *Gita* leads Arjuna, step by step, from distractions to illumination—from the mind that is caught up in the pulls of desire to the mind that is illumined by the light of *Buddhi*. In other words, it leads him from Mind to Super-Mind.

Does the *Gita* ask man to renounce the world in pursuit of spiritual objectives? Does it suggest that man must give up action in order to explore the realms of the Super-Mind? The uniqueness of the teaching of the *Bhagavad Gita* lies in the fact that it asks man to seek his spiritual objectives in the daily avocations of life—it says that man can come to supreme enlightenment not by running away from action but by performing all actions in the right manner. How can man come to recognize Right Action? The *Gita* says that as he frees himself from Reaction (*Vikarma*), he comes to the deep and profound experience of Inaction (*Akarma*). Inaction or *Akarma* is indeed the right background for the performance of *Karma* or Action—action that is true, action that is free from all contamination of self.

In the three principal definitions of *Yoga* given in the *Gita* we perceive the path indicated by Sri Krishna to attain the point of Right Perception from where alone Right Action can emerge. Speaking about *Yoga*, the *Gita* says that it is 'a dissociation from that which gives an association with sorrow.' What is it that gives to man an association with sorrow? Surely it is mind with its ability to compare and contrast which brings to the human individual a sense of sorrow. The problem of man's suffering is fundamentally the problem of mind caught up in the process of comparison and contrast. All his reactions emanate from this process. In fact, it is this process which constitutes the ceaseless movement of the mind, the movement which conditions the perceptive activity of man. The *Gita* deals comprehensively with the conditioning factors of the mind. It calls them *tamas, rajas* and *sattva*—inertia, activity and harmony, respectively. One of the clear instructions of Sri Krishna to Arjuna is that he should transcend these three attributes of the mind so that he can come to a clear and undistorted perception of men and things. To dissociate from that which gives an association with sorrow is indeed to be aware of these attributes and their functioning within one's own psyche. It is in this awareness that one understands the meaning of the second definition of *Yoga* to be found in the *Gita.* It states that *Yoga* is Equilibrium. The state of equilibrium is indeed the poise of inaction, and it can be achieved only when the mind is purged of its three attributes. So long as the mind is caught up in the process of an identification with, or a condemnation of, the movement of the three attributes, so long there can be no experience of equilibrium or silence. From the point of equilibrium whatever emerges is good and beneficent. The third definition of *Yoga* given by the *Gita* is : *Yoga* is skill in action. All actions become perfect when they emanate from the Ground of Inaction or the Ground of Equilibrium.

Modern man is indeed beseiged with great inner conflict, and it is this conflict which has caused the utter disintegration of his psychological life. The disintegration within has caused unhappiness without. He is verily in search of inner integration and perhaps, for this, there can be no better guide than the teaching of the *Bhagavad Gita.* The creation of an Integrated Individual—*Yukta*—is indeed the purpose of the intensely dynamic message of the *Gita.* The Poise of Inaction, where the opposites of the mind are transcended, is a state of psychological integration. The *Gita* deals with this problem in a very comprehensive manner, in discourse after discourse, until, in the last discourse, Arjuna sees the identity of the Individual and Cosmic Wills, and, with that perception, he arrives at the cessation of inner conflict and therefore to a state of perfect integration.

The message of the *Gita* has an immediate and practical

bearing on the problems of the modern age. It shows a way out of the complexities of the mind, to a complete and unfettered freedom of the Super-Mind. The *Gita* says that this path is not meant only for the few; it can be trodden by all who seek freedom from life's entanglements. In an age where the individual is becoming more and more insignificant due to the impacts of political, economic and social forces, the *Gita* brings to man a message of hope and cheer, for it shows to him *that* way of life which leads to the regaining of his lost significance. It indicates to him the path of creative living.

The spiritual regeneration of man is indeed the way to the creation of a happy society—this is verily the refreshing and the revitalizing message of the *Bhagavad Gita*.

Varanasi, India,
15 January 1966

ROHIT MEHTA

CONTENTS

CHAPTER I

THE DISTRACTED MIND

THE SOUL-STIRRING message of the *Bhagavad Gita* begins with the very First Discourse. Many a student of the *Gita* has skipped over the First Discourse, regarding it as one having no relationship with the main theme of this Great and Universal Scripture. It is true that the First Discourse gives a description—a vivid description—of the battlefield where the Great War of the Mahābhārata took place. But it is this vivid picture of the battlefield which supplies the appropriate background to the philosophy of life which the *Gita* enunciates. In fact, the way of life which the *Gita* propounds has an immediate relationship with the inner or psychological background of man. There is a continual warfare going on within the psyche of man. The battle of Kurukshetra was fought not merely five thousand years ago—it is being fought every day and every hour within the psychological domain of man. And so the description of the battlefield given in the First Discourse is symbolical of the inner battleground where the forces of 'Good' and 'Evil' are arrayed against each other. To skip over this description is to miss the very context in which the teaching of the *Gita* can be truly comprehended.

It is very significant that the *Bhagavad Gita*, as it has come down through the ages, is a narration by Sanjaya to the blind King Dhritarāshtra of what happened on the battleground of Kurukshetra. Most of us are like the blind King unable to see what is happening in the battle of life because of our close identification with the daily events. We would like this battle of life to cease even as the King Dhritarāshtra desired, in his heart of hearts, that the Pāndavas and the Kauravas gave up their fratricidal war. But his inability to dissociate himself from the designs of Dūryodhana resulted in the devastating war of Mahābhārata. And it was this identification with Dūryodhana which figuratively rendered him incapable of seeing the events of the war in their right perspective. Sanjaya who narrated the events to the blind King represents a perception which is absolutely objective and impersonal. In the battle of life most of us are confused as to the events that are taking place. This is because we are unable to dissociate ourselves from them. We, too, need a Sanjaya to give us an objectivity in our perception. The *Bhagavad Gita*, indeed, enables us to discover this Sanjaya within ourselves, for the central core of its message teaches us to look at the events of life with perfect objectivity. Such objectivity alone can reveal to man the real meaning of life.

Is it not significant that the very first verse of the *Bhagavad Gita* should refer to the request of the blind King to Sanjaya to tell him what happened on the battlefield of the Kurus? But even in this request one can see the psychological blindness of the King—blindness arising out of a close identification which prevented him from seeing things aright. In this first verse, King Dhritarāshtra asks Sanjaya:

> On the holy plain, on the field of Kuru, gathered together, eager for battle, what did they do, O Sanjaya, my people and the sons of Pandu?

The sense of mine-ness on the part of the King is evident even in this request to know about the happenings of war. Thus the fundamental theme of identification and dissociation which forms the central core of the teaching of the *Gita* is revealed even in the opening verse. In the *Gita* we are not concerned so much with the physical battlefield as with the field of psychological warfare. To the fascinating story of this psychological conflict, the First Discourse is indeed a fitting prelude.

After mentioning the names of the eminent commanders and warriors on both sides, Sanjaya gives a graphic description of the war-field. He refers to the blowing of conches first from the camp of the Kauravas and then of the Pāndavas. Sanjaya says: 'On all sides several conches blew' filling earth and sky with sound. It was this tumultuous uproar from the blowing of conches that, as it were, awakened Arjuna to the realities of the war. For, immediately after that Arjuna tells Sri Krishna, his Charioteer, 'Draw up my chariot, O Achyuta, between the two armies so that I may observe these men standing, eager for battle, with whom I have to contend in this strife of war.'

The teaching of the *Gita* was given by Sri Krishna to Arjuna on the field of Kurukshetra where the armies of the Kauravas and the Pāndavas were arrayed against each other and the warriors on both the sides were eager for battle. A very relevant question must arise in the minds of the students of the *Bhagavad Gita* as to how could the fighting forces of the Kauravas, itching for battle, have kept themselves in check so long while all the practical and metaphysical doubts of Arjuna were being cleared one by one? If we consider *Gita* in the context of an actual physical war between the Pāndavas and the Kauravas, the dialogue between Arjuna and Sri Krishna seems utterly incongruous. In the feverish background of a raging war, imparting of such teaching as contained in the *Gita* seems incredible and unbelievable.

Perhaps the Great War of the Mahābhārata was a historical fact. But the author of the *Gita* seems to have taken this war as only a starting point to develop the theme of the great Battle of Life itself. The description of the war does give a picturesque background to the consideration of the complex theme of the fierce battles of life. So the *Gita* and its message become meaningful only when they are seen, not so much with reference to the physical war, as with reference to the inner war raging within the psyche of man. The following words of Dr Annie Besant, appearing in the Preface to her translation of the *Bhagavad Gita*, may be of value in understanding the fundamental basis of this great Book of Life:

> ... as all the acts of an *Avatāra* are symbolical, we may pass from the outer to the inner planes, and see in the fight of Kurukshetra, the battle-field of the soul, and in the sons of Dhritarāshtra, enemies it meets in its progress.

Looking at the Kurukshetra war from a psychological standpoint, we perceive a new meaning in the teaching of the *Gita*. The way of life propounded by it becomes intensely practical, for it throws a new light on the problems of man's inner or psychological warfare. At no time in the history of mankind was man's inner warfare so intense as it is today. Therefore perhaps the message of the *Gita* was never so much needed by man as today in this age of increasing comfort and decreasing happiness.

But why has man's inner warfare assumed such large proportions as it has done in this age of science and technology? It is but obvious that man's inner warfare is largely, if not mainly, dependent on the condition of the human mind. Mind is indeed the cause of man's bondage as well as his liberation. The greater the development of the mind, the greater is the complexity brought into the field of man's living. With the growth of the mind, man becomes a citizen of two worlds—the world of outer circumstances and the world of inner ambitions. In the undeveloped condition of the mind, the distance between these two worlds is small, but with the growth and development of the human mind it becomes enlarged with the result that the reconciliation between the two worlds becomes intensely difficult. It is this ever-increasing distance between the two worlds, in which man tries to live at the same time, which causes tensions and anxieties, stresses and strains of everyday life. In the present-day civilization, the mind of man has grown immensely so much so that many a thinker has described our age as the Age of the Mind. It is in a mental civilization that we live today—and so the fundamental problem of our age is indeed the Problem of the Mind. How is mind to be freed from tensions and conflicts which seem to have increased with the growth of mental capacities? How is the human mind to come to terms with the two Wills—the Cosmic Will and the Individual Will? These are the most pressing problems of the day.

It is in the background of these problems that the modern man can evaluate truly the message of the *Gita*. For, the *Gita* deals with the Problems of the Human Mind—with the reconciliation between the Will of Man and the Will of the Cosmos. The *Bhagavad Gita* is a dialogue between Sri Krishna and Arjuna. And does not Sri Krishna represent the Cosmic Will even as Arjuna represents the Individual Will? It is with the conflict between these two Wills that the *Gita* is primarily concerned. The Kurukshetra war is only symbolical of this inner war of Two Wills. The last Discourse of the *Gita* practically ends with Arjuna's declaration where he says to the Lord : 'I shall do Thy bidding' or 'I shall act according to Thy Word'. It is in this declaration that we see the perfect reconciliation, nay, the absolute merging of the Two Wills. As Dr Radhakrishnan says in his commentary on the *Gita*: 'To will what God wills is the secret of divine life'. In his commentary he goes on to say:

> When Jesus cried 'May this cup pass from me', He was yet having His own preferences and asked for personal satisfaction. He wished to escape the bitter humiliation and death, but when He uttered: 'Thy will be done' (*Karishye Vachanam Tava*), he gave up His separate existence and identified Himself with the work of the Father who sent Him.

The whole message of the *Gita* constitutes a movement from: 'May this cup pass from me' to 'Thy Will be done'. From the assertion of the Individual Will to the discovery of an identity between the Individual and the Cosmic Will—this indeed is the psychological pathway traversed by the teaching of the *Bhagavad Gita*. If only the modern man could traverse that path he would know freedom from tensions and mental anxieties.

The blowing of the conches on several sides is indeed the beginning of the problem of human mind as discussed in the *Gita*. The difficulty of Arjuna seems to have started with his hearing of the tumultuous roar of the conches. It was the sound of the conches which made him aware of the situation in which he was—the situation which he wanted to understand clearly by having his chariot placed between the two armies. In the *Bhagavad Gita* Arjuna verily represents the Human Mind—the mind that is active and alert, the one that has explored the extent of its capacities and possibilities. The blowing of the conches on several sides comes to such a mind as a pull of distractions. It was not the blowing of a conch or two—but conches from all sides causing a certain amount of confusion.

Are not our minds too in that condition in the present age when conches of modern civilization are being blown from several sides demanding our attention? We are caught up in unceasing distractions, not knowing where to go. The conches of the modern civilization are so incessant in their blowing that we are utterly confused. Yet our confusion is still of a vague nature as was Arjuna's until his chariot was placed between the two armies.

Why did Arjuna ask for his chariot to be placed between the two armies? For the mind, the perception of any situation or problem becomes clear only when it sees the two opposites. The seeing of the opposites by the mind is one after the other so that it sees the one thing and then the other, and the other is seen as opposed to the former. Thus the placing of the chariot between the two armies is mind's search for a clarification of the problem. The mind comes to its alertness only when it sees the opposites with reference to any situation. A movement between the pairs of opposites is the normal movement of the mind. It feels secure so long as this movement is guaranteed. In the confusion caused by the blowing of the conches Arjuna seeks a clarification of the situation by assuring himself of an undistorted perception of the opposites.

It is very interesting to see Arjuna's reaction to the war-situation as soon as his chariot was placed between the two armies. When Arjuna asked Sri Krishna to place his chariot in such a way that he may 'gaze on those here gathered together, ready to fight, desirous of pleasing in battle the evil-minded son of Dhritarāshtra', Sri Krishna did what his friend and disciple wanted. Arjuna's chariot was drawn up between the two armies 'in front of Bhishma, Drona and all the chiefs', and having done this, Sri Krishna told Arjuna, 'Behold, these Kurus assembled here'. As soon as Arjuna looked up, he saw uncles and grandfathers, teachers, cousins, grandsons as also companions arrayed in the army of the Kurus ready and even eager to fight. This was a sight for which evidently Arjuna was not prepared. No doubt he knew who were in the army of the Kurus, but when he saw them face to face he was overcome by feelings of grief and sadness. And with this feeling of sadness he addressed Sri Krishna thus:

> When I see my own people arrayed and eager for fight, my limbs quail and my mouth is parched, my body trembles, and my hair stands on end. The bow, *Gandiva*, slips from my hand and my skin burns all over. I am not able to stand. My mind is reeling.

Why did Arjuna have this sense of sadness on his seeing his kinsmen in the army of the Kurus? Did he not know that they were in the opposite camp? He certainly knew that they belonged to the camp against which he was called upon to fight. Did Arjuna become sad because he was afraid of the war? Arjuna was no coward. He was the bravest among the brave. He had fought many a battle and vanquished fierce adversaries. He had certainly not become converted to non-violence. Why then this feeling of sadness? It is in dealing with this question that we see, in an unmistakable way, the psychological content of the teaching of the *Gita*. We have stated above that Arjuna represents the human mind in its active and alert condition—a mind that is conscious of its potentialities but not aware of its limitations. The human mind is always clever and logical when dealing with abstractions and generalities—but when it is face to face with a concrete reality it tends to develop cold feet. It is because of this that it avoids facing a problem. Arjuna knew who were in the enemy camp, but this knowledge had an element of an abstract nature. It is because of this that he said to Sri Krishna: 'I wish to look at those who are assembled here, ready to fight and eager to achieve in battle what is dear to the evil-minded son of Dhritarāshtra. These were brave words but then they were spoken before Arjuna faced the concrete reality. Hardly did Arjuna realize what he was asking for when he requested Sri Krishna to place his chariot between the two armies. In this position Arjuna was compelled to face a concrete fact for which he was not prepared.

While the human mind seeks a solution of the problem it is not prepared to pay the price for such a solution. The mind at all times wishes to retain a continuity of movement between two opposite points. If a solution can be found keeping this movement intact then the mind is willing to accept it. But any solution which threatens the continuity of this movement is most repugnant to the human mind. Here in the sadness of

Arjuna and in the slipping away of his bow we witness clearly the operation of the human mind when faced with a situation, the ultimate result of which would most assuredly be discontinuity and not continuity.

The mind of man is indeed very clever, for, it always finds suitable arguments for what it wants to do, or for what it does not want to do. Wanting to get out of an akward situation it deduces arguments which are sometimes too virtuous to be true! Arjuna in the predicament in which he was placed utters very noble sentiments in support of his desire not to fight. He says to Sri Krishna:

> These I do not wish to kill, though myself slain, O Madhusudana even for the sake of kingship of the three worlds; how then for earth? Slaying these sons of Dhritarāshtra, what pleasure can be ours, O Janardana; killing these desperadoes sin will but take hold of us.

Arjuna belonged to the warrior-caste and so the above words seem unnatural in his mouth. Evidently he was not against war, but in the present situation he felt a shudder at the idea of killing his kinsmen. It is the sight of his kinsmen, face to face, ready for battle which seems to have unnerved Arjuna. The kinsmen naturally represent points of attachment so far as Arjuna was concerned. On seeing them, the centres of psychological recognition are aroused in the mind of Arjuna. Although Arjuna had put forward noble arguments showing the futility of war, the real reason for his unwillingness to fight comes up when he becomes conscious of attachment to the people he is asked to kill. We have stated above that the human mind moves in the realm of continuity and that any break in this continuity is most repugnant to it. With the centres of psychological recognition awakened, mind, as represented by Arjuna, sees in the waging of the war a threat to its continuity. It is this threat to continuity which forms the main part of Arjuna's argument in support of his laying down the arms. For he says:

> Although these, with intelligence overpowered by greed, see no guilt in the destruction of a family, no crime in hostility to friends, why should not we learn to turn away from such a sin, O Janardana, who see the evils in the destruction of a family?

> In the destruction of a family, immemorial family traditions perish; in perishing of traditions, lawlessness overcomes the whole family.

Now the family with its traditions is indeed a symbol of continuity. In the family traditions one witnesses a continuing stream of customs and manners. Any break in this continuing stream appears to the human mind as confusion and lawlessness, resulting in the destruction of the very edifice which it has built up with toil and labour. In the killing of the kinsmen Arjuna sees this confusion and destruction, and so says to Sri Krishna: 'The abode of men, whose family customs are extinguished, O Janardana, is everlastingly hell.' In this verse, as in others forming part of the First Discourse of the *Gita*, one sees the plea of the human mind for the maintenance of a stream of continuity. Mind's security lies in uninterrupted continuity which is a movement between two opposites, without any break whatsoever. If the points of attachment, represented by the kinsmen, are wiped off, where lies the security for the mind? For the mind, it is a condition of utter lawlessness where customs and traditions are extinguished.

The family with its traditions typifies the past, and the movement of the human mind is rooted in the past. From the past to the future, in the never-ceasing stream of a continuous Time-process, in which the mind moves on. This indeed is its life—its denial is a veritable death from which the mind forever shudders. Arjuna who was a seasoned warrior knew that all wars meant destruction. But it is not against destruction caused by all wars that Arjuna speaks here. For in wars even though there is destruction there is not a break in continuity—but the Kurukshetra war was of a different category. It was a war where kinsmen, 'those for whose sake we desire kingdom, enjoyments and pleasures', were arrayed against each other, and so the result of the war would not only be destruction but a complete break in the stream of continuity. Arjuna expresses here something to which the human mind always gives utterance in moments of deep crisis.

The mind of man desires to keep intact its areas of attachment under all circumstances. It may agree to modifications within those areas—but to their total destruction it can never give its assent. The points of attachment are the centres from which the mind acts. To demand a dissolution of those points of attachment is to ask the mind to write its own death-warrant. The mind naturally puts up a resistance against it and this is what we find in the various arguments which Arjuna puts forward explaining his unwillingness to fight. The battle of Kurukshetra represents a fundamental transformation in the psychological life of man, for it is not with the mere modification of the areas of attachment that it is concerned—it aims at the total destruction of the very centre from which mind carries on its ceaseless chain of reactions. Seeing this, Arjuna recoils from the very idea of killing his kinsmen.

In Arjuna's despondency we have an interesting illustration of the mind of man cleverly putting on the robes of renunciation, displaying the façade of virtue and piety—and concealing its fear of insecurity which arises out of the destruction of the very centre from where alone it can act. In the Kurukshetra war the mind of man recognizes that it will have no foot-stool on which to rest its weary feet—that it will have nothing by which to hold on to the past represented by traditions and customs and that it will face the threat of complete obliteration. The last verse of the First Discourse graphically describes the condition of Arjuna. It says:

> Having spoken thus on the field of battle, Arjuna sank down on the seat of his chariot, casting away his bow and arrow, his spirit overwhelmed by sorrow.

The casting away of the bow and the arrow signifies Arjuna's unwillingness to fight. Is this not what most of us do in the battle of life? The mind of man forever evades the real issue, it seeks escape after escape from the actualities of life. But when all escapes are blocked and evasions are not possible the mind is compelled to face the stark realities of the problem. The placing of the chariot of life between two armies is indeed that position from where evasion and escape are impossible. The realities of the situation stare the human mind in the face. Unable to run away, it closes its eyes, even as the ostrich hides its face in the sand, hoping that because he does not see the problem, the problem will cease to exist! Even at this stage the mind seeks an escape. It thinks it can deceive life by the façade of renunciation and non-resistance. And that by so doing life will pass by leaving the mind undisturbed and therefore secure in its areas of continuity. But life is a hard task-master, it follows its path relentlessly, whether man co-operates with it or not. If man can see in the path of the Cosmic Will the fulfilment of his own Will, then life carries him into bliss unknown. But if by resistance or renunciation he puts himself in opposition to the Will of the Cosmos, then woe unto him, for life snatches him away leaving behind all his points of attachment to which he tenaciously clings. In the Eleventh Discourse, in Verse 32, Sri Krishna tells Arjuna in unmistakable terms the outcome of the problem of life which the latter faces. Sri Krishna says:

> Time am I, world-destroying, grown mature, engaged here in subduing the world. Even without thee, all the warriors standing arrayed in the opposing armies shall cease to be.

Why was Arjuna in a state of despondency if he had come to the decision of not engaging himself in the battle of Kurukshetra? If he had renounced his bow and arrow, why then this dejection and the overwhelming feeling of sorrow? This is because Arjuna's renunciation was more out of fear than out of the understanding of life. He was afraid of a break in continuity, of the dissolution of the very centre of attachment. The mind that acts out of fear is uncertain of its action. A decision born out of fear alone is not a wise decision. When the mind is not able to make its choice from a position of freedom, the result is always dejection and depression. The mind seeking to justify its action is indeed caught up in doubt and uncertainty. Does not Arjuna put forward clever arguments for the justification of his action? But the more he justifies, the more uncertain he is. It is because of this that in Verse 7 of the Second Discourse we find Arjuna telling Sri Krishna that,

> My heart is weighed down with the vice of faintness; my mind is confused as to duty. I ask Thee which may be the better—that tell me decisively. I am Thy disciple, teach me who am seeking refuge in Thee.

Arjuna asks Sri Krishna to tell him decisively because he is in a state of indecision. The dejection that Arjuna experiences is indeed due to the tension of indecision. The mind that is not able to make the right choice faces stress and strain. The despondency of Arjuna is a state in which most men and women of the present age find themselves. In the midst of tremendous distractions man does not know what to choose. He seeks evasion and escape from the situations that demand the making of a choice. To facilitate this the modern man has built up a huge edifice of distractions in the nooks and corners of which he tries to hide himself. But such escapism serves no purpose. The more a man seeks distractions the more does life press upon him with the problem of choice. Just as Arjuna, placed between the two of armies, was not able to make the right decision, so also is the case with the making of decisions in the Battles of Life. The *Bhagavad Gita* tries to enlighten us on this important aspect of life.

The First Discourse of the *Gita* prepares us for the understanding of this great gospel. To formulate one's problem without any ambiguity, to feel the tremendous impact of that problem, to see mind's justifications and explanations proving of no avail—this is indeed the first step towards resolving that problem. The First Discourse enables us to take this first step. Arjuna's despondency clearly and unmistakably reflects the dejections and the depressions of the men and women of the modern age.

CHAPTER II

THE STATE OF INTEGRATION

THE SECOND DISCOURSE of the *Bhagavad Gita* is most outstanding as it contains the quintessence of the entire message of the *Gita*. There are scholars who maintain that the *Gita* lacks cohesion because the different discourses have no interrelationship. But many will agree that the *Gita* presents a view of life which is gradually developed, discourse by discourse, until the culminating point is reached in the Eighteenth or the Last Discourse. There is a close interrelationship between the various chapters of the *Gita* so that the main theme of the book is presented in the most systematic manner.

The question may arise: If the theme of the book is gradually developed what is the purpose in giving the quintessence of the whole message of the *Gita* in its Second Discourse? It is like pointing the finger to Mount Everest and indicating its stupendous glory. But Arjuna's vision is blurred by the confusion in which his mind is caught. And so we find Sri Krishna helping him to clear his mind of all doubts till he reaches the stage when he is able to declare in the Last Discourse: 'Destroyed is my delusion. I have gained knowledge through Thy Grace, O Immutable One! I am firm, my doubts have fled.' While the Second Discourse gives the Great Vision of Life, the subsequent chapters give us the *modus operandi* of moving towards that Vision—they indicate to us the Path that leads to the Great Summit of Life so beautifully portrayed by the Supreme Teacher Himself.

We saw while discussing the theme of the First Discourse that Arjuna threw away the arms and in so doing placed before Sri Krishna many a learned argument, specially indicating the confusion that would arise due to a break in continuity caused by the killing of kinsmen. Sri Krishna, the great Teacher that He was, listened very patiently to what Arjuna had to say. After Arjuna had finished, Sri Krishna addressed him with a smile—not with annoyance or irritation, but with a smile. Dr S. Radhakrishnan says in his commentary on the *Gita* that 'the smile indicates that He saw through Arjuna's attempt at rationalization or what is now known as wishful thinking.' Probably in that smile of Sri Krishna there was something more than just amusement at Arjuna's attempt at rationalization, there is evident here a deep compassion for His disciple who was engulfed in confusion and bafflement. Sri Krishna tells Arjuna:

> Thou grievest for those that should not be grieved for, yet speakest words of wisdom. The wise grieve neither for the living nor for the dead.

The human mind is very clever at argument and rationalization. The great weapon in its armoury is: Verbalization. It knows how to dress up for any occasion. Its arguments flow endlessly. Most people are impressed by the arguments of the mind with its overpoweringly strict obedience to the principles of logic and the laws of structural thinking. But Sri Krishna's insight was much too penetrating to be taken in by Arjuna's clever rationalization. So he smilingly tells Arjuna that while he speaks words of wisdom, his actions belie those words of wisdom.

What indeed is the cause of Arjuna's grief? We saw in the first chapter that the cause of Arjuna's despondency was the prospect of a break in continuity that would definitely come about with the death of his kinsmen arrayed in the Kurukshetra battle. For the human mind a break in continuity is death in its most fearsome form. Therefore man is for ever afraid of death so long as he functions within the confines of the mind. Arjuna expresses this fear of death even though he covers it up with many a seemingly wise argument. He would rather renounce everything than kill his kinsmen on the battlefield of Kurukshetra. And yet behind this impulse of renunciation Sri Krishna perceives the fear of death and discontinuity gripping the mind of Arjuna. While sympathizing with Arjuna's turmoil Sri Krishna rebukes him for the discrepancy between his wise words and his unwise behaviour. Why is Arjuna's behaviour declared as unwise? The lack of wisdom in Arjuna's behaviour lies in the fact that he grieved for 'those that should not be grieved for'. Who are *those* for whom there should be no grief? Sri Krishna says, 'The Wise grieve neither for the living nor for the dead.' One associates grief with the dead but not with the living. It is strange that Sri Krishna should have mentioned both the living and the dead in this problem of grief. What is the significance of the word 'living' in the context of this question of grief?

The one question that is associated with Death is: Do the dead continue to exist? What happens to those who die? If there is a continuity of existence, what is the nature of that continuity? But apart from the question of the continuity of existence after death, there is another factor—the feeling of separation experienced by those who are left behind. Even though there may be assurances about the dead continuing to exist, these assurances do not solve the problem of separation with which the living are afflicted. The problem of separation is the problem of a break in continuity caused by death. This break in continuity is experienced by the living because the death of a loved one creates a gap in the life of those who are left behind—a gap which cannot be bridged by assurances regarding the continuity of existence beyond the portal of death. Thus death raises two fundamental issues—one of continuity and the other of discontinuity. While the issue of continuity is with reference to the dead, the issue of discontinuity or separation refers to the living. Sri Krishna says: 'The Wise grieve neither for the living nor for the dead.' The statement indicates that the wise understand the whole problem of death, with reference to both continuity and discontinuity, and so they are completely free from all grief. Arjuna feels acute despondency because he has yet to understand the problem of death in all its entirety. Is this not one of the most fundamental problems of the Human Mind? If the mind could know the significance of continuity and the secret of discontinuity, it would comprehend the meaning of life itself. It is to this problem of death with its twin phenomena of continuity and discontinuity that Sri Krishna turns in the Second Discourse while developing the fascinating theme of the Gospel of Life as enunciated in the *Bhagavad Gita*.

The inevitability of death and the continuity of existence through the recurring process of birth, death and re-birth are the two important themes with which the main teaching of the *Gita* begins. What is Arjuna afraid of? Does he think that death will be the end of these warriors whom he is likely to slay in the battle? If death is the end of man, how can he attack those who are worthy of reverence like Bhishma and Drona and slay them in battle? These are the questions that have distracted Arjuna from the battle of Kurukshetra. Sri Krishna leaves no stone unturned to satisfy Arjuna on all vital questions dealing both with death as well as life.

There have been numerous interpretations of the teaching of the *Bhagavad Gita*. Some scholars claim that the *Gita* indicates *Gnana Yoga* or the Path of Knowledge. Some others speak of the message of the *Gita* as belonging to *Karma Yoga* or the Path of Action. Still others have described the gospel of *Gita* as *Bhakti Yoga* or the Path of Devotion. No doubt there are verses in the *Gita* to substantiate all these different interpretations. Nevertheless, the *Gita* is *par excellence* a book dealing with the Yoga of Integration. It is with the integration of man that it is fundamentally concerned. Needless to say, in the process of psychological integration man has to be a pilgrim along all the three Paths—the Path of Knowledge, the Path of Devotion and the Path of Action. To the man of integration the *Gita* gives the name *Yukta*, one who combines in himself Knowledge, Devotion and Action.

It is most interesting to see how the very structure of the Second Discourse reveals this fact of an integrated approach of the *Gita*. In dealing with the despondency of Arjuna, Sri Krishna begins with the approach of Knowledge—this is what is known in the *Gita* as the teaching according to *Sānkhya*. In the *Gita*, *Sānkhya* is used as a description of the Path of Knowledge. While the Second Discourse begins with the approach of Sānkhya, the latter part of this chapter deals with the approach of Yoga. Once again Yoga is used in the *Gita* in the sense of *Karma* or Action, and not so much in the sense indicated by the System of Hindu Philosophy called by that name and attributed to Patanjali. Between the teachings of *Sānkhya* and *Yoga*, there are a few verses in the Second Discourse of the *Gita* where Sri Krishna reminds Arjuna of his duty. The *Bhagavad Gita* speaks of Duty as *Svadharma* meaning action which emanates from the perception of one's own nature. Sri Krishna asks Arjuna to show his supreme dedication to Duty, and reminds him not to lose sight of his true nature and not to be disloyal to the dictates of that nature. Sankaracharya in his *Viveka-Chudamani*, in Verse 31, says: 'The return to one's own true nature is designated as devotion.' In the verses that remind Arjuna of his Duty, arising from his true nature, the approach is that of Devotion or *Bhakti*. Thus the Second Discourse gives us that integrated approach of Knowledge, Devotion and Action which is so characteristic of the whole teaching of the *Bhagavad Gita*.

We have stated above that Arjuna's despondency arises out of the prospect of death and discontinuity which he sees as an outcome of the Kurukshetra war. Therefore it is these two factors that Sri Krishna elaborates as he expounds the teaching according to *Sānkhya*. Sri Krishna says to Arjuna:

> Certain is death for the born, and certain is birth for the dead; therefore over the inevitable thou shouldst not grieve.

Death is the one thing which cannot be avoided nor can it be postponed. It has to be regarded as *Aparihārya* or unavoidable. In other words, death is an unalterable fact of life. Since it cannot be altered, to grieve for it is utterly meaningless. Sri Krishna speaks here of the eternal flux which is the fundamental nature of all manifested things, for he says: 'That which is born must die.' That which has a beginning must have an end. This is a fact which must be accepted. An intellectual acceptance and the seeing of a fact are two different things. Most of us are able to recognize the inevitability of death at an intellectual level—but very few of us can see it as an unalterable fact. He who can see thus is truly wise for he grieves not for death.

While Sri Krishna describes the bodies of men as finite and therefore destructible, he also speaks of the re-birth that follows death. It is in this concept of rebirth that Sri Krishna refers to a continuity of existence in spite of the inevitability of death. Sri Krishna says to Arjuna:

> Nor I, nor thou, nor any one of these,
> Ever was not, nor ever will not be,
> For ever and for ever afterwards.
> Nay, but as when one layeth
> His worn out robes away,
> And taking new ones sayeth,
> 'These will I wear today!'
> So putteth by the spirit
> Lightly its garb of flesh,
> And passeth to inherit
> A residence afresh.

The mind of man for ever seeks to understand the problem of death. But it can give an explanation of death only within the framework of continuity. It can therefore know of death only in terms of an after-death condition and in terms of re-birth—any other meaning would be utterly incomprehensible to the human mind. And yet the mystery of death must remain inexplicable so long as it is approached through the framework of continuity—be it the continuity of after-death state, or be it the continuity in terms of re-birth.

Arjuna must have been familiar with the concept of re-birth for it has been a part and parcel of the Hindu thought throughout the centuries. While the principle of Re-incarnation is intellectually satisfying, it fails to give sufficient consolation to the human heart. The knowledge of after-death conditions and the concept of re-birth may lessen our grief for the dead but they certainly do not free the living from the pangs of sorrow and separation. Death is fundamentally a problem of discontinuity and therefore cannot be easily comprehended through the framework of continuity however logical and comprehensive such a framework may be. In the Second Discourse of the *Bhagavad Gita*, the main emphasis of Sri Krishna's teaching regarding the problem of death is on this aspect of discontinuity and not so much on the continuity of existence through re-birth.

Perhaps it may be asked: Where does Sri Krishna speak of discontinuity with reference to death in the teaching as contained in the Second Discourse? It is true we do not find anywhere in this discourse any mention about discontinuity, but we come across another word the full significance of which can be understood only when death is comprehended not in terms of continuity but as a phenomenon of discontinuity. While dealing with the problem of death, Sri Krishna speaks more of the 'immutable being' rather than of the mutable entity which is caught up in the cycle of birth and death. His unmistakable emphasis is on the Immortality of Spirit. It has to be understood that Continuity and Immortality are not only not identical but they belong to two different dimensions of existence. The one belongs to the Time-process while the other is Timeless. To know the distinction between the Immortal and the Continuous one must differentiate between the Eternal and the Ever-lasting. The Ever-lasting represents a continuity of time, but the Eternal is where the Time is not. That which is within the framework of Time has a beginning and therefore an end. The Continuous belongs to a Universe which may be expanding and yet it is finite. All manifested things are finite and therefore subject to the limitations of the Time-process. Hence, to speak of Immortality with reference to anything that is manifest is utterly meaningless. Immortality cannot be found in the realm of continuity—in fact it is where continuity ends that the Vision of Immortality comes. The human mind for ever confined within the frontiers of continuity can never know what Immortality is. While after-death condition and re-birth can speak to us of continuity—it is the actual moment of death which alone can reveal the secret of Immortality—because the moment of death is indeed a moment of discontinuity. And so the language of continuity, however subtle and polished it may be, can never explain the true meaning of Death. Seeing Arjuna baffled and confused because of the prospect of killing his kinsmen, among whom were such revered ones as Bhishma and Drona, Sri Krishna says:

> He who regardeth him as slayer, and he who thinketh he is slain both of them are ignorant. He slayeth not, nor is he slain.

Here Sri Krishna explodes the whole myth of the slayer and the slain. He is referring here to the Immortality of the Spirit.

Surely the above verse has no meaning in terms of re-birth, for re-birth can be only of one who dies. What is it then that Sri Krishna refers to in the above verse? This is made clear as we turn to Verse 20 of the Second Discourse which runs as follows:

> Never the spirit was born; the Spirit shall cease to be never;
> Never was time it was not; End and Beginning are dreams!
> Birthless and deathless and changeless remaineth the spirit for ever;
> Death had not touched it at all, dead though the house of it seems!

Deathlessness in the midst of death—that indeed is what the above verse proclaims. There is *something* which death cannot touch even though the house of that *something* may be utterly consumed by the fire of Death. It is that *something* which truly is Immortal for death cannot hold it in its grip. But that *something* is unborn and therefore never dies. The soul of man is immortal—but then the soul for ever is Unborn and Unmanifest. One can commune with the Unborn only in the moment of death. Rabindranath Tagore rightly says: 'Man is immortal; therefore he must die endlessly.' Not in continuity, but in a condition of endless death can one comprehend the secret of Immortality. It is to this secret of Immortality that Sri Krishna draws the attention of Arjuna, for He says:

> Weapons do not cleave this self, fire does not burn him; waters do not make him wet, nor does the wind make him dry. He is uncleavable, He cannot be burnt, He can be neither wetted nor dried, He is Eternal, All-pervading, Unchanging and Immovable. He is the same for ever. He is said to be Unmanifest, Unthinkable and Unchanging. Therefore, knowing Him as such, thou shouldst not grieve.

The Spirit is unmanifest and therefore unthinkable, for the mind can dwell in thought only on the manifest. The unmanifest is outside the purview of thought. The unmanifest has no parts which the mind can examine one after the other. The unmanifest is the whole—not the whole made up of the parts, but the whole which transcends the totality of the parts. Therefore, the unmanifest can be known only as a whole, but such a perception is not possible for the mind to have through its process of mentation, however subtle and abstract it may be.

It is only in the hour of death when even the last veil of the manifest is rent as under that the Vision of the Unborn and the Unmanifest is vouchsafed to man. Sri Krishna tells Arjuna: 'Knowing him as such thou shouldst not grieve.' He asks Arjuna to rise to the Vision of the Unborn and the Unmanifest if he would unravel the secret of death. This is indeed to look at death not through the framework of continuity but through that interval of discontinuity where alone the secret of death resides. Sri Krishna says:

> Beings are unmanifest in their origin, manifest in their midmost state, O Bharata, unmanifest likewise are they in dissolution. What room then for lamentation?

When the real nature of things resides in the Unmanifest, why should there be sorrow and grief when the Manifest ceases to be? The Manifest is but partial and fleeting, it is the Unmanifest which is the whole and the immutable. Thus the whole problem of death disappears when one communes with the Unmanifest—such indeed is the teaching of the *Gita*. Arjuna's lamentation is false because he wants the flux of the Manifest to cease. But this cannot be, for the Manifest for ever is vulnerable. It is in the death of the Manifest that the Unmanifest is revealed, and the Unmanifest never ceases to be, for, It is Eternal and Timeless.

The *Bhagavad Gita* says that the Vision of the Timeless imparts to man that quality of perception whereby the succession of time ceases to be restrictive. With the vision of the Timeless all actions in time are rendered devoid of the element of bondage. It is because of this that Sri Krishna, having explained to Arjuna the approach of *Sānkhya* or Right Perception, speaks to him now of *Yoga* or Right Action. Sri Krishna says:

> The teaching set forth to thee is in accordance with *Sānkhya*; hear it now according to *Yoga*, imbued with which teaching, O Partha, thou shalt cast away the bonds of action.

It has to be remembered that the teaching of *Yoga* is not unrelated to the teaching of *Sānkhya*. Sri Krishna is not talking of two absolutely different and unrelated things. In fact, at one place in the *Gita*—in the Fifth Discourse, Verse 4, Sri Krishna says: 'Children, not sages, speak of *Sānkhya* and *Yoga* as different.' And so, *Sānkhya* and *Yoga* can be described as Right Perception and Right Action respectively. Where the perception is right, the action that emerges is free from the element of bondage. How does Right Perception perform this miracle of Action?

What indeed is Right Perception? Needless to say, where the mind is distracted there can be no true perception of things. It is the undistracted mind which is a pre-requisite for Right Perception of things. The *Gita* refers to this undistracted condition of the mind by the phrase *Vyavasāyātmikā Buddhi;* meaning determinate reason or resolute understanding. In the Second Discourse, Verse 41, the *Gita* says:

> The determinate reason is but one-pointed, O Joy of the Kurus, many branched and endless are the thoughts of the irresolute.

The irresolute are distracted and, therefore, unable to see things as they are—they are devoid of Right Perception. They are caught up in the non-essentials of life and are ever seeking for new 'toys' with which to play. They are directed hither and thither by rewards and punishments, motivated as they are by greed and fear. A distracted mind functions merely on the surface unable to probe the deeper layers of existence. Such a mind obviously cannot have Right Perception of things and can never establish a communion with the Unborn and the Unmanifest. What is it that distracts the mind? The mind is indeed distracted by the functioning of its own attributes. Mind's field of knowledge is defined by these attributes; in other words, mind gathers knowledge through the functioning processes of its own attributes. Unless the mind is freed from these attributes there cannot descend into it a 'resolute understanding' or the *Vyavasāyātmikā Buddhi*. It is the field of knowledge established by the action of the mind which hinders the Right Perception of things. The *Bhagavad Gita*, therefore, asks Arjuna to rise above the attributes of the mind, for it says:

> Vedas deal with the three attributes, be thou above these three attributes, O Arjuna, beyond the pairs of opposites, ever steadfast

> in purity, not caring for acquisition and preservation, and be possessed of the Self.

The Vedas in the larger context of the term would mean knowledge. Now, the field of knowledge is restricted by the three attributes of the mind. Arjuna is asked to rise above these three attributes of the mind—in other words to come to a comprehension of life which is not of the mind but which transcends the limitations of the mind. It is only in this condition that he would come to the understanding of the Unborn and the Unmanifest, to the perception of the Timeless in Time. What are the three attributes of the mind? They are according to the *Gita, Tamas, Rajas,* and *Satva,* Inertia, Activity and Balance, or to put it differently, Thesis, Anti-thesis and Synthesis. The mind has its own patterns of habit, its own causes of conflict and its own contents of conclusion. This is the whole field of the mind. In this field it lives, moves and has its own being. The whole process of gathering knowledge is within this field. This indeed is its sphere of continuity. Arjuna is asked to break through this circle of continuity if he would know the secret of death and life too. He is asked to go beyond the pairs of opposites. Now to go beyond the pairs of opposites is to leave behind the frontiers of the mind, because the field of thought has opposites as its boundaries. The mind forever moves between two opposing points and the area between these two points is its field of knowledge. On any subject, mind's knowledge consists in defining the opposite. The more clearly it is able to define the opposites the more effective is its knowledge regarding the subject it investigates. To transcend the pairs of opposites is, therefore, to go beyond the frontiers of mind's knowledge and enter a realm of true understanding—the realm of Right Perception. It is from this point, poised between the two opposites, that true action can emerge—action which is free from all factors of bondage. To such action does Sri Krishna refer in the following famous verse of the *Gita*:

> To action alone has thou a right and never at all to its fruits; let not the fruits of action be thy motive, neither let there be in thee any attachment to inaction.

3

It is to Pure Action that Sri Krishna draws the attention of his friend and disciple. He is asked to act, but not to react. The mind caught up in the movement of the opposites is always subject to reactions. It never knows what Pure Action is. Sri Krishna tells Arjuna: 'Let not the fruits of action be thy motive.' In other words, the action must be motiveless, directed neither by greed nor by fear, neither by the allurement of reward nor by the dread of disfavour.

It is most significant to note that dealing with the subject of Pure Action, Sri Krishna asks Arjuna 'to perform action dwelling in union with the Divine.' The Divine is obviously the transcendental—the Unborn and the Unmanifest. To act in union with the Unmanifest is indeed to act from a point where all mentation has ceased, where all movement of the mind between the pairs of opposites has come to an end. This is the state of *Buddhi* or Pure Reason according to the teaching of the *Gita*. Pure Reason or Intelligence is not the product of the mind. It dawns upon the mind that has come to a poise between the two opposites. It is only the mind so poised that can dwell in union with the Divine. It is only to such a mind that the perception of the Unborn and the Unmanifest comes. Speaking about this poise of the mind, the *Gita* says: 'United to Pure Reason, one abandoneth here both good and evil deeds.' One can understand the abandoning of the evil deeds, but it is difficult to reconcile oneself to the idea of an abandonment of good deeds as well. It has to be remembered that the concept of good which the mind has is always in opposition to evil. Thus Good and Evil are but the opposites of the mind. The un-enlightened mind moves between these two opposites, clinging to its good and therefore resisting what it calls evil. So long as the mind has one point to rest its feet on, so long it feels safe, for, from one point it can always create its apposite and thus establish its sphere of continuity in which to carry on its movement for ever. But the man of Pure Intelligence is one in whom both the points of the mind have been discarded so that the mind is delicately poised ready to receive even the subtlest intimation from that which lies beyond its frontiers. For such a mind there is a complete abandonment of good as well as evil deeds, for, whatever emerges out of that poised condition is absolutely good—not good as opposed to evil.

It is most interesting to note that while Sri Krishna instructing Arjuna in *Yoga* or Action, he is not concerned with describing the nature of right action so much as defining the source of such action. The condition of poise to which he refers in this discourse is indeed the source from where alone right action can emerge. Sri Krishna wants Arjuna to come to that condition of poise so that the clouds of despondency may disperse and he may, dwelling in union with the Divine, know what right action is. Now this communion with the Divine or the Unmanifest is a direct experience—it is not one which can be had through an intermediary. Sri Krishna speaks of this in no mistakable terms, for He tells Arjuna:

> When thy mind shall escape from this tangle of delusion, then thou shalt rise to indifference as to what has been heard and should be heard. When thy mind, bewildered by *Shruti*, shall stand unmoved, fixed in contemplation, then shalt thou attain unto *Yoga*.

Yoga in the *Bhagavad Gita* refers to a condition pre-requisite for Right Action—in other words, it is the source of action from which any pattern may arise—it may be a pattern of war or it may be a pattern of peace. But such a condition can come into being only when the mind is freed from all authority, even the authority of the scriptures. Sri Krishna tells Arjuna that his mind is bewildered by scriptures and that he must rise to 'indifference as to what has been heard and should be heard'. He wants Arjuna to keep his mind unmoved even in spite of all the injunctions of the scriptures so that he may be able to bring to bear upon the problem facing him, a mind, unconditioned and unbiassed, free from all authority. It is such a mind freed from all conditioning factors which alone can commune with the Pure Source of action—action which does not bind, being devoid of all elements of reaction. Before Arjuna can act rightly, he must come to the stillness of mind for this indeed is the Pure Source, uncorrupt and uncontaminated, the root-base of action that is right.

But Arjuna wants Sri Krishna to tell him as to what are the characteristics of a man who has come to such stillness of intelligence so that he too may come to that state and thereby know what Right Action is. The very first distinguishing characteristic of a man of still mind given by Sri Krishna is 'content in Self by Self'. What does this mean? It really points to a condition of a man who is self-contained. Be it remembered that a self-contained individual is not a self-satisfied or a self-complacent person. A self-contained individual is one who is free from all desires to become something or somebody. His psychological existence is not dependent upon any external factor. He acts not for self-fulfilment but for the expression of that Fullness which he experiences within himself. He is an integrated person, poised between the opposites, and, therefore, free from all conflicts and cravings that come in the wake of a process of psychological becoming. It is only the self-contained individual who can act rightly, for there are no centres of psychological reaction within the psyche of such a man. The last section of the Second Discourse is intensely fascinating and illuminating because it gives an elaboration of the character of the self-contained individual. To create a self-contained individual is indeed the very purpose of the *Gita*, for such an individual knows no conflict of wills.

It is most interesting to note that throughout the description of the self-contained individual, Sri Krishna again and again emphasizes the condition of poise between the opposites. He says that such an individual has a 'mind untroubled in the midst of sorrows and is free from eager desire amid pleasures'. Normally a man is worried in conditions of sorrow and is full of dreams of expansion in the circumstances of pleasure. But a condition of being neither elated in pleasure nor depressed in restrictive circumstances demands a poise, a state of equilibrium where the human mind has to walk on the razor-edged path, ever watchful lest it should fall into either of the extremes. The *Bhagavad Gita* says that an individual 'who neither likes nor dislikes, of such a one the understanding is well-poised'. To meet the situations of life without justification or condemnation, without indulgence or repulsion is indeed a difficult undertaking—and yet it is only there that one can discover the true basis for right action. Right Perception and Right Action are two sides of the same medallion—one cannot exist without the other. When the mind is well-poised then there is the perception of the Whole, and is not such perception the very foundation for right action?

But such a condition of Poise cannot be brought about by an act of conscious renunciation. The state of neither indulgence nor denial is not arrived at by the following of a prescribed code of behaviour. The condition of Poise is an inner state which comes into being naturally and spontaneously, for, it is not the product of man's conscious effort. It comes; it cannot be brought about. But how does it come? The *Bhagavad Gita* in the following verse gives a penetrating insight into this whole problem of man's perception and action. It says:

> The objects of sense turn away from the embodied soul who abstains from feeding on them, but the taste for them remains. Even the taste turns away when the Supreme is seen.

It is easy to discard the objects of sense-delight. It is also possible to make oneself utterly insensitive to sense-impacts. But man's psychological problem resides neither in the objects nor in the senses—it abides in the mind. To run away from sense objects is comparatively easy—this is what the abstemious persons do. But while the sense-objects may be cast away—the mind that dwells on them remains. The mind that indulges in its own tastes and relishes will for ever remain distracted. In fact, one who consciously renounces something is caught up in an act of indulgence, for, he indulges in that which is the opposite of the one he has discarded. Therefore the man of conscious renunciation is verily a man of strong indulgence—he feeds not the senses, but his mind is tethered to a point from where it derives secret indulgence through an outer display of denial and renunciation. The *Gita* says that the relish of the mind disappears only when the Supreme is seen. The Supreme is the Transcendental—the Unborn and the Unmanifest. When can the Supreme be seen? Can the mind by its conscious effort ever see the Supreme? It is only when the mind abandons all its efforts that the Vision of the Supreme can dawn upon human consciousness. The dawning of that Vision and the purging of the mind of all its tastes and relishes are a simultaneous process. All conscious efforts, however noble they may seem, are rooted in motives. It is the motive which constitutes the relish of the mind. How can mind be freed from motives through efforts that are themselves rooted in motives? It is only when all motives subside—even the ridding of the mind of all its relish—that the Vision of the Supreme can come as if in a flash, illumining the entire path of man's consciousness.

The great Indian poet Kalidasa says in one of his plays that 'they whose minds are not disturbed when the sources of disturbance are present, are the truly brave'. The mind that appears to be calm when sense-objects are taken away is a mind that has yet to know what true Poise is. The silence of the graveyard is not to be mistaken for the utter tranquility of the mind that is poised. But how is this state of tranquility to be arrived at? Once the Lord Buddha posed a problem to His disciples. It was a problem of untying a knot. When the disciples gave their answers to the problem, the Lord Buddha said: 'If you want to untie a knot, all that you have to do is to know how the knot was tied'. In this answer we have a clue to the problem with which the *Bhagavad Gita* is concerned. The problem to which we have come is: How to free the mind of all its distractions? How to uncondition the mind so that it is not carried away by its motives? Now to uncondition the mind all that one needs to do is to see how the mind gets conditioned. To observe the conditioning process of the mind is itself the beginning of mind's de-conditioning. In the following two verses of the *Bhagavad Gita* there is presented to us a keen and a penetrating observation of the mind and its conditioning processes. The verses read as follows.

> Man, musing on object of sense, conceiveth an attachment to these; from attachment ariseth desire; from desire anger cometh forth; from anger proceedeth delusion; from delusion confused memory; from confused memory destruction of reason; from destruction of reason he perishes.

Here we have an analysis of the mental processes such as we do not come across even in profound treatises of modern psychology. The *Gita* says, from musing on objects, an attachment for them is born. It is not the coming in of thoughts that matters as the dwelling on them. In other words, it is the giving of abode to thoughts in one's mind that causes attachment, for, the mind, dwelling on thoughts, forms an association with them. It is this association, the keeping of company, which produces an attachment. From attachment is born naturally a desire—the desire to defend those thoughts and to prevent them from going away. Such defence mechanism of the mind is assuredly the begetter of anger. Truly speaking all anger is rooted in fear—the fear of losing something which one is trying to protect. The fear that the thoughts whose company we cherish may slip away gives rise to anger—anger against all challenges of life. From anger arises delusion—the losing of a sense of proportion. It is quite obvious that the angry man has moved away from the right perspective of things. He is unable to see things as they are. The man who has lost a sense of proportion is truly a victim of confused memory. The term 'confused memory' is most significant. It indicates the overlaying of the factual memory with psychological memory. Where such overlaying takes place there the past projects into the present preventing one from seeing things as they are. The man of confused memory is unable to think clearly, for his mind is conditioned and coloured by the impacts of psychological memory. Needless to say, where clarity of thinking is lost there the mind decays. There has begun a complete psychological degeneration in the life of such an individual. Here we see clearly the whole process by which mind is conditioned. To be aware of this process is indeed to free the mind of all the distracting factors. The mind that constantly deconditions itself is a sensitive mind, open to receive the subtlest intimations of the Unborn and the Unmanifest. Such a mind is free from the opposites of attraction and repulsion, and therefore utterly peaceful, devoid of all conflicts.

It is in the clarity of mind, and there alone, that Intelligence can take its birth. Now such clarity of mind is a state of total attention so that whatever the mind sees, it sees with a completeness of attention, because from it all centres of distractions have vanished past resurgence. Such total attention is the begetter of peace and therefore of happiness. The *Gita* says:

> There is no Intelligence for the non-harmonized, nor for the non-harmonized is there concentration, for him without concentration there is no peace, and for the unpeaceful, how can there be happiness?

The secret of happiness is the peace or the quiet of the mind. But a distracted mind never knows what peace is. It is only the mind capable of total attention that knows what peace and quiet are. It is only such a mind that can act with intelligence for it has a right perception of things. Therefore the problem of problems for a man thrown in the battle of life is to deal with the distracting factors of the mind so that he can come to a totality of attention and thereby know how to act intelligently under all situations. The *Gita* has described the distracted mind beautifully by the phrase: the 'wind carrying away a ship upon the waters'. Our minds are being carried away by the winds that blow from all sides. Our ship of the is a prey to the passing winds—it has no steadiness, it knows no quiet at all. How can such a mind act in an intelligent manner? How can it comprehend the secret of life or the meaning of death?

But once again the question arises: How is this flighty mind to be brought to a state of silence? If neither indulgence nor resistance can bring peace and quiet, what else can? If the pairs of opposites are to be transcended, how is one to meet the challenge of life? These are indeed practical questions of life. If indulgence and resistance are both ruled out, is there a third way of approaching life? The *Gita* indicates this third way of meeting the challenges of life in the following verse:

> He attaineth Peace, into whom all desires flow as rivers flow into the ocean, which though ever being filled remaineth unmoved—not he who desireth desires.

The way indicated in the *Gita* in terms of the above verse is neither submission nor resistance, but acceptance of life as it is. Any action with reference to the challenges of life is possible only from the point of acceptance. If life is not accepted as it is then all responses to the demands of life are meaningless; it is like a undertaking a journey without establishing the right starting point. To accept life as it is constitutes the only correct point of departure for undertaking one's journey into the untrodden lands of life. The above verse of the *Gita* indicates the path of accepting life as it comes. Such acceptance is not to be mistaken for submission. In submission there is an outer pattern of acceptance with an inner feeling of resistance. Thus submission introduces an element of ceaseless conflict between the outer pattern and the inner content. But acceptance indicates no such conflict, for here life is received as it comes and such receiving is made the starting point of right relationship with all that life brings. The ocean receives the rivers as they flow into it bringing with them the content of immense diversities. The ocean shows forth neither indulgence nor resistance with reference to any stream that flows in, bringing its own waters, whether clear or muddy. The ocean is neither elated nor is it depressed at the prospect of what the river brings. The ocean is full and yet is ready to receive what comes. It remains unmoved even though countless streams may flow into it.

The *Gita* suggests that the individual whose mind is receptive and yet not selective is truly integrated—he is at peace with himself and so is at peace with all. The peace and silence of the mind are to be brought about not by submission nor by resistance. Acceptance is the only path that leads to that deep silence in which alone communion with the Unborn and the Unmanifest is possible. The Way of life is to be found in this communion, for, it is there and there alone that the Whisper of the Soul is heard. The Path of Action which the *Gita* indicates has its starting point in Acceptance.

To accept life as it is, constitutes the right starting point for Action with reference to that life. It is only such acceptance which brings man in communion with the Unborn and the Unmanifest—the communion which enables him to see the Whole and the right relationship of the Part with that Whole. The truly integrated man, the man of steady intelligence, is he in whose life the Part occupies its rightful place in the beautiful pattern of the Whole. When this happens there is no conflict between the Will of Man and the Will of the Cosmos. When the Part occupies its rightful place in the pattern of the Whole then can man say with Arjuna: 'Let Thy Will be done for destroyed is my delusion.' To accept life as it comes and to make it the starting point for right action—this indeed is the path indicated by the *Gita*. This is the path of the individual will finding its complete fulfilment in the cosmic will. This indeed is the quintessence of the teaching of the *Bhagavad Gita* as revealed in its Second Discourse.

The *Bhagavad Gita* indicates a way of life which is intensely revolutionary, for, it speaks not merely of an extension of consciousness but most assuredly of an expansion of consciousness. What *Gita* indicates is not just a difference of degree in the way of one's living—it points to a difference of kind, a fundamental difference such as is seen between a variation and a mutation, to use the language of biology. The following verse of the *Gita* bears ample testimony to the above fact:

> That which is night for all beings, for the disciplined man is time for waking, and what is the time for waking for other beings is indeed night for the Sage who seeth.

The Sage is awake when all others are asleep—this shows a dimensional difference between the life of the Spirit and the life of worldly activities. As Dr S. Radhakrishnan says: 'The spiritual is not an extension of the ethical; it is a new dimension altogether, dealing with things eternal'. The *Bhagavad Gita* deals with spiritual realities and not with mere ethical principles. The moral behaviour of the *Gita* emanates from spiritual perception and not from the law laid down by a religious authority. The above verse unmistakably points to a new dimension of life into which Sri Krishna initiates his great friend and disciple Arjuna. The *Bhagavad Gita* is not a book dealing with a code of ethics—it is a book dealing with spiritual perspectives. It is a book dealing, *par excellence*, with spiritual revolution and not a mere tinkering with ethical and moral patterns of behaviour. The latter would constitute an act of merely decorating the prison walls of one's existence while the former indicates the breaking through all walls and emerging into the open spaces of life. The *Bhagavad Gita* is a book of spiritual revolution and not of mere moral reformation. It demands from the pilgrim of life a spirit of fearless adventure. For this adventure of life, the pilgrim must leave behind all his abodes and stand utterly 'homeless', stripped of everything. The *Bhagavad Gita* leads us on to this pilgrimage of life, giving us as it were a Staff of Nothingness with which to clear our way through the deep forests of daily living.

Into this fascinating story of the Soul's pilgrimage through life we are initiated as we turn to discourse after discourse of this priceless book. It opens to us new dimensions of living enabling us to scale new heights of human endeavour and to probe greater depths of human existence where the mystery of life stands revealed in all its grandeur for man to see.

CHAPTER III

THE BEING AND THE BECOMING

THE UNIQUENESS in the teaching of the *Bhagavad Gita* lies in the fact that it asks the spiritual aspirant not to leave the world and retire into a forest for the practice of spiritual life but to live it where one is, even in the midst of one's mundane duties. In fact, the *Gita* says that to live is to act, because, not even for one moment can man exist without action. The *Gita* says:

> No one, even for an instant, can remain really actionless.

To live is to act—even the so-called non-action is a form of action. Man cannot escape relationship, as existence and relationship are synonymous. Now this relationship which is a part of existence finds its expression in action. It does not matter what the nature of that action is—it may have physical forms or it may be encased in non-physical expressions. Action being inseparable from existence is one of the cardinal principles of life enunciated by the *Gita*. It is interesting to note that the *Gita* makes a distinction between Action and Activity. It says: 'man winneth not freedom from action by abstaining from activity.' It is possible for a person to refrain from activity—but even then he cannot free himself from action, for the state of non-activity is also a form of relationship with the environment in which he lives.

There is another distinction which the *Gita* has made and which is worth noting in understanding the whole problem of spiritual life. This distinction is between *Sanyasa* and *Tyaga*, between Renunciation and Non-attachment. The *Gita* is all the time concerned with the content of action and not with the pattern of action. It emphasizes the motive of action, not so much the manner of activity. Renunciation deals with the outer pattern of behaviour while Non-attachment is an inner state, a condition of mind. One can display renunciation by doning a saffron robe or by adopting a particular code of behaviour. It can be demonstrated by a denial of physical comforts or by putting on a certain regalia of outer observances. But all these outer proofs have no meaning whatsoever so far as spiritual life is concerned. In spirituality it is the condition of mind that matters, not the colour of one's robe.

The *Bhagavad Gita* is most unambiguous with regard to the essential nature of spiritual life, for, it says:

> Who sitteth, controlling organs of action, but dwelling in his mind on objects of senses, that deluded man is called a hypocrite.

Man's spiritual stature is to be judged from the condition of his mind and not from his demonstrable code of behaviour. In fact, a really spiritual man is unostentatious; there can never be a display or demonstration in a life that is truly spiritual. Any display, whether of material possessions or of spiritual accomplishments, is essentially vulgar. Surely there is nothing more crude and vulgar than the display of one's so called virtue. The more one displays one's spiritual conduct, the less spiritual content is there in the inner make-up of such an individual. The *Bhagavad Gita* calls such a man a hypocrite, a man of false conduct.

In the Second Discourse, the *Gita* speaks of the Unborn and the Unmanifest as holding the key to the understanding of life and death. The *Gita* indicates that a communion with the Unborn and the Unmanifest is possible only when the mind transcends the pairs of opposites and remains perfectly poised, receiving life as it comes without justification or condemnation. Perhaps it may be stated that in asking one to accept life as it comes, the *Gita* is enunciating a gospel of utter passivity. Nothing can be farther from the truth. The *Gita* advocates the path of acceptance not as a substitute for action but as the right starting point for true action. Any action that misses the right starting point is bound to be wrong and therefore a cause of bondage. Arjuna was baffled and could not make the right choice because he had moved away from the right starting point of true action. What indeed is the right starting point for true action? It is a condition of non-attachment where the mind is unswayed by the pairs of opposites. Sri Krishna tells Arjuna :

> The world is bound by action, unless performed for the sake of sacrifice; for that sake, free from attachment, O son of Kunti, perform thou action.

In terms of the above verse, the bonds of action are severed only when action is performed as a sacrifice. What is this sacrifice about which the *Gita* speaks? In one verse of the Third Discourse there is mention of the sacrifice of the Creator out of which Creation came into existence. The *Gita* says: 'In ancient days, Prajāpati, the Creator, created men together with His sacrifice.' The Eternal Sacrifice of God is indeed one of the most fascinating themes in the mystic lore of all great religions. The idea that all creation exists only because the Author of that creation has sacrificed Himself is one of the most inspiring concepts in the religious tradition both of the East as well as the West. In Hindu religious thought, this theme is woven round the Sacrifice of Prajāpati, the Lord of all creatures. Writing on this subject, C. Jinarajadasa says in his essay entitled *The Eternal Sacrifice of God* as follows :

> In India, in a great dramatic story and ritual, perhaps clearer in some ways than the other rituals, this same mystical fact of the Divine Sacrifice is commemorated. They say in ancient Hindu tradition that Prajāpati, the Lord of all creatures, before creation began, voluntarily laid himself down on the altar to be slain, for it was only by His being so slain that creation could come into existence. He called upon His elder children, the great Angels, and He laid himself down upon the altar. According to His command they dismembered and slew Divinity, and by the death of the God, by His martyrdom and sacrifice, came the creation of the universe. From the dismembered parts of Prajāpati there arose the hills and the plains, the planets and the stars. There arose from his members the life of the mineral, the plant, the animal and man. We are told that it is only because God, in the beginning of time, so died to His full and free nature, that you and I have our separate individual existences.

In Hindu tradition man is asked to bring the dismembered parts of God together and resurrect Him. While in the Christian tradition the resurrection of God is looked upon as a miracle performed by God Himself, in Hinduism the resurrection of God is a miracle to be performed by man. This is possible only when man engages himself in sacrifice so that out of the dismemberment of man as man there takes place the miracle of the resurrection of God Himself. The Hindu thought has described the Sacrifice of god as an ever-continuing process. This is reflected in the following statement of the *Gita* :

> The Eternal, the all permeating, is ever present in sacrifice.

Since the Eternal is ever present in sacrifice, it is in sacrifice and there alone that one can commune with it. Sri Krishna asks Arjuna to engage himself in Action that is Sacrifice. Now the real meaning of sacrifice is to be a witness to. Action that is sacrifice thus means an action to which one is a witness. To be a witness to one's own action—this verily is the injunction of the Teacher to His disciple. Action that is sacrifice can come into being only when the actor ceases to exist. This idea has been most graphically brought out in the following verse of the *Gita* :

> The righteous who eat the remains of sacrifice are freed from all sins, but the impious who prepare food for their own sake—verily they eat sin.

What are the remains of sacrifice? Surely it is the 'I' from which all 'I-ness' has vanished, it is the self which has been emptied of all its self-hood. If to sacrifice is to be a witness to oneself then in such sacrifice the 'I' is bereft of all 'I-ness'. He who seeks nourishment from self that is devoid of self-hood, he surely is released from all sins. But he who prepares food for himself, he who seeks nourishment from his own self-hood—he verily eats sin—such is the beautiful exhortation of Sri Krishna to Arjuna. According to Him, it is sacrifice which is the sustaining force of all Creation.

Very often sacrifice is understood to mean duty. Where action is done out of a sense of duty there the element of compulsion is always present, even though it may be imperceptible. The presence of compulsion obviously denotes a motive—for man can be compelled to do something only when he seeks a satisfaction of some motive, however nobly worded that motive may be. In the world we see actions which are visibly selfish, which are motivated by overt selfishness. But in the world we also see actions, which, though not overtly selfish, have their selfish intentions hidden under the cloak of duty. Both these categories of actions are performed out of necessity. Surely where the necessity to act is present there the action is polluted by attachment. It is action, free from all necessity, and, therefore spontaneous, which alone can be called action without attachment. Once again it is the self-contained individual who alone knows what action without attachment is. Sri Krishna tells Arjuna that 'by performing action without attachment, man verily reacheth the Supreme'. Now action without attachment is action done not out of necessity but out of spontaneity. The *Gita* here refers to Janaka who attained to perfection by action —but the action of Janaka had no tings of compulsion or necessity in it. He acted without any corrupting influence of the self. It is such actions that truly sustain the world even as the sacrifice of the Creator sustains the creation.

Dealing with this subject of non-attached action, the *Bhagavad Gita* lays down a fundamental principle of social transformation. It says:

> Whatsoever a great man does, the same is done by others. Whatever standard he sets, the world follows.

Here we see the creative and dynamic role of the individual in the shaping of human societies. The individual is not a product of the society—rather the society is the product of the individual. The society can rise only to the heights set by the individuals comprising it. This teaching of the *Gita* is comparable to the Superior Man of the Chinese philosophy. As Carlyle said, 'The history of humanity is the biography of its great men'. But the Superior Man of the *Gita* is one who acts with complete non-attachment since he is not deluded by such egoism as 'I am the doer'.

Sri Krishna tells Arjuna that He himself is under no necessity to act—and yet He engages Himself in action. This is indeed the Great Sacrifice of the Supreme for the sustenance of the world. The whole world would perish if the Creator were to bring to an end His Great Sacrifice. It is said that God created man in His own image. If this be so then man too must act in the likeness of His Creator. Man can indeed be a collaborator with God—but for this he must link up his sacrifice with the Great Sacrifice of God Himself. He must collaborate with Him in the sustenance of the world. In the Hindu Mythology there is an incident described where Sri Krishna, out of compassion for His people and with a view to protecting them, lifts up the mount Govardhana and balances it on His little finger. Seeing this the cowherds, the companions of Sri Krishna, lift up their sticks so as to help Sri Krishna in keeping aloft the mount Govardhana. Here in this story we see the merging of the little streams of man's sacrifice in the Great Sea of the sacrifice of God Himself. The dismembered Godhead must find His resurrection in Man—and this happens only when man engages himself in sacrifice—in action that is free from all attachment. Sri Krishna tells Arjuna:

> As the ignorant act from attachment to action, O Bharata, so should the wise act without attachment.

But what is this action without attachment? Can there be an action without the actor? If the actor disappears then who is it that acts? These are questions of deep metaphysical import, but the *Gita* deals with them in a very simple manner. The *Gita* says that he who knows the nature of properties and the modes of their functioning is free from attachment in all that he does. If only man would allow nature to work in a free and unfettered manner he would save himself from many a complexity of life. It is man's interference with nature that creates the problem of good and evil. If man could be a witness to the functioning of nature within himself then would he be able to help Nature and work on with her. The *Gita* says that the wise know that the *Gunas* work among the *Gunas*—and so long as man can allow the *Gunas* to work among the *Gunas* so long is he giving to nature the freedom that it needs to express the fundamental quality of things. The sub-human entities give themselves up to Nature unreservedly, and so Nature looks after them and fashions out of their living exquisite expressions of beauty. Man, however, comes on the scene of creation with the mistaken notion of being a subduer of Nature. However, man's true role is to be a collaborator with Nature by anticipating the further move of Nature and by creating conditions where Nature could move speedily along its appointed way. To anticipate the movement of Nature and then to allow Nature to work in a free and unfettered manner along that path—this truly is the destiny of man. And this indeed is the non-attachment to which the *Gita* refers. To be a witness to one's actions is watch nature working freely without the slightest interference from man. To see *Gunas* working among the *Gunas*—this is true non-attachment, for, here man becomes the true witness to his own actions.

Dealing with the subject of Non-attachment, Sri Krishna introduces a concept which almost runs throughout the teaching of the *Gita*. He tells Arjuna:

> Surrendering all actions to Me, with thy thoughts resting on the Supreme Self, from hope and egoism freed, and of mental fever cured, engage in battle.

For non-attachment in action, the above verse lays down a condition which is 'freedom from hope and egoism'. It also says that one must be cured of 'mental fever'. Being cured of mental fever obviously means a condition of mind where it is absolutely calm and still—there is no agitation within it, for, all agitation would produce heat and fever. But this calmness of the mind, the state of being cured of mental fever, is possible only when there is freedom from hope and egoism. Surely it is hope which is the motive power behind the whole process of becoming. It is the desire to become something which brings into existence the element of hope. It is obviously a looking into the future. Now the one who looks into the future is the 'I'—the entity which seeks a continuity through the passage of time. Thus while egoism is the entity that looks into the future it is hope which is as it were the window through which a peep into the future is sought to be undertaken. Hope and egoism are thus a joint phenomenon—one cannot exist without the other. It is once again hope and egoism which prevent a man from engaging in action which is free from attachment.

But what indeed is the basis of man's hope? Why does he indulge in this act of looking into the future through the glasses of hope? It is quite obvious that hope is an attempt on the part of the ego to seek security. It is with hope that man tries to bridge the gulf between the known and the unknown—the known being the past and the unknown being the future. Man for ever seeks security. He shudders at the idea of insecurity. But can there be any security in the world of manifestation? Eternal flux is the very nature of manifestation—the *Gita* says: 'That which is born must inevitably die.' If that be the case, is not the so-called security of the manifested world something utterly insecure? The question is: Where does man's security lie if the world of manifestation is in a state of eternal flux? Sri Krishna shows to Arjuna this path of real security by telling him: 'Surrender all actions to Me.'

In the *Bhagavad Gita* we find again and again this word 'Me'. What does this word 'Me' mean? Was Sri Krishna asking Arjuna to give blind obedience to his Teacher? Did He indicate that the Guru was the only security for the disciple? Unless we clearly know what the word 'Me' implies, we cannot understand the full implication of the teaching of the *Gita* which almost centres round this word. For the understanding of this word, we must turn to Verse 24, of the Seventh Discourse of the *Gita* which says:

> Those devoid of reason think of Me, the Unmanifest, as having manifestation, knowing not My supreme nature, imperishable, most excellent.

The immutable centre of endless mobility—this is indeed the 'Me' of the *Bhagavad Gita*. Sri Krishna refers not to the Manifest but undeniably to the Unmanifest and the Unborn. The surrender about which the *Gita* speaks is the surrender to the Unmanifest, the Unborn, the Unknown—and not to the manifest and the known. A surrender to the known is always with a motive, with the element of hope projected into it. It is such a surrender to the known which has been the basis of spiritual exploitation throughout the ages. By introducing the word 'Me' the *Bhagavad Gita* speaks of the Unknown and the Unmanifest. Right Action, action without attachment, can emerge only out of such a surrender to the Unborn and the Unmanifest. In action without attachment, it is not the 'I' who is the actor—the actor is the Unmanifest Itself. Where the known is the channel through which the Unknown acts—this is the true nature of Non-attachment.

It is in the Unmanifest that the original nature of man resides. It is in manifestation, the field of becoming, that man develops an acquired nature. In course of time this acquired nature becomes so powerful that man forgets his own original nature. However, the original nature can never be obliterated; sooner or later it bursts forth breaking the encasement of acquired nature. That is why the *Gita* says: 'All beings follow their own nature—of what avail is restraint?' Here nature is to be understood not as habit but as the essential quality of men and things. The essential quality can never be altered. It is something unalterable in the midst of endless change. The man who acts through his acquired nature is given to attachment and aversion which the *Gita* declares as the 'obstructors of the path'. Attachment and repulsion, the pairs of opposites, are the expressions of the acquired nature. The man of non-attachment acts from his original nature and, therefore, his actions are natural and spontaneous, utterly devoid of motive. The *Gita* gives us a cardinal doctrine of true action in the following verse where it says :

> Better is one's own law though imperfectly carried out than the law of another carried out perfectly. Better is death in the fulfilment of one's own law, for to follow another's law is perilous.

The *Gita* obviously speaks here of the law of one's own being. This is one's own true quality, one's fundamental and original nature. The law of another refers to the nature that has been acquired. The acquired nature is the product of man's attachment and resistance. The acquired nature is always for self-preservation and self-propagation. It is rooted in the desire for security and continuity. The acquired nature is indeed the law of another, for, it has been built up out of the compulsions of outer circumstance. The *Gita* says: 'Better is death in the fulfilment of one's own law, for to follow another's law is perilous.'

The Becoming which does not emanate from the Law of one's own Being is frustrating and therefore perilous. That alone is right action which is spontaneous, emanating from one's original nature and therefore utterly motiveless.

Here Arjuna asks Sri Krishna very pertinent questions: 'What is it that induces man to stray from right action?' 'How is it that even though man knows that something is wrong yet moves in that direction?' 'Is there something which compels man to do wrong?' Sri Krishna replies that there is a compelling force which is made of *Kāma* and *Krodha,* of attachment and repulsion. He describes this as the 'all-consuming, all-polluting' fire generated by the element which is *Rajas* or the ceaseless activity of the mind. The never ceasing activity of the mind constitutes the inner compulsion of man. Just as fire is covered by smoke and a mirror by dust, so is the right understanding of man covered and enveloped by this ceaseless activity of the mind, moving between the points of attachment and repulsion. Mind's movement is caused by the desire to become something. It is this becoming which strays the man away from the path of Right Action. Senses and thought, both concrete as well as abstract, are fields in which the mind moves on, immersed in the process of becoming. Obviously man cannot come to right understanding unless he transcends the limitations of the mind. It is to this limiting factor of the mind that Sri Krishna refers in the following verse:

> The Sages say that senses are great; greater than the senses is the mind; greater than the mind is intelligence, but greater than the intelligence is He (the Supreme).

The *Gita* refers to Intelligence or *Buddhi* as greater than the mind. While mind gathers knowledge it is *Buddhi* which brings understanding. There are fundamentally two categories of knowledge—knowledge by ideation, and knowledge by being. Mind can know a thing only from outside and hence its knowledge is structural. But true understanding can come only when the duality of the observer and the observed vanishes—this is knowledge by being. Sri Krishna asks Arjuna to transcend the mind, as thus alone can he be free from the compulsions of becoming, the compulsions which lead him away from the path of Right Action. But how is Mind to be transcended? It is to this that the Gita turns, indicating as it does, in the subsequent chapters, the path that leads to illumined understanding where alone all doubts are dispelled and man stands firm even in the raging storms of life.

CHAPTER IV

THE SECRET OF RIGHT ACTION

MAN is indeed a meeting place of two streams—the ascending and the descending. Physical science studies the ascending stream in its structural aspect, while psychology is concerned with the functional expression of this ascending stream. But the descending stream is the subject-matter of religion, or more truly of mysticism. It is the descending stream which gives quality to human life. Without it life would be bereft of qualitative richness. In the ascending stream there is a variety—but this variety tends to be monotonous and mechanical without the living touch that comes only through a contact with the descending stream. It is because of this that forms begin to decay and there sets in a degeneration of man and a disintegration of society. At all such times it is the new impulse, the new descent, call it mysticism or what you will, which revitalizes both the individual and the society. In such revitalization, forms that are old and *effete* are destroyed, and the forms that show forth potentiality of future growth are nourished and protected. This concept of the Descent of a New Spirit is to be found in all the great religions of the world, but perhaps nowhere has there been such a clear indication of this concept as in Hinduism. The concept of Descent is known in Hinduism as *Avatara.* Sri Krishna refers to this concept of *Avatara* or Descent in very clear and unmistakable terms in the following two verses appearing in the *Bhagavad Gita :*

> Whenever there is decay of righteousness, O Bharata, and exaltation of unrighteousness, then I create myself—I incarnate myself in some form. For the protection of the good and the destruction of the wicked, for the sake of firmly establishing righteousness, I am born from age to age.

The *Avatara* is a new mystic impulse, a living touch with Reality, which comes when forms become degenerate and *effete*. The history of human civilization bears testimony to this Miracle of Descent in moments of man's trial and tribulation. A question may arise : How can the Unborn be incarnated, how can the Unmanifest become manifest? If it so becomes, does not the Unmanifest cease to be unmanifest, and by so doing does it not become subject to the process of birth and death? The Unmanifest for ever remains unborn. The *Avatara* or Incarnation does not transform the Unmanifest into the Manifest. What then is the secret of Incarnation? Perhaps the simile of the Sun may to a certain extent unravel its mystery. The Sun sends out millions of rays every moment, and yet the sending out of these rays does not cause any diminution of the Sun. The Sun remains at its place, a glorious symbol of effulgent light—and yet it illumines the dark corners of the far-off earth. It takes the whole Solar System with it, tending and nourishing the various forms of life existing in its far-flung empire. While it is engaged in this stupendous task, it has time enough to ripen a bunch of grapes in an obscure corner of the earth. The bunch of grapes probably feels that the Sun exists for itself and for no one else—such is the fullness of attention which the Sun bestows upon the bunch of grapes! Surely the Sun has not left its place and yet has given the warmth of its presence to the bunch of grapes waiting to be ripened. The mysterious phenomenon of *Avatara* or Incarnation is indeed of this nature. The Unmanifest does not become manifest and yet its presence is felt through the ray of light it sends out to vitalize and nourish the manifested universe. In so doing the Unmanifest suffers no diminution. Through the ray It sends out there is felt the fullness of Its presence, bringing life and vitality to the erstwhile dead and dying forms. The following verse of the *Gita* explains this phenomenon of the *Avatara* more clearly:

> Though I am unborn and Myself is imperishable, though I am the Lord of all creatures, yet establishing Myself in My own nature I am born through My own Power *(Maya)*.

Although the Unborn is established in Its own nature, It takes birth through the power of *Maya*. The power of *Maya* is indeed the power of projection. The Unborn does not leave its place but projects itself into manifestation. It is like the radiation of the Sun due to which millions of rays are projected to nourish and protect the units of life, seeking growth even in the remotest corner of the Solar System. The Sun's rays fall on the rich as well as the poor, on gardens and parks as also on slum areas—and yet the Sun is unaffected and untouched by the spot it touches through its rays.

Sri Krishna deals with this subject of *Avatara* or Incarnation to elucidate further the theme of Non-attachment in action. For He says:

> The fourfold order was created by Me according to division of qualities and functions; know Me to be the author of them, though actionless and changeless.

Sri Krishna says that even though He is the author of the fourfold order of social organization with the division and co-ordination of functions based on psychological aptitudes, He Himself is unaffected by this action. Sri Krishna points out to Arjuna that he who knows 'Me' as such, acting and yet actionless, is himself free from all bondage arising from action. To know that state in which there is action in the midst of actionlessness—this is indeed the true Ground for Right Action. Inaction is the Ground in which alone action without attachment can arise. But what is this Inaction; is it different from non-action; is it a negation of all action? Sri Krishna says:

> What is action, what inaction—even the wise are herein perplexed. Therefore I will declare to thee the action by knowing which thou shalt be freed from all evil.

Thrown in the turmoils of life, we are confused and perplexed as to what constitutes right action in a given situation. To act or not to act is very often the dilemma in which man finds himself. Many a time it is action which imparts a complexity to a situation, but, not infrequently, it also happens that non-action makes confusion worse confounded. What is man to do? Sri Krishna formulates this extremely difficult problem in a clear manner in the following verse :

> One must understand what action is, and likewise one must know what wrong action is. One must also understand what inaction is. Mysterious indeed is the path of action.

In discussing the whole subject of Right Action, Sri Krishna introduces three terms : *Karma* or Action, *Vikarma* or Wrong Action, and *Akarma* or Inaction. What is the significance of these three terms? Perhaps if we know what *Vikarma* or Wrong Action is, we would be able to understand both Action as well as Inaction. *Vikarma* is sometimes translated as unlawful action. Perhaps Reaction would be a more appropriate term to understand the significance of *Vikarma*. Most often, in response to the challenges and the impacts of life, we do not act, we only react. Be it remembered that action never binds, it is only the reaction that binds. Man is caught up in a chain of reactions. He mistakenly thinks that it is action which binds, and therefore seeks freedom from action. There can never be freedom from action, for, to live is to act. There can, however, be freedom from reaction. A reaction is caused by the stimulation of the centres of one's psychological memory. In all reactions the present is responded to in terms of the past. In other words, a reaction arises due to one's inability to see things as they are. It is only in the background of distorted perception that all reactions come into being. In reactions it is the actor, the entity seeking continuity, that operates, polluting action with the unholy touch of the 'I'. Therefore, unless all reactions drop away there is no possibility of Action or *Karma* coming into existence. Needless to say, the state where all reactions have dropped away is described by the *Bhagavad Gita* as Inaction or *Akarma*. True Action arises in the Ground of Inaction. The *Bhagavad Gita* says :

> He who seeth inaction in action, and action in inaction, he is wise among men, he remains integrated even while performing all action.

The above verse indicates the joint phenomenon of action and inaction. In such a phenomenon action emerges naturally and effortlessly from the Ground of Inaction. It is effortless action which alone is devoid of motive and therefore shows forth a quality of non-attachment. In a spontaneous action the whole being of man is present, and so, even while acting he is completely integrated. In such an action one sees the miracle of the totality present in the unit, of the whole inhabiting the part. The state of inaction is a condition of wholeness, of integration. Action or expression is, however, always partial. So the action which is torn away from the background of inaction shows forth disintegration or lack of cohesion. It consists of parts that are scattered like a jigsaw puzzle completely bereft of a wholeness of design. It is obvious that in such a scattered condition the part fails to occupy its rightful place. It is when the part does not occupy its rightful place that evil is perpetrated. And so the action that does not emerge out of the Ground of Inaction is evil; it contains elements of attachment and therefore is a cause of bondage.

What indeed is this state of inaction which gives wholeness to action? The *Gita* says :

> He whose undertakings are free from desire and ideation, whose actions are burned up by the fire of wisdom, him the wise have called a Sage.

Here the burning away of actions obviously means the burning away of *Vikarma* or reactions. When do reactions burn away? The *Gita* says that it is possible only when all undertakings 'are free from desire and ideation'. Mind consists of a composite process of *Kāma* or Desire and *Sankalpa* or Ideation. Thought-desire is indeed the basis of mind's movement. If one's undertakings are to be free from desire and ideation then surely it means that the mind has to be completely free from its movement. In other words, the state of inaction corresponds to the stillness of the mind. The flower of Wisdom can bloom only in a mind that is utterly silent, and it is only the wise that know what Right Action is. The *Bhagavad Gita* describes this man of non-attachment, the man who is free from desire and ideation, as one who is 'ever content, nowhere seeking refuge'. Such a man seeks no dependence on any one or on anything for his psychological existence. He needs no props or crutches for he is self-contained and therefore is self-reliant. True contentment comes only from self-reliance. But a man of contentment is not to be regarded as a passive, dull and self-complacent individual. Contentment is a condition where the movement *of* the mind has ceased, but for him a totally different movement has begun, and that is the movement *in* the mind. Therefore, the silent mind shows forth both stillness and dynamism at the same time. Speaking further about the man of non-attachment, the *Gita* says :

> Hoping for naught, his consciousness calm and controlled, having given up all possessions, performing actions by the body alone, he doth not commit sin.

The man of non-attachment has given up all possessions—not so much material possessions, as the possessions of the mind. The mind that clings to ideas and ideations is a greedy mind, it is caught up in hopes, and, therefore, in frustrations. In its actions there is an element of psychological fulfilment. The *Gita* says that the man of non-attachment performs 'actions by the body alone'—his mind ever calm and quiet. In the well-known Buddhist book, the *Voice of the Silence*, H. P. Blavatsky writes thus on this subject of action and inaction :

> Both action and inaction may find room in thee; thy body agitated, thy mind tranquil, thy Soul as limpid as a mountain lake.

To perform action by the body alone is to become a channel of the Universal Mind, the personal mind having become calm and quiet. The man of non-attachment is one who receives life as it comes and makes such receiving as the starting point for Right Action. Of such a man the *Gita* says :

> What God's Will Gives
> He takes, and is contented.
> Pain follows pleasure,
> He is not troubled:
> Gain follows loss,
> He is indifferent.
> Of whom should he be jealous?
> He acts, and is not bound by his action.

If freedom from reaction is a precondition for arriving at the state of inaction, the question is : How does one become free from reactions or *Vikarma*. It is quite obvious that any conscious effort of a positive nature to free oneself from reactions is itself a reaction. In this attempt one set of reactions is replaced by another set—may be of the opposite kind. A reaction cannot be eliminated by establishing another reaction. Freedom from reaction requires a process of negation or disassociation. Reactions drop away when the spiritual aspirant becomes aware of them. The approach of awareness is a negative approach. It is by constant negation, the declaring of 'not this, not that' (*neti, neti*), that one can come to the experience of spiritual plenitude. Inaction or *Akarma* is the highest state of negation. But in the moment of complete negation comes also the experience of Transcendental Fullness. In fact in the condition of inaction there is a paradox of Emptiness and Fullness. Thus man must engage himself in a process of ceaseless negation if he is to come to the state of Inaction from where alone Right Action can emerge. It is to this process of negation that the *Gita* refers when it talks of different kinds of sacrifices. A sacrifice is fundamentally a negating process. If to sacrifice is to be a witness, then surely it is possible only through an act of negation or disassociation. In speaking about sacrifices, the *Gita* deals with this process of negation or disassociation by referring to a variety of sacrificial offerings and sacrificial fires. All these sacrificial offerings, whether they are different senses, or in-breathing and out-breathing, whether they are material possessions or religious austerities—whatever be their nature, they indicate negation and disassociation. However, the greatest of all sacrifices is the sacrifice of Knowledge according to the teaching of the *Gita*. It is said :

> Better than the sacrifice of any objects is the sacrifice of knowledge.

What does the sacrifice of knowledge mean? Has even knowledge to be negated in order to come to Wisdom? It is true that knowledge is a barrier to understanding. The most cherished possession of the Mind is the knowledge which it has acquired. The accumulation of knowledge is indeed like a self-enclosing wall, shutting the individual away from all fresh and vital contacts with life itself. An existence behind such a self-enclosing wall is utterly dull and stagnant. An accumulation of knowledge makes the mind heavy with inertia, rendering it unpliable and therefore insensitive. How can the mind, burdened with knowledge, ever comprehend the new? The reactions to which human mind is attached are obviously rooted in knowledge. It is from the centres of knowledge that one reacts. Knowledge is the symbol of the past. How can the past which is dead understand Reality which is ever alive and vibrant? After all what is the content of mind's knowledge? Mind can know only the structure of things—it can never comprehend the significance of things. Thus mind's knowledge is hollow and superficial. It has been rightly said that 'he who knows and knows that he does not know is a Wise man'. To be aware of the hollowness of mind's knowledge and therefore to negate it, declaring it as *neti, neti,* is indeed the beginning of wisdom. It is only when knowledge is negated that one can stand on the threshold of the Unknown, and it is the Unknown that holds the key to the mystery of life and death as well. Man is freed from *Vikama* or Reactions only when knowledge itself is negated, for in this negation the very centre of reaction is dissolved, bringing the individual to the sublime state of Inaction from where alone right action can emanate. Therefore, very rightly the *Gita* says that 'better than the sacrifice of any objects is the sacrifice of knowledge'.

But does the sacrifice of knowledge mean making the mind dull and insensitive? The *Gita* says that man can come to Wisdom only by the sensitivity of his entire being—body, emotions and mind. It says :

> Learn that by humble reverence, by inquiry and by service can thou come to Wisdom.

Does not service demand a sensitivity of the body—an utter refinement of the senses? How can one whose senses are unrefined engage in acts of service? Once again is not humble reverence a state of emotional sensitivity? It is only when the heart is sensitive and refined that there flows from it spontaneous reverence—and reverence which is not spontaneous is no reverence at all. A cultivated reverence is rooted in fear and therefore is motivated by self-gratification. What is inquiry but a condition of an alert and sensitive mind? How can a dull mind inquire? A mind that inquires must be open—not open to something but in a state of openness—so that it is able to perceive truth from wherever it comes. The verse concerning reverence, inquiry and service, coming as it does immediately after the question of the sacrifice of knowledge, naturally induces one to conclude that the *Gita* speaks of a state of extraordinary sensitivity, a refinement of one's entire being, and not of a dull, emaciated and insensitive condition of human consciousness. It is quite obvious that the human mind can become sensitive only when it is free from the burden of accumulated knowledge. A mind that gathers knowledge but does not accumulate it is verily alert and sensitive. It is like a mirror which reflects every image that comes within its range but does not hold on to it. If the mirror were to retain the images that are cast upon it then it would cease to be a mirror. The sensitive mind acts like a mirror—it reflects but does not gather dust. The mind freed from the dust of knowledge is like a quiet lake into which is reflected the Wisdom of the Ages. The spiritual man is verily the man of wisdom—the man whose mind is emptied of all the contents of acquired knowledge and is therefore ready to receive the Fullness of Reality itself. It is the man of wisdom who acts, but never reacts. Sri Krishna asks Arjuna to be a citizen of this land of Wisdom, for He says :

> Even if thou art the most sinful of all the sinners, yet shalt thou cross over all sin by the raft of wisdom. As burning fire reduces fuel to ashes, O Arjuna, so doth the fire of wisdom reduce all bonds of action to ashes.

The *Gita* says: 'Verily there is no purifier in this world like Wisdom.' Wisdom may be described as the illumined state of human consciousness. It is a state of enlightenment which comes into existence because of the descent of a new ray of light from across the regions that lie beyond the frontiers of the mind. The *Gita* says that with the raft of wisdom one can cross over all sins. This implies that he who acts wisely is free from bondage. He is actionless even in the midst of action. Sri Krishna tells Arjuna that the man who is full of faith obtains wisdom.

But what indeed is faith? Surely faith is a surrender to the

Unknown. Faith has no relevance in terms of the known. With reference to the known one can speak of belief; it is the Unknown that demands faith. If the man of faith obtains wisdom then surely he is the one who has come face to face with the Unknown. Sri Krishna knows that the mind of Arjuna is beset with doubts. Now all doubts have their roots in fear. Among the many fears with which the path of man is strewn there is nothing so overpowering as the fear of losing the known. But unless the known is given up, the Unknown cannot be seen, and it is the Unknown which is the begetter of Faith. Sri Krishna tells Arjuna: 'Cut asunder all doubts with the sword of wisdom' so that he may become a Man inspired by Faith, ready to accept the challenge of life, whatever be its nature. If we could cut asunder all doubts then we too would become men filled with Faith. But the dispelling of doubts demands a coming to grips with the problem of fear. The spiritually integrated man of the *Gita* is a fearless person.

In the Seventeenth Discourse while describing the divine properties of the spiritual man, Sri Krishna gives first place to *Abhaya* or Fearlessness. How can a man who is beset with fears ever act with non-attachment? Fear has its basis in the pairs of opposites—and the mind caught up in the play of the opposites can never know what Right Action is. Freedom from fear is the path shown to us by the *Bhagavad Gita*. Sri Krishna leads the pilgrim, step by step, to the summit of Spiritual Experience as He unfolds, in Discourse after Discourse, the many facets of the *Yoga* of the *Bhagavad Gita*.

CHAPTER V

THE CO-EXISTENCE OF OPPOSITES

In the *Bhagavad Gita* one of the things that strikes a student is the bafflement of Arjuna on every point that Sri Krishna places before him. His mind is active and alert and so is full of doubts and questionings. Every now and then Arjuna asks Sri Krishna to tell him conclusively what he should do. The First Verse of the Fifth Discourse similarly contains this request of Arjuna, for he says:

> Renunciation of action, thou praiseth, O Krishna, and then also non-attachment in action. Of the two which one is the better? That tell me conclusively.

The constant question before Arjuna is : What to choose? Sri Krishna was a Great Teacher, and so He never tells Arjuna what to do with any air of finality. He never exercises His authority over Arjuna. In fact, he places before his friend and disciple, alternative after alternative and discusses the full implication of each alternative. He shows immense patience and is therefore ready to explore every point that Arjuna raises. Surely Sri Krishna could have laid down the law and told Arjuna 'conclusively' what he should do. Arjuna would have carried out the behest of his friend and Master. One of the unique features of the *Gita* is that it indicates the irrelevance of conclusions of thought and shows the importance of the process of thinking.

Most people demand conclusions and are satisfied when these are offered. In our entire dealing with life we prefer to move from the base of our conclusions. But conclusions by themselves have no value whatsoever. To act from conclusions is to adopt a static approach for the understanding of that which is intensely dynamic. Life has a dynamism which cannot be comprehended by the static approach based on conclusions. It is not the conclusion that matters; it is the process of thinking that is of fundamental importance. Without examining the process of thinking to adopt conclusions is utterly meaningless. Such conclusions are no better than mere words. They are the verbalizations of the mind. They are like artificial flowers, beautiful to look at but containing no fragrance. The fragrance, or the lack of it, depends upon the process of thinking by which those conclusions have been arrived at. It is true that in the *Gita*, Sri Krishna again and again declares what is true and what it false, but each time He examines the whole process of thinking by which truth or falsehood is postulated. This investigation into the process of thinking is certainly one of the unique features of the *Bhagavad Gita*.

The Fifth Discourse begins with Arjuna's query as to which is better : Renunciation of action or performance of action without attachment. These two approaches once again represent *Sānkhya* and *Yoga* respectively. *Sānkhya* with its emphasis on *Gnana* or Knowledge speaks of the renunciation of action while *Yoga* with its emphasis on *Karma* advocates the performance of action but with a spirit of non-attachment. The reply that Sri Krishna gives to Arjuna's inquiry is most significant, for He says :

> Action rightly renounced brings freedom;
> Action rightly performed brings freedom.

One may follow either of these paths. It has to be remembered that renunciation of action is not the shunning of action—it is not running away from action. When does a person run away from action? He does so when he is afraid of the implications of action. Truly speaking in the running away from action there is still an involvement in action, because to run away from action is to take shelter in the opposite which is non-action. There is a fundamental difference between non-action and inaction. Non-action is within the sphere of reactions as it constitutes a negative reaction. To react and to consciously refrain from reaction are two opposites—they are inseparable since one is contained in the other. Sri Krishna states in the above verse that rightly renounced action can be equated with rightly performed action. This is like two sides of a medallion. Where there is right renunciation, there is right performance also. Rightly does the *Gita* say :

> That place which is gained by *Sānkhya* is reached by *Yoga* also. He truly seeth who seeth that *Sānkhya* and *Yoga* are one.

There is no conflict between *Gnana Yoga* and *Karma Yoga*—nay, one is incomplete without the other. The relation between the two is that of Experience and Expression. *Gnana Yoga* is indeed the Right Perception of things—the seeing of things without any projection of the mind. Wisdom arises only when the projections of the mind drop away. All reactions are rooted in mind's projections. Thus *Gnana Yoga* is fundamentally concerned with the dissolution of the centres of reaction so that the true condition of Inaction may arise. This is indeed right renunciation—it is a state where all reactions have dropped away but action has not yet emerged. It is a condition where the performer of action has disappeared; and is this not the right background for the performance of pure action? The state of right renunciation exists not in Time but in the Timeless Moment. It can be experienced but cannot be described. All descriptions need the framework of Time and Space; how can that which is beyond Time and Space be put into this framework? The *Bhagavad Gita* says :

> He who acteth, placing all actions in the Eternal, abandoning attachment, is unaffected by sin as a lotus leaf which remains untouched by water.

To act and to place all actions in the Eternal—that is the secret of non-attachment. Action is obviously in the realm of Time, but the Eternal is where the Time is not. To bring the quality of Timelessness in Time—this truly is the secret of Right Action. One who can act thus is like a lotus leaf which remains in water and yet is untouched by it. The action of such an individual is complete, leaving no residue whatsoever. Emerson has very beautifully expressed this idea of complete action in the following lines:

> Teach me your mood, O patient stars :
> Who climb each night the ancient sky,
> Leaving on space, no shade, no scars,
> No trace of age, no fear to die.

In the entire discussion concerning non-attachment in action, the *Bhagavad Gita* has laid stress on the abandoning of the fruit of action. It is the fruit of action which for ever distracts a person even in the midst of action. It thus prevents a complete action from coming into existence—an action which on space 'leaves no shade, no scar, no trace of age'. It is the mind that introduces the element called the fruit in action. Needless to say, the mind is not interested so much in action as in the fruit that may come as a result of the performance of that action. Mind seeks its own fulfilment through the fruit which it anticipates. So the *Gita* speaks of 'mentally renouncing all actions'. True renunciation is indeed of the mind. When the mind is serene, the action that is performed is always complete, leaving no trace behind. It is the serenity of the mind that truly is the pre-condition for the performance of action which is free from all attachment. The *Gita* says:

> Even here on earth everything is overcome by those whose mind remains balanced. The Eternal is incorruptible and balanced; therefore they are established in the Eternal.

What is it that corrupts the human mind? Surely the mind that is subject to modifications is a corrupt mind. The mind that receives what life brings and yet is free from all modifications is indeed a balanced mind. The *Gita* says that such a mind is 'established in the Eternal', for the Eternal is incorruptible, it is perfectly balanced since nothing can cause modifications in it. Thus to place all actions in the Eternal is to perform them in a state of perfect balance, not allowing, through the anticipation of fruit, even the slightest modification. That which causes modification is the anticipation of joy or the fear of sorrow arising out of the performance of a particular action. Normally a person performs action in the hope that it will bring him happiness. But the happiness that comes is a decaying happiness—it wears out with the passage of time. Such happiness is born in time and therefore dies also in time. But when actions are placed in the Eternal then the happiness that comes is of an entirely different order. The *Gita* describes it as 'happiness exempt from decay'. The Eternal is beyond the decaying influences of time; it has no future to offer in which dreams of happiness can be realized. In the Eternal, the beginning and the end are the same, and so there is no question of realizing happiness as a result of performing certain action. If the beginning is devoid of happiness then there cannot be happiness at the end. The end is only an elaboration of that which is in the beginning. If there is no joy in the performance of action then there cannot be the reaping of joy as a result of such action. As the *Gita* says the happiness that depends upon the time process is a decaying happiness. Sri Krishna tells Arjuna:

> The delights that are contact-born, they are verily wombs of pain, for they have a beginning and an end, O Kaunteya—not in them may rejoice the wise.

The contact-born delights are those that are caused by modifications in consciousness. The delights that are dependent upon contacts are fleeting even as all contacts are fleeting. The contact-born delights always create cravings because the objects that produce contacts are continually moving away—they are a part of life which is for ever in a state of flux. The Lord Buddha said 'Impermanent are all component things'. Now all manifestation consists of component things—it is built up of compounds which are subject to dissolution and decay. Therefore, delights that are born out of contacts with manifested things are wombs of pain. But the delights that arise out of a communion with the Unmanifest are for ever exempt from decay. When one touches the Intangible in the tangible, when one sees the Infinite in the finite, when one is established in the Eternal even while living in time—then does one know happiness that is exempt from decay. The *Gita* says:

> He who is able to endure here on earth, ere he be liberated from the body, the force born of desire and anger, he is integrated, he is a happy man.

To be able to endure is to stand firm and unmoved even in the midst of impacts that come from the opposites of the mind.

The opposites of the mind are desire and anger, indulgence and denial, attachment and repulsion. When the mind stands unmoved between these two points then is man truly balanced and therefore supremely happy. If this happens, then, here and now, on this earth, man can know joy indescribable. His joy does not depend upon anything external, he is rooted within himself. It is the happiness with dependent origination which is undependable. It passes away leaving a craving behind. But the happiness that emerges from within is free of all contamination due to the process of time and is therefore incorruptible. It is only when the corruptible puts on incorruptibility, or when the mind is free of all contamination arising out of contacts with component things, that there comes to man happiness which is outside the reach of the decaying processes of Time.

But how can the corruptible put on incorruptibility? The incorruptible is the true and the original nature of man. But the corruptible is the acquired nature—the nature that is built up out of the modifications caused by external impacts. When the acquired nature is put aside then the mind that was corrupt is rendered incorruptible, reflecting the original nature of man. The *Gita* says:

> The Peace of the Eternal lies near to those who know themselves.

It is the man who knows himself who truly comes to Peace that passeth all understanding. It is only the man who knows himself, who can perform actions that are free from all attachments. To know oneself is to be liberated, for there can be no real liberation save from the thraldom of one's acquired nature. This liberation comes only when, according to the *Gita,* man has 'cast away desire, anger and fear'. Desire and Anger are the two opposites of the mind, but where does fear come in? Fear constitutes the motive behind the casting away of Desire and Anger. When renunciation is with a motive, it is no renunciation at all. In casting away desire or anger, there is very often the motive of fear—the fear of losing something or the fear of not gaining the desired object or objective. The losing of something which one cherishes evokes from man that element of resistance which is anger. Similarly the fear of not gaining the desired objective generates that element of craving which is called *Kāma* or Desire. Thus fear is the motivating factor behind the patterns of renunciation, be it the renouncing of desire or be it the casting away of anger. When even this fear is cast away then is man truly balanced, establishing himself in the Eternal and therefore experiencing Peace and Happiness.

The Fifth Discourse ends with the following significant verse:

> Having known Me, as the enjoyer of sacrifice and of austerity, mighty Ruler of all worlds, and Lover of all beings, he goeth to Peace.

As has been already pointed out earlier, the 'Me' in the *Bhagavad Gita* refers to the Unmanifest and the Unborn. Now the Unmanifest is the container of all opposites. In fact the opposites co-exist in the Unmanifest even as they exist one after the other in the Manifest. The 'Me' is here described both as the enjoyer of sacrifices and the enjoyer of austerity. The enjoyer of sacrifices is the recipient of offerings, and the enjoyer of austerities is the renouncer of everything. The Unmanifest is both the participant as well as the spectator, both the actor as well as the witness. As the above verse says, the Unmanifest, the 'Me', is both the Ruler of all worlds and at the same time the Lover of all beings. Here we see the co-existence of opposites—the co-existence of Justice and Compassion—the Ruler symbolizing Justice and the Lover showing Compassion.

How does man come to the experience of the Unmanifest, the Unborn, the Infinite and the Eternal? How can man come to the comprehension of the opposites existing together? In one of the *Upanishads*, the Sage Yāgnvalkya gives a very significant reply to the question which we have been discussing. He says:

> O King, when the Sun and the Moon are set, when the fire is gone out, and all those external sources of the world's light have failed, and the world itself is wrapped about in darkness, then alone does the light of the soul shine forth—the true, inextinguishable, and Eternal Light of Man.

His Light shineth even in our darkness. To see the light of Eternity shine even in the darkness of Time—this is what the *Gita* and the *Upanishads* have indicated throughout the centuries as the path that leads to happiness which is exempt from decay. It is only when the sources of external light fail that the Light of Eternity can be seen. It is only when the light of the world is negated that the Light of the Infinite is vouchsafed to man. In the Sixth Discourse, Sri Krishna takes Arjuna further in the understanding of this path of negation for it is in the complete negation of the manifest that the indescribable Beauty of the Unmanifest is revealed in all its glory to the sight of man.

CHAPTER VI

THE MIDDLE WAY

In the religious and philosophical literature of the world one comes across very often two streams of thought which may be described as the Occult and the Mystic. The Occult deals with the Invisible even as the Mystic deals with the Intangible. Occultism is concerned with the extension of consciousness. In Mysticism, however, the main concern is with the expansion of consciousness. The Occultist explores the sphere of continuity in the realms both physical as well as the super-physical. The Mystic is primarily interested in probing the depths of discontinuity, in communing with the Timeless, not by running away from the Time-process, but, by being aware of the point of intersection between the Time and the Timeless. Along the line of Occultism the effort is to exhaust the potentialities of thought. In the Mystic approach the emphasis is on transcending the processes of thought. One can see these two lines of thought represented in the *Bhagavad Gita* through *Sānkhya* and *Yoga*. *Sānkhya* moves along the path of knowledge where the thought-process is explored to its utmost limit. *Yoga* is concerned with Action, not with reaction nor with mere activity. Action in terms of *Yoga* arises from the Ground of Inaction, a negative state where all mentation has come to an end. Almost the very opening verse of the Sixth Discourse refers to this negative state; for it says,

> That which is called renunciation know thou that as *Yoga*, O Pandava, nor doth anyone become a *Yogi* with the formative will unrenounced.

According to the above verse, one who is a *Yogi* or Mystic has to be completely free from *Sankalpa* which may be translated as positive thought or the formative will. It is the positive thought which interprets the impacts and the challenges of life and in terms of that interpretation plans for the future. The positive thought is an effort of the mind to meet life's challenges with advance preparation. To meet life's challenges without prior preparation is for the human mind utterly unthinkable. But how can the intensely dynamic and ever-changing patterns of life be approached with a prior preparation? It is the function of the formative will or positive thought to build up, in advance, defences and fortifications to meet the challenges of life. But such an approach of the formative will or the positive thought is utterly static. By the time the formative will builds up its defences, life has moved on. Life's challenges are for ever new, changing from moment to moment. Man, by the instrument of positive thought, tries to meet the challenge of today with the preparations of yesterday. There is no wonder that all such preparations are ineffective. The *Yogi* or the Mystic is one who has left behind the positive thought and is established in absolute negativity. This state of negativity is indeed the Ground of Inaction. The negative mind is not a passive mind—it is extraordinarily sensitive. Inaction is not to be mistaken for non-action. Inaction is not away from activity. It arises in the midst of activity and transforms activity into action. This idea is made plain in the following verse of the *Gita*:

> For a sage who is seeking *Yoga*, activity is called the means; when he is enthroned in *Yoga*, serenity is called the means.

The sage seeking *Yoga* is one who is moving in the direction of inaction. The *Gita* says that such movement is possible only in the field of activity, not away from it. The abandonment of activity leads to non-action. He who makes activity the field and observes the movement of the actor in that field comes invariably to inaction. The *Gita* says that for the man of inaction, which is verily the condition of being enthroned in *Yoga*, it is serenity which is the field; and it is in the field of serenity that right action is born. The *Gita* speaks in no mistaken terms about the mark of one who is 'enthroned in *Yoga*', because it says that such a man has renounced completely the formative will—he is a man in whom all mentation has totally ceased. The cessation of all movement of the mind is thus the condition of being enthroned in *Yoga*.

One of the most revolutionary concepts enunciated in the *Gita* is that man is his own saviour. His salvation is not outside him, not in following an external authority. The *Gita* says: 'Let a man raise himself by himself.' What is meant by raising oneself by oneself? This is indeed the doctrine of self-transcendence. The self or the sense of 'I-ness' is verily the product of the mind. Self-transcendence is thus the process of transcending the mind. The *Gita* says that the mind can be transcended only with the help of the mind. The man of self-transcendence is ever calm and collected. He is *Kutastha* or absolutely unwavering. He is completely free from all subjective projections and is therefore able to look at things with an equanimity. Usually we project into the things of the external world our own psychological grades of significance. The whole of the manifested world is full of diversities. However, we do not merely see differences—we give to these differences certain distinctions. In other words, we give status to differences and varieties. The ascribing of status is undoubtedly an act of subjective projections. The *Gita* says that the man of Wisdom is one 'to whom a lump of earth, a stone, and gold are the same'. To see these as same does not mean that there are no differences in them.

To be aware of differences and yet not to give them distinctions is a true sign of wisdom. Each thing is distinct in its own place, and therefore to indulge in distinctive comparisons is to move away from right perception of things. It is by ascribing status to functions that we lose a sense of proportion. Each thing has its inherent status which is revealed not through a process of comparison but by seeing that thing in its own place. In comparison we destroy the inherent worth of a thing. The *Gita* says that the wise man is not given to this process of comparison. He does not see things through the glasses of his subjective projections. He does not project his own significance into things, and therefore is able to perceive the true significance of all things. By not comparing a lump of earth, a stone and gold, he sees the inherent significance of these objects.

The objects of the external world do not cause any modifications in the consciousness of one who is enthroned in *Yoga*. He is *Kutastha,* unmoved and changeless, in the midst of differences and is therefore able to bring a totality of perception in his relationship with things, persons and ideas. In such totality of perception the inherent worth of everything is made manifest to the perceiver. One can show forth right perspective in one's relationship only when one sees the inherent worth of all that constitutes one's environment. Needless to say, in right perspective there is a perfect sense of proportion.

The *Bhagavad Gita* indicates to us that the spiritual man is one who displays a perfect sense of proportion in all that he does. In fact, an action in which a sense of proportion is lost can never be pure and uncorrupt. It is always vitiated by a sense of attachment, as the loss of proportion is invariably caused by the pulls of indulgence and denial, of justifications and condemnations. Sri Krishna tells Arjuna that:

> Verily *Yoga* is not meant for him who eateth too much, nor who abstaineth to excess, nor who is too much addicted to sleep, nor even to wakefulness, O Arjuna.

To avoid excess in everything and thus to tread the Middle Path is the injunction given to him who desires to scale the heights of spiritual realization. But the question is: How is one to know what is an excess and what is not? How can one draw a line between too much and too little? Surely there can be no set standards laying down what constitutes excess and what does not. To avoid excess is to come to a point from which one can never err—however, it is a point which has position but no magnitude. The Middle Path is indeed a line which has length but no breadth. Such a line cannot be defined nor can it be described. To define is to set limits, and the very setting of limits gives a breadth to that line. To describe the Middle Path is to introduce a space between the opposites of indulgence and denial, and with the introduction of space these very opposites begin to function, bringing in their train modification and distortion. Elaborating the theme of avoiding excess, the *Gita* says:

> For the man who is temperate in food and recreation, who is restrained in his actions, whose sleep and waking are regulated there ensues for him *Yoga* which destroys all sorrow.

The destruction of sorrow by treading the Middle Path—this is what the *Gita* indicates to one who aspires to comprehend spiritual verities. But once again the Middle Path is not the striking of a compromise between the two excesses: it is not a little of indulgence and a little of denial that makes up the Middle Path. Indeed the Middle Path is not a compromise between two excesses—it is the transcending of excesses. It is that negative state of perfect balance which the *Gita* describes as 'the lamp that flickereth not in a windless place'. The flame is so delicately poised that even the slightest movement of the air produces a flicker in it. But when all movement of air has ceased, the flame is absolutely steady. Such steadiness is the characteristic of a *Yogi* or a Mystic. He is perfectly poised showing forth the beauty and grace of exquisite relaxation. Such a state of poise is free from the excesses of tension and dullness. That which emerges from the state of poise is always graceful. A man of non-attachment is always perfectly poised, never tense nor dull. In poise there is an element of impersonality—but it is an impersonality which gives birth to true intimacy. Intimate and yet impersonal—that is the mark of a *Yogi*. He is like a steady flame which while it gives warmth is for ever unmoved and unmodified.

It is this man of poise who knows what Supreme Delight is. Such delight is not of mind, for mind delights in excitement and superficial enjoyment. The Supreme Delight, however, is born of depth, of enormous depth, and therefore, has a quality of dynamic silence. The *Gita* says that this Supreme Delight can be understood only by Intelligence or *Buddhi*. The mind knows the delights that are sense-born; but the Supreme Delight comprehended by *Buddhi* is not born of the senses. It comes from a communion with the Intangible and the Unmanifest. The happiness born of the mind has always an element of craving in it—there is a desire for 'more' and 'still more' always present in it. And so the pleasures of the mind become the means for getting more pleasures. But the Supreme Delight about which the *Gita* speaks is of that quality 'which having obtained there is no greater gain beyond it'. The man who is established in this Supreme Delight is not 'shaken even by the heaviest sorrow'. The experience of Supreme Delight is an end in itself. There is no seeking of something else through the realization of it. Why do the joys of the mind not have this quality of completeness?

As has been pointed out earlier the movement of the mind is always between the two poles of duality. The mind invariably moves from one extreme to the other—it knows only the way of excess never of poise. It does not know what joy by itself is—its joy is only the opposite of sorrow. So in the joy of the mind there is always present the shadow of pain. Man is engaged in the frustrating battle of chasing away the shadow—but the shadow will ever cling to the substance so long as the substance is opaque. Instead of dealing with the shadow one must deal with the substance itself. Instead of struggling against pain one must examine the content of joy—for, it is the content of joy which casts its shadow—the shadow to which man has given the name of pain. It is from the opaqueness of the mind that the duality of joy and sorrow, of pleasure and pain, arises. The *Gita* gives here a very strange definition of *Yoga*, for it says:

> Let that be known by the name of *Yoga*, this dissociation from an association with pain.

The true *Yogi* is one who has dissociated himself from that which gives the association of pain. What is it that gives an association of pain? Surely it is the mind with its process of comparison and contrast. In comparison, the contrast is involved; and so the mind that compares always brings an association of pain. If we can see a thing as it is—not broken up by the process of comparison—then we shall be filled with joy from moment to moment. It is comparison and contrast which render the mind opaque, and the opaqueness of the mind is truly the generator of pain and sorrow. A dissociation from that which gives association with pain is brought about by a renewal of the mind. In such renewal the mind becomes transparent because of the casting aside of all its opaqueness. The opaque mind is filled with its own memories, with the residue of past experiences. In our day to day existence, it is the long shadows of memory which are for ever cast on our pathway rendering it dark and often dismal. The *Yogi* or the Mystic is never despondent because through the transparency of mind he finds his pathway always bright and illumined. Even in the darkness of the earth, he sees the light of heaven. He is able to declare that 'His Light shineth even in our darkness'. It is said of the Mystics that they 'sing of sunrise in the darkness of the night' and they 'see the vision of man's ascension in the tragedy of his crucifixion'. The mind that is transformed from its state of opaqueness to that of transparency is indeed an illumined mind. But what is really meant by a transformation from opaqueness to transparency? The *Gita* describes this condition as:

> Abandoning without reserve all desires born of positive or deterministic thinking.

The abandoning of positive thinking without any reserve—that is the injunction of the *Gita*. This means that the mind has to be emptied of all its content, because any content that clings to the mind will once again cast a shadow preventing the aspirant from seeing clearly what lies on the pathway of life. The *Gita* says 'with the mind abiding in Self', let not the aspirant think of anything. The cessation of all thought is indicated as the true condition of *Yoga*.

But how is one to come to this condition where all mentation has ceased?

The Sixth Discourse of the *Bhagavad Gita* is known as the *Yoga* of Self-subdual. It is needless to say that the subdual of the self is truly the subdual of the mind, since self is indeed the product of the mind. The mind in its effort to seek continuity gives birth to the entity known as self. To subdue the mind is therefore to subdue its entire process of continuity. The mind by its processes of thought strengthens the self or the 'I'. Self-subdual therefore indicates that state where all projections of the mind have ceased. But how is one to arrive at that state? The *Gita* says:

> As often as the wavering and unsteady mind runneth away, so often reining it in, let him bring it under the control of the Self.

The mind constantly wavers and is thus for ever unsteady. The wayward mind is obviously a divided mind, distracted hither and thither by the pulls of numerous vested interests.

The *Gita* says that every time the mind moves away, it should be brought back. The question is: Where should it be brought back? According to the *Gita,* it should be brought under the control of the Self. But the Self is the Unborn and the Unmanifest. The Self is the Great Unknown. What is really meant by the statement that the mind must be brought under the control of the Great Unknown? Surely when the mind is freed from the limiting factors of the Known, then does it come under the control of the Unknown. Freedom from the known is thus the path indicated by the *Gita* for the control of the mind. The mind that abides in the SELF is the mind that has surrendered itself to the Unknown. In such surrender there is perfect control for all movement of the mind has ceased. The Unknown or the Unmanifest is devoid of differentiation—in fact, differentiation appears only in manifestation. Obviously it is differentiation which distracts. Now the mind that has surrendered itself to the Unknown and the Unmanifest is free from distractions for it is no longer in the realm of differentiation. The *Gita* says:

> He who, established in unity, worshipeth Me, abiding in all beings, that Yogi liveth in Me, whatever be his mode of living.

He who has established a communion with the Unmanifest is able to see the One in the Many. He has come to a perception of Unity in the midst of Diversity. The relationship that subsists between Unity and Diversity is comparable to the relationship that exists between the Point and the Circle. All circles of the past, the present and the future, exist in the Point, not one after the other but all at once. And so he who can commune with the Point for him the future is now. The true security for man lies not in the manifest but only as he abides in the Unmanifest. The mind that is vulnerable to the impacts of the Unknown is utterly secure. The *Gita* says:

> He who seeth Me everywhere, and seeth everything in Me, I am never lost to him; nor is he lost to Me.

As has been previously stated in 'Me' in the *Bhagavad Gita* refers to the Unmanifest and the Unborn. He who sees the Unmanifest in the Manifest, and the Manifest in the Unmanifest

—he is truly secure. William Blake, the English poet, has given expression to this idea in the following lines of his:

> To see a world in a grain of sand,
> And heaven in a wild flower,
> Hold infinity in the palm of your hand,
> And eternity in an hour.

The man of such vision approaches life with perfect equanimity. To him all things are equal—which means, equally significant. He who sees the intrinsic significance of everything, for him there is nothing low and nothing high. Seeing the true significance of all things, he is full of reverence to all. The mind of such a man is freed from the limiting factors of comparison, because the Unmanifest is incomparable. The mind freed from comparison is perfectly poised as it experiences no pulls of distractions.

Having listened to this soul-stirring philosophy of Sri Krishna, Arjuna raises a fundamental question. He says:

> This *Yoga*, which Thou hast declared to be by equanimity, O Madhusudana, I see not a stable foundation for it, owing to restlessness. For the mind is verily restless, O Krishna, it is impetuous, strong and difficult to bend; I deem it as hard to curb as the wind itself.

The *Yoga* by equanimity—that is what the Sixth Discourse speaks about. Equanimity can come only when the mind is able to see the intrinsic worth of everything. But for this the mind must arrive at a state of perfect stillness. Arjuna, however, says that his mind is utterly restless. He says it is impetuous because of the violent movements that surge within it; obstinate because of heavy inertia; and strong because of the judgements and evaluations to which it is committed. How is such a restless mind to be brought to a condition of rest? Most of us would join with Arjuna in asking this question. What is the reply that Sri Krishna gives to this great problem of problems. He says:

> Without doubt, O mighty-armed, the mind is hard to curb and restless; but it may be curbed by constant practice and by dispassion, O Kaunteya.

Sri Krishna says that the mind can be controlled by practice and dispassion. But what indeed is a controlled mind? Surely it is not a mind that is tethered to something. A tethered mind is bound to be restless. A controlled mind is indeed a free mind—free to wander anywhere and everywhere, and yet, in spite of its wanderings, it is not held by anyone.

In Hindu Mythology there are stories about the performance of Horse-sacrifices by those Kings who aspired to become Paramount Rulers of the surrounding kingdoms. The tradition was that a well-trained horse belonging to the aspiring king would be left free to move about. If any feudal chief dared to capture it and tie it, then the would-be Paramount Ruler would declare a war against that Chief and defeat him. The King could enjoy the title of a Paramount Ruler only if he could defeat chief after chief who had dared to capture his horse. The condition for being a Paramount Ruler was that his horse should be able to move about freely without let or hindrance. In this Horse-sacrifice there is as it were a reflection of what is meant by the control of mind. Like the horse of the King, the mind of man must be able to move freely in the entire field of the senses called *Indriyagrāma* in the *Bhagavad Gita*. It is only the mind thus moving freely without being caught in any object, person, or idea which can be described truly as a controlled mind. The mind tethered to nothing, and nothing clinging to the mind—that is what a free and controlled mind is. A mind running away from sense-objects is surely not a controlled mind. The free mind is not free *from* something—it is just free. That which is free from something is most assuredly bound somewhere else. The question is : How to have such a controlled mind which can move about with complete freedom in the entire field of sense-objects without being caught anywhere?

Sri Krishna tells Arjuna that it is through Practice and Dispassion that one can control the mind. Now Practice and Dispassion are mutually contradictory—for practice demands participation, while dispassion indicates non-participation. Are these two mutually contradictory factors to co-exist, or have they to come one after the other?

If Practice and Dispassion are to come one after the other then surely that is what every one does. To go on with one's own avocations so long as one can be active and then to retire from the daily run of activities due to the inability of the physical body to engage in any work—this is what every one does. Yet most of us are caught in the whirlpool of the mind's restlessness all throughout our lives, during our period of activity and also during our period of non-activity. Obviously when Sri Krishna speaks of Practice and Dispassion as the instruments of mind-control, He does not suggest a time-lag between the two. The have to come not one after the other, but simultaneously, as a joint phenomenon. In other words, Practice and Dispassion must co-exist if one is to come to a perfect control of the mind. This idea of the co-existence of Practice and Dispassion is indicated in the Upanishadic story of the Two Birds. The story speaks of the two birds, seated on the same branch of a tree, but out of the two birds, one eats the fruit of that tree while the other watches in silence. To be a participant and yet at the same time a watcher—this is what the *Gita* suggests through the co-existence of Practice and Dispassion. Practice is possible only by being a participant in the daily activities aimed at sustenance or betterment, whether individual or collective. But Dispassion suggests a stepping out of activities; it indicates a condition of being a witness to what is happening.

Now when one participates in activities, what is it that participates? It is not merely the body, it is also the mind. In fact, the mind plays a very determining role in all that the man does. In practice or participation it is the mind that is in action. And so if Practice and Dispassion are to co-exist, it means that one must observe the mind in action. It is in the mirror of relationship, and there alone, that the mind can be observed. Sri Krishna tells Arjuna that if he seeks mind-control then the most effective way is to observe the mind in its process of action or relationship. The control of mind is not by resistance nor by indulgence, but by observation. To be a witness to the operations of one's own mind—this is the unique method which the *Gita* suggests for dealing with the restlessness of the mind.

In the Sixth Discourse where Sri Krishna speaks of the *Yoga* of Self-subdual, we are told that *Yoga* is attainable 'by properly directed energy'. Now the proper direction of energy is possible only when one observes that energy—whence does it come, whither does it go and how does it operate? The motive, the movement and the manner of mind's operations—it is these that need to be observed. It is this observation which will indicate to man the proper direction of his energy. The energy can be said to be properly directed only when it follows the path emanating from one's own original nature. *Svabhava* and *Svadharma*, Essence and Expression, these need to be understood. When one is engaged in *Svadharma* then one's energies are properly directed. But *Svadharma* is possible only when one is established in one's *Svabhava*. To know one's own original nature is therefore of fundamental importance in the attainment of *Yoga* where one's energies are properly directed. But the original nature of man had been overlaid with what the mind has accumulated in the course of its movement through time. Unless we observe what mind has accumulated, how it has brought about those accumulations, and what aim does its seek to accomplish through these accumulations, we cannot come to the understanding of our true nature. At present our energies are dissipated in protecting and safeguarding mind's accumulations. There takes place a constant depletion of energy whereas for spiritual living there must be a continuous release of more and more energy. Such release of energy is not possible if mind is tethered to something—the release is possible only when the mind is completely free. But for the freeing of the mind one needs to observe the whole process by which it gets entangled in limitations. To observe the conditioning processes of the mind is to begin the process of its release from this very conditioning itself.

It has to be remembered that the control of mind is not easy—it is one of the most difficult things to do. Arjuna is not oblivious of this fact. He asks Sri Krishna : 'what happens to a man who fails in spite of his best efforts.' The Master assures the disciple that it is not the success or the failure that matters—what matters is the right effort. Man can never come to ruin or destruction by engaging in right effort. But the right effort has concern not so much with manner as with motive. In the performance of motiveless action man ever goes to bliss and never to woe. It is the *Yogi* or the Mystic who alone knows what a motiveless action is. The *Bhagavad Gita* says :

> The *Yogi* is greater than the ascetic; he is greater than the man of knowledge; he is greater than the man of action—therefore do thou become a *Yogi*, O Arjuna.

The ascetic who performs austerities is inspired by a sense of devotion. Through self-denial the devotee aspires to please his deity. Sri Krishna says that the *Yogi* is greater than the man of devotion. He is greater than the man of knowledge. He is also greater than the man of action. What does this mean? It surely indicates that the *Yogi* is an integrated individual combining in him all the three—devotion, knowledge and action. In the completely harmonized individual that the *Yogi* is, there is a perfect blending of knowledge, devotion and action. The *Yoga* of Integration is the fundamental characteristic of the Mysticism of the *Bhagavad Gita*. One may say that it is the mysticism of *Karma* or action—action that is rooted in *Bhakti* or self-surrender; the surrender that emerges from *Gnana* or knowledge; the knowledge which gives an undistorted vision of reality, the perception of the Unmanitest..

In the Discourses that we have so far considered the *Gita* has dealt with the problems of action. The *Gita* now initiates us into the understanding of true knowledge, the attainment of which will enable us to probe the secrets and mysteries of that supreme self-surrender where the Will of the Individual is merged in the Will of the Cosmos.

CHAPTER VII

COMMUNION WITHOUT A CONTACT

There is a fundamental difference between Knowledge and Wisdom. Knowledge is arrived at as a result of the operational activities of the Mind. The acquiring of Knowledge is a gradual process. It is a collection of parts to which the Mind sometimes gives a framework of synthesis through the process of abstraction. The synthesis of the mind is the collecting together of similarities and thereby building up a synthetic product called the Universals. Knowledge being a product of the mind contains only structural data, it does not matter what the subject of mind's investigation is. Wisdom, however, is completely different. Wisdom is not arrived at through an extension of knowledge. Knowledge even when indefinitely extended still remains knowledge. Just as an extension of the lower dimension, however indefinite it may be, cannot bring into existence a higher dimension, similarly Knowledge can never become Wisdom. There is a qualitative difference between Knowledge and Wisdom—it cannot be bridged by any quantitative extension, however varied and long it may be. While knowledge is a process of gradual accumulation, Wisdom indicates sudden awakening. Wisdom is the perception of the Whole even as Knowledge is the seeing of the parts. The perception of the Whole is always sudden, not split up in time-succession. The totality can be seen in time-succession because it is brought about by putting the parts together. But the Whole is not the sum of the parts—it is immanent in the parts and yet transcends the parts. To perceive the Whole in the Part—this verily is Wisdom. As the *Bhagavad Gita* says : 'To see the inseparate in the separated' is indeed the true hallmark of Wisdom. The Inseparate is not a synthetic product manufactured by the mind—it is for ever present in the separated. The intimation of the Whole or the Unmanifest comes through that intangible *something* which imparts to the manifest the peculiar grace and beauty which are so elusive and yet so real. Knowledge gives to the human mind a conceit born of possessions; wisdom is for ever humble, for it possesses nothing. How can the intangible be possessed? It can be experienced, but it cannot be clung to. A communion without a contact—that alone is possible with reference to the Intangible. He who has such a communion knows the secret of life and the mystery of death. Sri Krishna tells Arjuna :

> I will declare to thee this wisdom in its completeness, which, having known, there is nothing more here needeth to be known.

When one comes to wisdom in its completeness then one comprehends the Wholeness of things. In the perception of the Whole one communes with the source from whence all created things emerge. This is indeed the vision of the Mystic. It is not the man of supernatural or occult powers that necessarily comes to this vision, for, communion is not to be found more easily on super-physical planes than on the physical. Sri Krishna draws attention to this fact when he tells Arjuna :

> Among thousands of men scarce one striveth for perfection; of the successful strivers, scarce one knoweth Me in essence.

It is true that very few in the world seek the path of perfection—the path that leads to the development of super-natural powers or *Siddhis*. But even though one may develop these powers, one may not perceive the Essence of things. What is needed is not 'more' powers but a sensitivity of perception. The man of sensitive perception can know here and now the hidden mystery of all things. This mystery resides in the manifest, and yet is not to be found by dissecting and analysing the structure of things. When in the tangible one is able to have the intimation of the intangible—then is revealed to one's sight the great mystery of life. In the Seventh Discourse, the *Gita* deals with the fascinating subject of the Tangible and the Intangible. In the following verse, Sri Krishna describes the whole field of the manifest. He says :

> Earth, water, fire, air, ether, mind, reason and egoism—such is the eightfold division of My Nature.

Here Sri Krishna obviously describes the whole range of manifestation. Earth, water, fire, air and ether constitute manifestation at the physical level, while Mind, Reason and Egoism refer to non-physical expressions of manifestation. Mind and Reason represent two aspects of the process of mentation—concrete and abstract; to put it differently, they indicate impulsive thinking and logical or mathematical thinking. Egoism is obviously the content of all thought—it is the process of continuity which is the basis of all thought. The eightfold manifestation referred to in the above verse is described by Sri Krishna as the 'division of My Nature.' Manifestation is thus the spectrum in which the white light of the Unmanifest is split up into its variegated colours. But the spectrum has a derived existence, and not an intrinsic one. It has a dependent origination. It lives, moves and has its being in that White Light which is imperceptible to the eyes. In other words, the Manifest derives its existence from the Unmanifest, and so while the former is partial the latter is the Whole. Sri Krishna tells Arjuna that the eightfold division of His Nature is something inferior, and so he asks him: 'Know My other Nature, the higher, the life-element, O mighty-armed, by which the universe is upheld.' Obviously the universe is not upheld by that which constitutes the manifest—the source of its sustenance lies in the Unmanifest. As has been stated above this Unmanifest reveals itself as the Intangible or the Elusive in the fields of manifestation. Through an awareness of the Intangible one establishes a communion with the Unmanifest and the Unborn. Sri Krishna says :

> I am the source of the forthgoing of the whole universe and likewise the place of its dissolving.

The source of all things is for ever the Unmanifest. One may dissect and analyse the manifest as much and as long as one likes, but this examination part by part will never bring us nearer to the comprehension of the Source. The process of mentation operates within the confines of the Manifest. It is only when the mentation ceases that the Unmanifest can be communed with. When all mentation ceases then is the mind rendered supremely sensitive. It is only the sensitive mind that perceives the Intangible. Sri Krishna refers to the Intangible in the following verses of the *Bhagavad Gita*:

> I the sapidity in waters, O Son of *Kunti*, I radiance in moon and sun, the Word of Power in all the Vedas, the sound in ether and the virility in men. Pure fragrance in earth and brilliance in fire am I; life in all beings am I, and austerity in ascetics. Know Me, O Partha, as the eternal seed of all beings.

The Eternal Seed of all beings—that is the description of the 'Me' in the *Bhagavad Gita*. The Seed is Eternal meaning thereby Timeless. Thus it is the Timeless which is the source of all that happens in Time. How can one understand the significance of the Time-movement unless one communes with the Source which is Timeless? The communion with this Source is possible only through an awareness of the Intangible. Are not the sapidity in water or the radiance in moon and sun or the fragrance in earth or the brilliance in fire, something intangible and elusive? One can be aware of these things but one cannot hold them in the palm of one's hand. And yet that which the mind and the body cannot hold is indeed the Source of all manifested things.

All that is manifested partakes of the three attributes—the *Tamas*, the *Rajas*, and the *Sattva* which are Inertia, Activity and Balance respectively. Sri Krishna says: '. . . these know from Me: not I in them, but they in Me.' In this sentence we are given a clear indication of what constitutes Immanence as well as Transcendence. Sri Krishna says that the attributes are 'in Me, but not I in them.' It is but evident that everything emanates from the Unmanifest or the Transcendental. Thus the Three Attributes are an emanation from the Unmanifest—they are the spectrum caused by the splitting up of the White Light. But while the attributes emanate from the Unmanifest, surely the Unmanifest cannot abide in the Manifest. The Unmanifest can and does contain the manifest, but how can the manifest contain the Unmanifest? In the manifest there may be and are the intimations of the Unmanifest—but how can the manifest provide an abiding place for the Unmanifest? And so while the

Reality is immanent, it is at the same time transcendent. The Formless cannot be caught in the Form, the Transcendent cannot be imprisoned in the Immanent. The Creator is more than His Creation; He is immanent in His creation only as the musician is immanent in his music. The music, however, beautiful it may be cannot contain the musician. While the music resides in the musician, the musician does not reside in his music. The musician for ever transcends his music. Sri Krishna says :

> All this world deluded by these natures made by the three qualities, knoweth not Me, above these, inexhaustible.

The Unmanifest is above the three qualities and the natures emanating from them. The Transcendental is inexhaustible even as the Sun is inexhaustible inspite of the millions of rays that emanate from it to illumine the dark and distant corners of the vast solar system. The manifest is only a symbol giving an intimation of the Unmanifest. He who regards the symbol as the substance is surely caught up in an illusion. Sri Krishna says, '...they who come to Me, they cross over this illusion.' It is only he who communes with the Unmanifest, he alone pierces through the illusion so that he no longer mistakes the symbol for the substance. He who knows the Manifest as the symbol of the Unmanifest, he truly is wise.

The search for Reality is indeed a state of deepening awareness—the awareness of the Intangible in the midst of the tangible. Sri Krishna says there are various categories of seekers—those in distress as well as those who crave for knowledge. There are also those whose search is motivated by more and more acquisitions, whether wealth or power or supernatural capacities. The *Gita* says that it is only the search by the wise that has a purity and innocence about it, and the wise are free from the burden of knowledge and therefore truly humble. Sri Krishna says while referring to these different categories of seekers that 'noble are all these, but I hold the wise as verily Myself.' Here Sri Krishna suggests that the wise are rooted in the awareness of the Unmanifest and the Unborn. He says :

> Nor am I of all discovered, enveloped in My creative Illusion. This deluded world knoweth Me not, the unborn, the imperishable.

It is only when the delusion created by the mind is rent asunder that there comes the true discovery of the Unborn and the Imperishable. The delusion about which the *Gita* speaks is indeed the product of mind's projections. The wise are free from delusion because they have transcended the movement of the mind which operates between the pairs of opposites. The *Gita* tells us :

> By the delusion of the pairs of opposites, sprung from attraction and repulsion, O Bharata, all beings walk this universe wholly deluded, O Parantapa. But those men of pure deeds, in whom sin has come to an end, they, freed from the delusive pairs of opposites, worship Me with absolute steadfastness.

The men of pure deeds are described by the *Gita* as those in whom sin has come to an end. What is meant by sin coming to an end? What after all is sin? An act which is exaggerated is obviously sinful. Such exaggeration comes when one loses a sense of proportion. To give to each object, event or idea its proper grade of significance is to come to a cessation of sin. But the seeing of a proper grade of significance demands a vision of the Whole. This vision of the Whole comes only to an individual whose mind is freed from the delusive pairs of opposites. The mind is caught in the delusion of dualities—it sees the one as opposed to the other. Thought itself is the product of opposites. Paul Roubiczek in his book *Thinking in Opposites* says that one of the basic characteristics of our way of thinking is that 'we are forced to think with the help of opposites.' Since opposites are invariably involved in the thought-process, right perception is possible only when all mentation comes to an end. In fact, the cessation of sin is identical with the cessation of the thought-process. In such cessation the vision of the Unborn and the Unmanifest is vouchsafed to the man of spiritual aspirations.

The Path of Knowledge has two components—the knowledge of the Manifest and the awareness of the Unmanifest. The knowledge of the Manifest has been indicated in the *Gita* under a threefold classification. It speaks of *Adhi-bhuta*, concerning the elements, of *Adhi-daiva*, concerning the gods, and *Adhi-yagna*, concerning the sacrifice. *Adhi-bhuta* clearly refers to physical manifestation even as *Adhi-daiva* indicates astral manifestation. *Yagna* or sacrifice presupposes certain aspirations which induce the sacrificer to perform sacrifices, and so *Adhi-Yagna* clearly points to a manifestation which is mental. He who is aware of himself as operating in this threefold realm of manifestation, he is harmonized in his consciousness and therefore comes to a state of communion with the Unmanifest. Towards the close of the Seventh Discourse these three new terms—*Adhi-bhuta*, *Adhi-daiva* and *Adhi-yagna*—have been introduced and so Sri Krishna gives a further clarification of these terms to Arjuna in the Eighth Discourse.

The Seventh Discourse is described as the *Yoga* of Discriminative Knowledge or as the *Yoga* of Knowledge and Wisdom. It makes a clear distinction between Knowledge and Wisdom—for it speaks both of knowing the Manifest and of comprehending the Unmanifest. If Knowledge is tuition from without, Wisdom is tuition from within. Sri Krishna prepares Arjuna for receiving tuition from within—but before he comes to this intuitive perception, his mind must be capable of seeing objectively all that happens in the world of manifestation. As we enter the *Bhagavad Gita* in its Eighth Discourse, we find Sri Krishna leading Arjuna to this objective perception of the entire course of Cosmic Evolution.

CHAPTER VIII

THE INVISIBLE AND THE INTANGIBLE

THE fundamental theme of the *Bhagavad Gita* is most assuredly the Manifest and the Unmanifest. From the very first question of Arjuna, after his throwing away the bow and the arrow in utter dejection, Sri Krishna refers to the necessity of clearly understanding the eternal flux of the Manifest and the imperishable nature of the Unmanifest. He deals with the problem of action in its relationship with the Unmanifest. He again and again points out that a communion with the Unborn and the Unmanifest is of supreme importance as without it right action is impossible. But the question is : What is this communion with the Unmanifest? It is to this that Sri Krishna turns as He speaks of Knowledge and Wisdom in the Seventh Discourse. The same theme is continued in the Eighth Discourse. Sri Krishna draws the attention of Arjuna to the fact that it is only by observing the movement of manifestation that one can truly comprehend the nature of the Unmanifest. It is in this connection that He introduces the terms : *Adhi-bhuta, Adhi-daiva* and *Adhi-yagna*, for, these cover the whole field of manifestation.

Arjuna seeks clarification on this question of manifestation, and it is with this question of Arjuna that the Eighth Discourse of the *Bhagavad Gita* opens. The question is :

> What is Brahman or the Absolute? What is the Self, and what is Action? O Purushottama, What is said to be the domain of the elements? What is called the domain of the goods?

To the above three terms, there is added one more in this

verse, and, it is *Adhi-Atman*. In replying to this question, Sri Krishna refers to the *Kshara* and the *Akshara*—the Perishable and the Imperishable respectively. In the *Gita*, a distinction is made regarding the *Brahman* and the *Purusha*. *Brahman* is the Absolute Godhead, without attributes, while the *Purusha* is God with attributes. This distinction is similar to what one finds in the Upanishads. Dr S. Radhakrishnan says in his *Bhagavad Gita* :

> The distinction between Godhead and God, the Absolute and the Personal God, Brahman and Isvara, is clearly enunciated in the *(Mandukya) Upanishad*. The personal God is Cosmic Lord, while *Brahman* is the Supra-cosmic Reality.

The *Bhagavad Gita* says that '*Brahman* or the Absolute is the indestructible.' IT is, as Dr Radhakrishnan says, 'the immutable self-existence on which all that lives, moves and has its being rests.' Thus *Brahman* is the Ground of the entire manifestation. The *Gita* further tells us that '*Svabhava* is known as *Adhyatma*' meaning thereby that 'the manifestation of *Brahman* as the individual soul is called the *Adhyatma*.' The SELF is the spirit in man and nature—the touch of the *Brahman* on the entire field of manifestation. Arjuna asked Sri Krishna three questions, viz. What is *Brahman*? What is Self? What is Action? We have seen what the *Gita* means by *Brahman* and what it means by the term Self. *Brahman* is the Absolute and the Immutable. The Self is the individual soul that emanates from the Ground of *Brahman*, partaking of the quality of *Brahman* Itself. Now Action is the very process of emanation—the 'emanation that causes birth of beings.' Dr Radhakrishnan says :

> The Immutable which is above all dualities of subject and object, becomes, from the cosmic end, the eternal subject, *adhyatma*, facing the eternal object which is mutable in nature, *prakriti*, the receptacle of all forms, while *karma* is the creative force, the principle of movement. . . . The subject-object interaction which is the central pattern of the cosmos, is the expression of *Brahman*, the Absolute Spirit which is above the distinctions of subject and object.

Brahman which is above all distinctions of subject and object brings subject and object into existence. The subject is the *Purusha* or *Isvara*, while the object is the *Prikriti*, the Primordial Matter. The relationship between the *Purusha* and the *Prikriti* is verily *Karma* or Action about which the *Gita* speaks in the third verse of the Eighth Discourse. The subject may be interpreted to mean both *Purusha* and *Jiva* or the Individual Soul, for, there is a fundamental principle of creation which says : As Above, so Below. If the subject is taken to mean *Jiva* or the Individual Soul, then its relationship with the objective environment must be described as Action. In other words, Action is the relationship between subject and object, both at the Universal as well as the Individual levels.

But Arjuna's question was not confined to seeking a clarification only of *Brahman*, Self and Action; he wanted to know as to what was meant by knowledge of elements and knowledge of the shining ones—in other words he wanted a clarification of *Adhi-bhuta* and *Adhi-daiva*. He also wished to understand as to what was meant by knowledge of sacrifice or *Adhi-Yagna*. To these three further questions, Sri Krishna replies as follows:

> Knowledge of Elements concerns the perishable nature, and knowledge of the Shining Ones concerns life-giving energy; knowledge of Sacrifice tells of Me, as wearing the body, O Best of Living Beings.

Matter, Force and Mentation—these three are mentioned in the above verse as belonging to the manifested universe. Elements are of a perishable nature—they constitute the matter of the universe. It is the Shining Ones that supply the force behind all material formations. The Shining Ones are of the astral region as the very word astral shows. Emotion is indeed the force behind all material happenings. Sacrifice, as was mentioned in the last chapter, indicates aspiration, and, as such constitutes the world of the mind. Sri Krishna says that Sacrifice 'tells of Me, as wearing the body.' Obviously the knowledge of Sacrifice is therefore the knowledge of the manifested world and not of the Unmanifest. Speaking about the subject of manifestation, Sri Krishna says :

> The worlds upto the world of Brahma (are of them that) come and go, O Arjuna, but he who cometh Unto Me, O Kaunteya, he knoweth birth no more.

The worlds upto the world of Brahma, which means even up to the subtlest of the worlds or planes, are subject to creation and dissolution. In other words they belong to the realm of manifestation. But Sri Krishna says that 'he who cometh unto Me,' for him there is no more birth and death, for, he has transcended the Time-process. The Unmanifest is not of Time and therefore is outside the purview of birth and death. Creation and Dissolution are within the realm of manifestation—the Unmanifest being unborn is ever deathless. The *Gita* says :

> From the Unmanifest all the Manifested stream forth at coming of day; at coming of night they dissolve, even in that called the Unmanifest.

The *Bhagavad Gita* speaks of two categories of the Unmanifest. That which is invisible to one's normal perception is regarded by man as Unmanifest. But there is another category of the Unmanifest which remains unmanifest even when one is able to penetrate the invisible realms. The one is Invisible and the other is Intangible. Or to put it differently, the Unmanifest as Invisible is the Subjective, while the Unmanifest as Intangible is the Transcendental. The Invisible seems unmanifest because of the limitation of one's perception. If the range of perception is extended then the invisible would appear as manifest before one's eyes. That which is invisible belongs to the subjective level of one's consciousness. But when the subjective is objectivized then that which was invisible enters the realm of one's visibility. The process of subjective becoming objective belongs to Time-succession. But that category of the Unmanifest which is Intangible does not need a time-process for its perception. It is not by an extension of sense-response that the Intangible can be experienced. A contact with the Invisible is possible by a scientific clairvoyance, but a communion with the Intangible requires intuitive clairvoyance. Making a distinction between the two categories of the Unmanifest, the *Gita* says :

> But beyond this Unmanifested, there is yet another Unmanifested Eternal Being who does not perish even when all existence perish.

> This Unmanifested is called the Imperishable. Him they speak of as the Supreme Status. Those who attain to Him return not. That is My supreme abode.

The *Gita* here speaks of the Unmanifested in Time and the Unmanifested which is Timeless or Eternal. The unmanifested in Time seems a contradiction in terms, for, time operates in the realm of manifestation; how can Time be posited with reference to the Unmanifested? Time is relative and as such its measurement depends upon one's scale of observation. Man's scales of observation are of different kinds—in fact, man grows in his scales of observation. This growth is a gradual process dependent upon the extension of one's perceptive. Powers spoken of in Occult sciences fulfil but one purpose, and that is to extend man's perceptive range. Clairvoyance and clair-audience, mental-telepathy and psychometry, pre-cognition and retro-cognition—all these are extensions in man's sensorial perception. Science, both physical and Occult, is concerned with cognizing that which is outside the range of sense-perception. In other words, it is concerned with the Unmanifest as Invisible —the Unmanifest which exists in the gradually unfolding Time-process. But the *Gita* speaks of the 'higher' Unmanifest which is the Eternal Unmanifest residing not in Time but in the Timeless Moment. This is the Supreme Abode of Reality. The *Gita* says :

> This is the Supreme Person, O Partha, in whom all existence abide and by whom all this is pervaded.

While all existence abides in this Supreme State of the Unmanifest, the latter is not dependent upon the former, for the *Gita* says, it 'does not perish even when all existence perisheth.' But how is one to commune with this Supreme Unmanifest which is beyond all the decaying processes of Time?

The *Gita* here indicates a path which is most remarkable and at the same time intensely startling. The *Gita* says that a man can come to such a communion only if he knows how to die. To know how to die is to come to the true understanding of the Unmanifest, for, death alone opens the door into the Unknown and the Unmanifest. He who can enter this doorway knows for himself the Mystery of the Unmanifest. The *Gita* tells us :

> ...he who casting off the body, goeth forth thinking upon Me only at the time of the end, he entereth into My being—of that there is no doubt.

There is a common belief among the Hindus that the last wish of man, before his death, determines the nature of his future. Thus according to this belief it is the last thought of man which has an important bearing on his future. Perhaps this may seem very strange, for, man may do whatever he likes during his life-time and start uttering the name of God on his death-bed so as to assure for himself a happy future. It is very often forgotten that the last thought of man will depend upon how he has lived his entire life. If his experiences have remained incomplete then his thoughts will doubtless centre round the completion of those experiences when he is lying on death-bed. The *Gita* tells us in clear terms that

> Whosoever at the end abandoneth the body, thinking upon any being, to that being only he goeth, O Kaunteya, being ever absorbed in the thought thereof.

It is the content of thought that matters, not merely its structure. One may repeat the name of God a hundred times, but it is where the mind abides that determines the future. Sri Krishna says : 'If only man could think upon Me at the time of death' then would he enter the state of Supreme Bliss. But the 'Me' cannot be thought about since it is beyond thought. The 'Me' which is the Unmanifest can never become a subject of mentation. Therefore, paradoxically, to think upon 'Me' is to come to a cessation of all thought. If at the moment of death, man could come to a state of complete cessation of thought, then would he know the blissful condition of the Unmanifest where alone the mystery of death and life can be unravelled. But the cessation of thought demands completion of experiences. It is incomplete experiences which perpetuate the thought-process. And the perpetuation of thought-process is indeed mind's circle of continuity. Death is most assuredly a moment of discontinuity. He who carries on the continuing process of thought does not know what death is even though he may be physically dead. Death is not a physical event : it is a psychological state of complete negation. Whenever man comes to this state, he knows what death is. In fact, even though alive, he enters the mansion of Death. He who dies from moment to moment, he is for ever ready for the physical event of death. Death has no sting for him nor has grave any fear. It is the man who dies from moment to moment who truly is deathless. The *Gita* tells us how to die so that we may enter the realm where birth and death have no sway. Sri Krishna says :

> Fire, light, day-time, bright fortnight, six months of the northern declension of the sun—then going forth, the men who know the Eternal go to the Eternal.

It needs to be remembered that 'how' to die depends upon 'when' to die. The *Gita* gives a fivefold condition suggesting 'when' man should die; and if he knows when to die, then surely he will know how to die. The *Gita* says: fire, light, day-time, bright fortnight and six months of the northern declension of the sun—these are the right moments to die. What does this mean? Is it suggested that just because a man dies during these moments he goes to the state of Supreme Bliss? Be it noted that the message of the *Gita* has to be interpreted in psychological and not physical terms. What then is the psychological significance of the above fivefold conditions? Man must die when the fire is lit and not extinguished. The fire being lit is a condition of alertness. One cannot enter the mansion of death in a state of passivity or indolence. The *Gita* says, man must die while there is the light of the sun. Now the light of the sun indicates a state of illumined mind—it is a state where the mind possesses a clarity of thinking. The day-time suggests a period of action so that the mind's alertness and clarity are maintained in the midst of activity. Sri Krishna says that the happy death must be in the bright fortnight. Now the bright fortnight represents the Moon in a condition of its increasing phases. The Moon signifies Love and the bright fortnight suggests that period when Love conquers everything.

The mind that has alertness and clarity in the midst of daily activities, the mind that is filled with abiding love—it is this which is an appropriate moment of death. But that is not all. The *Gita* says that the right moment of death is during the six months of the northern declension of the Sun. The Sun moving northwards—*uttarāyana*—is regarded as a very auspicious moment by the Hindus. The Sun moving northwards is a period when the sky is utterly cloudless—the whole sky discloses a vast openness of space. The alertness and clarity of mind and the feeling of abiding love are possible only when the consciousness is like the cloudless sky. It is the consiousness that has vast space which alone can contain impersonality and intimacy, clarity and Love at the same time. The consciousness that has vast space is utterly pure, for, there is nothing that clings to it. The right moment of death arrives only when the mind is absolutely free with no distraction of an incomplete experience of the past. A free mind is like a mirror which reflects but does not gather dust. The blowing away of dust from the surface of mind's mirror is indeed true psychological death. In that state of death the mind is no longer engaged in its activities of splitting up an experience into its diverse parts. At the moment of psychological death, the mind becomes a pure receptacle receiving the wholeness of life. The mind that receives the wholeness of life comprehends the mystery of the Unmanifest. The *Gita* says :

> He who constantly meditates on Me, thinking of none else, by him, who is an ever-harmonided *Yogi*, I am easily reached.

The Unmanifest can be comprehended only when the mind is capable of total attention—*Ananyachetāh*. In that totality of attention where the mind is freed of all distractions, there is vouchsafed to man a vision of the imperishable and the infinite.

CHAPTER IX

THE SUDDEN AWAKENING

In her priceless book entitled *The Voice of the Silence*, H. P. Blavatsky asks the spiritual neophyte to see that his mind has both breadth as well as depth. The broadening of the mind takes place as man establishes newer and newer contacts with his environment, physical, emotional and mental. The more such contacts an individual has, the more does he grow in breadth of vision. This represents the development of mind along the plane of quantity. But a mere quantitative growth is not enough—the mind must grow in quality also. This qualitative development comes as the mind grows in depth. The deepening of mind enables it to contact a new quality of living. This is what constitutes a renewal of the mind. For the broadening process what is required is the development of a scientific mind, but for the deepening of consciousness what is of fundamental importance is the bringing into existence of a religious mind. A mind that is broad but not deep is a superficial mind, similarly a mind that has depth but no breadth has a very limited capacity of transmitting its experiences to others. In the Ninth Discourse of the *Bhagavad Gita*, in the very opening verse, Sri Krishna tells Arjuna :

> To thee, who dost not cavil, verily shall I declare this profoundest Secret, metaphysical wisdom with physical science combined, which, having known, thou shalt be freed from evil.

The *Gita* speaks here of *Gnana* and *Vignana*, metaphysical understanding and scientific knowledge. Sri Krishna says that both these are necessary if one is to be freed from evil. To be free from evil is to know the appropriate grade of significance of everything concerning the manifested world. To be able to put each object and each event in its rightful place is to be released from evil. There is nothing good or evil *per se*. It is the mind with its projected grades of significance that brings the element of good and evil into existence. A thing that is torn from its natural context is indeed evil. The natural context is verily the Whole; and therefore when a thing is isolated from the background of the Whole it is then that it becomes evil. To know the right relationship of the Part and the Whole is to transcend the duality of Good and Evil. Now Science, both physical and super-physical, deals with the part even as Metaphysics, which includes religion and mysticism, is concerned with the Whole. Sri Krishna tells Arjuna that an understanding both along scientific as well as metaphysical lines is necessary if he is to free himself from evil. He says that the Sovereign Secret can be known only by 'direct experience.' This experience is not to be arrived at through the cogitations of the mind. The mind sees everything through its veil of interpretation. It never sees a thing directly, but always through the glass, darkly. The direct experience is possible only when the veil of mind's interpretation is rent asunder. But to remove mind's veil of interpretation is to render mind, mindless. It is indeed true that only when the mind becomes mindless that man can come to that direct experience where alone the Secret of Life is communicated to him. The Reality is for ever Formless and is therefore capable of incarnating in countless forms. But forms, however beautiful they may be, are only a partial expression of Reality. As has been expressed in Chinese philosophy, 'The Tao that can be expressed is not the Eternal Tao.' All forms emanate from the Formless, but they can never exhaust the Formless. The Formless, while it is immanent in forms, it at the same time transcends all forms. The *Gita* says :

> By Me, the Formless, all this world is pervaded; all beings have root in Me, I am not rooted in them.

Now the mind can comprehend only forms. Its knowledge consists only of forms. The understanding of the Formless is an intuitive experience—it comes to the mind, the mind cannot go to it. It is only when the movement of the mind ceases that there comes the direct, intuitive experience which unveils the mystery of the Formless. But the Formless is to be comprehended through the Forms. It is because of this that man must have both the Knowledge of the Form and the Awareness of the Formless. The one needs a scientific mind, while the other requires a religious mind. The one is cognized by the breadth of the mind, the other is understood through the depth of the mind. And the deepening of the mind is a process where the mind is emptied of all its contents. The depth of the mind indicates enormous space in it—and it is only the mind that has space that can have an intimation of the Formless. Sri Krishna says that while the formless is 'the support of all beings, it is not rooted in beings.' He tells Arjuna :

> As the mighty air, moving everywhere, ever abides in Space, know thou that in the same manner all existences abide in Me.

The Space is unaffected by the air that moves in it. In fact, even though suns and moons abide in Space, the Space remains absolutely untouched by them. The Space is the all-pervading, infinite and universal background in which all phenomena take place. Although there is an endless movement of form going on in Space, the Space is for ever stable and immutable. This simile indicates, that 'while God causes things to exist, He does not exist in them.' As Dr Radhakrishnan says : 'No finite process can ever finally and fully express the Absolute.' In the *Gita* one finds a beautiful inter-weaving of the two concepts of Immanence and Transcendence. The Creator is more than His creation—this is what the *Gita* indicates with remarkable clarity. Sri Krishna tells Arjuna :

> The foolish disregard Me, when clad in human semblance, ignorant of My supreme Nature, the great Lord of Beings.

Most human beings mistake the symbol for the substance, the image for that which is the Infinite. The mind of man is forever a worshipper of images, be they the images in stones or images in thought. The conceptual image is the most subtle, and therefore man very often mistakes the subtle image for the Reality itself. We cognize the outer appearance and miss the

Inner Reality. The images of the mind should be used to transcend the very image-making process. Sri Krishna says : 'Being and Non-Being am I, Arjuna.' How is one to see the Infinite in the Finite, the Eternal in the everlasting? To know this is to be firmly established on the Rock of Ages, remaining unmoved even in the midst of endless movement. But how is one to come to this state? The *Gita* says :

> To those who worship Me alone, thinking of no other, I bring full security, both in the attainment of what they have not, and in the maintenance of what they have.

True security comes to man only when he gives up all thought of security. Man's insecurity arises out of a two-fold consideration. He feels insecure because of the fear that what he has may be taken away from him. But he also feels insecure because he may not get what he desires to have. The material and the ideational insecurity—these two continually cause fear in the heart of man. Sri Krishna says men need have no worry about their material or spiritual progress—for He is prepared to grant them full security provided there is no place in their minds for any one except Myself. But as the 'Myself' is beyond all thought what Sri Krishna indicates by the above condition is the rendering of the mind completely free from all processes of mentation. The mind that has given up all thought of its security is the mind that is utterly free from all movement of duality. Through security the human mind seeks for ever its continuity. To give up all thought of security is to ask the mind to write its own death-warrant. The moment of mind's death is indeed the moment of the descent of the Divine Grace. Dr Radhakrishnan says in his *Bhagavad Gita*:

> If we cast ourselves entirely on the mercy of God, He bears all our cares and sorrows. We can depend upon his saving care and energizing grace.

The mind of man is always averse to accepting its own defeat. Even when it is defeated, it explains away the defeat by throwing the blame on some one or the other or on some event over which it had no control. Acceptance of defeat is most humiliating to the human mind. It is therefore utterly confident of its own powers which it regards as limitless. How can such a mind surrender itself to the Unknown? It moves confidently to organize its own security—but the walls of security constructed by it, with such toil and labour, collapse again and again. The waters of life dashing against these walls of security undermine their very foundations. All efforts of the mind to seek security are fruitless and frustrating. A surrender to the Unknown is the only security for man—and when he thus surrenders, the Unknown protects him and nourishes him, giving him that completest security which none but the Unknown can grant. Man must ever remain restless until he finds rest in Thee, so says a Christian hymn. There is no rest for man in the realms of the Known—he must abide in the Unknown, for there, and there alone, lies his true security.

Now the surrender to the Unknown brings us to that intensely fascinating subject of Devotion. Devotion has meaning only with reference to the Unknown, as devotion to the known is always with a motive. Loyalty and devotion are two different things. Loyalty is to the known—but devotion is and can be only to the Unknown. Devotion pre-supposes a sense of humility—not a mere humility of behaviour but a humility of being. Such humility comes only when the mind sees the futility of all its efforts. It comes only when the mind is aware of its limitations. A recognition of mind's limitation and an awareness of it are two different things. A recognition is mind's verbalization and therefore belongs to the same category as mind's knowledge. The mind may regard this as a part of its knowledge and so add to its storehouse of conceit and confidence. Thus a recognition of limitation does not bring in its train humility. It is only an awareness of limitation that makes the mind feel humble. When the mind recognizes its limitation, it at the same time tries to cover it up with achievements along some other lines. But an awareness of limitation results in accepting the situation as it is without any effort at condemnation or justification. It is only such a mind aware of its limitations that can know what a surrender to the Unknown is. The mind that so surrenders is a religious mind possessing an exquisite fragrance of devotion.

In true devotion the subject-object duality vanishes. In fact, here there is neither a devotee nor a deity but only devotion. In such devotion, the size or the nature of offering does not matter. The offering to the Unknown can be the smallest of things, and yet it will be acceptable to the Unknown provided both the devotee and the deity are absent in such an offering. In fact so long as the devotee is present, so long the deity also remains, for, the deity is the god created by the devotee in his own image—it is a projection of the devotee's mind and therefore the Known. The devotee worshipping a deity is indeed the mind making an offering to the known. And the offering to the known is always with a motive. Such offering has a pattern of surrender but without a content of surrender. In such acts of devotion the size of offering matters the most, for, the pattern must appear as demonstrative as possible.

But in that act of devotion where the devotee and the deity are absent, there the offering is to the Unknown. The mind having become aware of its limitations is for ever humble. It has nothing big to offer : it is content to offer whatever it has. It is not ashamed to offer even the smallest of offerings. The *Gita* says :

> Whoso shall offer Me in faith and love a leaf, a flower, a fruit, water poured forth, That offering I accept, lovingly made with pious will. Whate'er thou doest, Eating or sacrificing, giving gifts, Praying or fasting, let it all be done For Me, as Mine.

It needs courage to offer just a leaf, a flower, a fruit or water poured forth. The shallow and the superficial mind desires to make a great show in its devotion. In this show it is the devotee who all the time exhibits himself. The devotee knowing the nature of the known desires to offer that which, according to him, will please the unknown. But the Unknown has no attributes—how can one make a selection of what to offer and what not to offer? To offer what one has and what one is—this is all that is possible with reference to the Unknown. That is why Sri Krishna says whatever you offer is acceptable to me so long as the offering has been lovingly made with a pious will. A pious will is devoid of all motive. The offering of love is always with a pious will, for love demands no reward. Love is its own fulfilment—it does not seek fulfilment through something and from someone. Sri Krishna says that true devotion consists in living a life of offering made lovingly and with a pious will. For such a man of devotion there is no fear, nor does he seek security. He is utterly secure in his insecurity. When the seeker for security himself has vanished, how can there be a search for security? When the mind becomes mindless then all search for security ceases. In the adventures with the Unknown, how can there be even a thought of security? It is the man seeking security who is worried about the bonds of action. Such bonds do not exist for a man who has surrendered himself to the Unknown. Sri Krishna tells Arjuna : 'Thus shalt thou be free from the good and evil results which are bonds of action.' To be free from all results, whether good or evil, is truly to show a state of non-attachment. So long as the selective process of the mind continues, calling some results as good and others as bad, so long is man caught up in the pairs of opposites. To accept the results without naming them as good or bad—this is the real state of devotion. Only such a man can offer whatever he has and whatever he is to the Unknown. A communion with the Unknown has a power of bringing about a fundamental transformation in the human individual. The *Gita* says :

> Even if the most sinful worship Me with undivided heart, he too must be reckoned as righteous, for he hath rightly resolved.

According to the *Gita* it is the right resolution which entitles a man to be reckoned as righteous. What does right resolution mean? Right resolution is indeed identical with pious will. In the term 'pious will' one finds a co-existence of the positive and the negative character of the mind. Will denotes a positive effort : piety indicates a state of absolute negativity. What is it that renders a thing impure? Surely when something clings to an object, then the object becomes impure. Similarly when something clings to the mind then the mind is rendered impure. The mind which is free from attachment is truly pious, and the movement in such a mind can be described as pious will or right determination. The condition of absolute negativity comes only from moment to moment—it has no extension in time, because the moment negativity is extended in time, that very moment it becomes impure. This moment of negativity is so potent that it establishes its nucleus in the consciousness of man. This nucleus gathers strength and builds up its vital and vigorous organism. The *Gita* says that even the most sinful person should be regarded as righteous if he has rightly resolved. Even though the co-existence of the positive and the negative character of the mind may last for a split-second, it is a moment fraught with tremendous possibilities. He whose consciousness touches this point, even for a second, is a man of right resolution. In the bosom of his consciousness is formed a nucleus of spiritual living. It may take time for the nucleus to build strong and vital organism—nevertheless the process has begun. The spirit is born, the structure will come into existence because of the impelling force of the spirit. The *Gita* further says :

> Swiftly does he become an embodiment of righteousness and obtain lasting peace.

Even the most sinful becomes an embodiment of righteousness when he comes to the point of right resolution. The *Gita* says that the transformation is swift, for the new spirit that is born permeates the entire being of such a man transforming his behaviour patterns. A man is to be considered righteous not because of a particular pattern of behaviour. It is the content of behaviour that matters—and such pure content descends at the moment of right resolution—a condition where the mind though alert is in a state of absolute negativity. A keen perception without evaluation—that is the condition of mind at the moment of right resolution. The pure content swiftly builds its own structure. This is the miracle of spiritual living which is experienced by all, sinner as well as the saint, provided he comes to the state of Pious Will.

The Supreme secret which Sri Krishna promised to transmit to Arjuna is verily a secret. It cannot be handed over by one person to the other. It has to be discovered, and the discovery comes in the state of total surrender to the Unknown and the Unmanifest. It is to this subject of total surrender that the *Gita* turns as it develops further its Gospel of true Devotion.

CHAPTER X

THE SPLENDOUR OF SPLENDID THINGS

THE Tenth and the Eleventh Discourses of the *Bhagavad Gita* have a peculiar significance with reference to the whole message of Sri Krishna as conveyed to Arjuna. These two Discourses deal respectively with the Sovereignty and the Transfiguration of the Lord. They are described in the *Gita* as *Vibhuti Yoga* and *Viswa-darshana Yoga* respectively. The Tenth Discourse, giving a detailed description of the *Vibhutis* or the Glories of the Lord, speaks of the all-pervading nature of the Reality. The Reality is intangibly present everywhere. It is indeed the soul of all things. The living quality in all that is manifested is due to the imperceptible touch of the unmanifest. The *Gita* has all along laid emphasis on the unmanifest as the Supreme Reality, regarding the manifest as its expression only. To miss the significance of the *Avayakta* or the unmanifest is to overlook the very core of the teaching of the *Gita*. It is true that the manifest contains wonderful glories of the Lord—but these are only the garment of nature. The real Splendour and Majesty of the Unmanifest can never be revealed in the manifest, for the manifest is only a fraction of the Unmanifest. The last verse of the Tenth Discourse of the *Gita* makes this clear. It says :

> ...What need is there, O Arjuna, for such detailed knowledge by you? I support this entire universe pervading it with but a single fraction of Myself.

If the glories of the manifest are but 'a single fraction' of the unmanifest, what must be the Majesty of the Unmanifest itself? Rightly have the *Upanishads* said that from IT the speech and the mind return unable to hold it. How can the Mind hold THAT which for ever is formless? Sri Krishna never allows Arjuna to forget the character of His real nature which is Unborn and Unmanifest, for, in this Discourse, in the third verse, He once again tells his friend and disciple that,

> He who knows Me, the unborn, without beginning, also the mighty Lord of the worlds, he, among mortals is undeluded and freed from all sins.

He who knows Him as the unborn he truly is undeluded. The glories of the manifest emanate from the unmanifest. While Sri Krishna, at the request of Arjuna, narrates the glories of the Manifest, He at the same time tells Arjuna not to forget the background of the Unborn in which alone all manifestation is rooted. As Dr Radhakrishnan says : 'When we learn to look at things as derived from the One Transcendent Reality, we are delivered, from all groping and bewilderment.'

Manifestation by itself poses numerous questions for which no answer can be found in the manifest world. It is Unmanifest which contains answers to the problems which are raised through the movement of the manifested things. The *Bhagavad Gita* says :

> Understanding, knowledge, freedom from bewilderment, truth, self-control and calmness, pleasure and pain, existence and non-existence, fear and fearlessness, Non-violence, equal-mindedness, contentment, austerity, charity, fame and ill-fame are the different states of beings which proceed from Me alone.

Fear and Fearlessness, Fame and Ill-Fame—all proceed from the unborn and the unmanifest. How can fear and ill-fame belong to the unborn? If sin and evil also emanate from the Unmanifest then why should man get himself involved in fighting the evil? The Unmanifest is the essence of all things—it is the pure energy which vitalizes all forms. It is the same energy which runs through what is known as 'Good' and what is called 'Evil.' The electric current which runs through a refrigerator is not different from that which runs through an electric chair on which a murderer is electrocuted. All states of being, proceed from the Unmanifest. The Unmanifest is neither good nor evil—it is pure energy. The unborn is the essence of all things—it is this which forms the central theme of the Tenth Discourse. Arjuna asks Sri Krishna to tell him in detail about the glories of the unmanifest as pervading the manifest. Sri Krishna says :

> I, O Arjuna, am the self seated in the hearts of all creatures. I am the beginning, the middle and the very end of beings.

The self seated in the hearts of all creatures is indeed the soul of all things—the energy that vitalizes all creatures. The manifested universe has a dynamic quality in it, for, the vitalizing energy is present not merely at the time of creation—it is present in the beginning, in the middle and even at the end. There is no moment of Time when the Timeless is not present. It is to show that the Unmanifest is the essence of all things that Sri Krishna points to the best and the most eminent among the created things as representing Him, the Unborn. For example, He says that among the gods He is Vishnu, among the radiances He is the effulgent Sun, among the Vedas He is the Samaveda, among the senses He is the mind, among the utterances He is the single syllable '*Aum*', of offerings He is the offering of silent meditation and among the unmovable things He is the Himalaya. Sri Krishna selects here as it were the most representative things among the various categories of created objects as symbols of Himself. To say that among the unmovables He is the Himalaya is to show that He is the very essence of 'Unmovableness.' In what Sri Krishna says in this Discourse, one is reminded of Plato's Divine Ideas. Plato maintained that behind all chairs there is the Idea of Chairness which gives birth to all the chairs of the past, the present and the future. All manifested chairs approximate to the Idea of Chairness, and as evolution proceeds, this approximation draws nearer and nearer to this Idea. When Sri Krishna says that among the unmovables He is the Himalaya, what is indicated is that the Himalaya, as it were, represents the Idea of Unmovableness so that every unmovable thing in the world tries to approximate to the Idea symbolized by the Great Himalayas. It is interesting to note that Sri Krishna regards *Japa Yagna*, the sacrifice of silent repetitions, as the very essence of all sacrifices. Very often people consider *Japa Yagna* to be the easiest of all disciplines. This is because they have taken to repetition and overlooked the silence which is the essential part of that sacrifice. *Japa Yagna* does not consist in merely repeating certain Names. There is no doubt the element of repetition present in *Japa Yagna*—but it is a silent repetition. It is not the silence of voice that is so important as the silence of the mind. The repetition of names with a silent mind—this is the fundamental basis of *Japa Yagna*. Surely this is not easy—it is one of the most difficult things to do. It is the experience of most of us that in an act of repetition, the mind always wanders. Repetition becomes so mechanical that the mind follows its path of distraction. To be undistracted even in the midst of repetition is very hard and arduous. To repeat and yet not to allow repetition to become mechanical is something extremely difficult. And yet this is the very essence of *Japa Yagna*. It demands that repetition be carried on in the background of the silent mind—the mind in which there is no flicker of movement. The *Japa Yagna* demands a totality of attention in the midst of repetition.

It is possible to keep a totality of attention when one is confronted with something New—but in front of the old, mind always wanders. And in repetition one is dealing not with the new but with the old. *Yagna* is sacrifice, and to sacrifice is to be a witness to. Thus *Japa Yagna* really means to be a witness to one's patterns and motives of thought and action in the routine of every-day life. The routine of daily existence is a repetitive process—to see oneself in the midst of this routine as a witness is verily the essence of *Japa Yagna*. This is the most difficult thing, and, therefore, Sri Krishna says that among the sacrifices he is the 'sacrifice of silent repetitions'.

Sri Krishna says : 'Of purifiers I am the wind.' The description of wind as the purifier seems a little strange. One associates the process of purification with fire, not so much with wind. How is wind the purifier? Wind signifies movement. One notices that the very movement of the river purifies the stream. The river is ever pure because of the continuous movement of water. It is the stagnant water which stinks and is impure. Many streams fall into the river, each bringing its own character. They may be muddy or clear—the river carries all these and keeps itself pure by virtue of its movement. Thus it is movement which is the cause of purification. The silent mind is a pure mind. Such a mind is not to be mistaken for a stagnant mind. In the silent mind there is a movement—it is not a movement *of* the mind, but a movement *in* the mind. The mind that receives the current of life without any indulgence or resistance, is ever pure. In such a mind there is an uninterrupted flow of life. The mind does not seek to collect the waters of life—it allows the waters to flow on. It is this movement of life which indeed keeps the mind pure and uncorrupt. The wind as the symbol of movement is verily the purifier. In fact, movement is the very essence of purification.

Sri Krishna while describing His *Vibhutis* says : 'Of the sciences, I am the Science of the Self.' The Science of the Self is indeed the supreme science, for without it all sciences are bereft of meaning and significance. As Dr Radhakrishnan says: 'Without it, the departmental sciences become misleading.' The common view with regard to science is that it is an objective investigation into the nature of the universe and the man. In arriving at any objective view, two factors have to be kept in mind. One is the selectivity of the senses and the other is the selectivity of the mind. It is true that the limitation of sensorial mechanism prevents a scientist from coming to an objective perception of things. And so he is at all times engaged in breaking down this sensorial limitation. This he does by inventing delicate and sensitive instruments which are able to pick up vibrations which are beyond the capacity of sensorial mechanism. But while sensorial limitation can be broken down to a certain extent this by itself does not bring the scientist to a really objective view of life. The extension of sense-response, by means of instruments, may serve to a certain extent the purpose of objective perception so long as the scientist is dealing with material things. But when one enters the field of psychological phenomena, an extension of sense-response is hardly of any avail, because added to the sensorial limitation is the limitation of the human mind which interprets sense-reports. For a real objective perception, it is the breaking down of the limitation of mind which is of greater importance than the extension of sense-response. The sense-reports by themselves do not constitute man's knowledge. It has to be remembered that knowledge is arrived at only when mind interprets sense-reports. If its interpretation is faulty then the knowledge arrived at is also false. In other words, there can be no real objective view of life so long as the subjective factor of the mind projects its own shadow on the screen of perception. Therefore, the true science is that which deals with the subjective factor of the mind whereby its projections are completely eliminated. This is the Science of the Self and, therefore, Sri Krishna says that among the sciences 'I am the Science of the Self'.

Describing Himself in terms of His glories of manifestation Sri Krishna says: 'I the Supporter, whose face turns everywhere.' He who acts from the Ground of the Unmanifest is indeed a *Visvatomukhah*, because he has his face turned on every side. The face turned on every side is a condition of a perfectly open mind. The man of open mind sees all points of view, for, his face is turned on every side. He does not see different points of view one after the other—he sees them all at once. To see the different points of view all at once is to have a right perspective. It demands a mind which is extraordinarily alert. But its alertness is rooted in absolute negativity. Sri Krishna talks here of the highest state of the human mind, a man whose face is turned on every side is one whose mind is illumined by *Buddhi*.

Sri Krishna tells Arjuna that '. . . all devouring death am I and the origin of all to come.' The Unmanifest is indeed the 'all-devouring death' for it is the Great Unknown. Human mind is unable to probe its depths. It shudders at the spectacle of total destruction which it brings. But while death is the destroyer, it is also the builder of new forms. In fact, death and regeneration are the two sides of a medallion. They co-exist, for, the moment of death is also at the same time the moment of the renewal of life. That is why Sri Krishna says that I, the Unborn, am all-devouring death, and the origin of all to come. The shape of things to come lies concealed in the bosom of the Unmanifest.

In mentioning the *Vibhutis* or the glories, Sri Krishna gives a very peculiar description of Himself in the following verse :

> I am the gambling of the cheat, and the splendour of splendid things am I; I am victory; I am determination, and I am the goodness of the good.

To be the gambling of the cheat and also the goodness of the good seems utterly paradoxical. And yet the fullness of the Unmanifest, when expressed in forms, must needs use the language of paradox. In the vocabulary of the mind there is no word like 'co-existence.' The mind knows only sequence—it cannot visualize a condition where two things can occupy the same space at the same time. Between two things there must be an interval either of space or of time—so says the human mind. Space and time are the framework in which mind is able to function, since they give Name and Form to things perceived. How is perception possible when the framework of Time and Space is eliminated? The mind can function only within the limits of opposites. If the opposites co-exist then how can Name and Form be distinguished? Such a condition is utter chaos and nothingness to the mind. How can the Lord be 'the gambling of the cheat' and also 'the goodness of the good'. It has to be remembered that the Lord does not say that He is the cheat nor does he say that He is the good. He talks of the goodness in the good and the gambling in the cheat. The good is static; it is goodness that is dynamic. The good is exhaustible; it is goodness which is inexhaustible. The good is relative; it is goodness which is absolute. Goodness is the source of the good that existed in the past, that exists in the present and will come into existence in the future.

The Lord says: 'He is the goodness of the good.' This expression is akin to the Platonic *Archetypes*. The *Archetype* is like a Centre from which all circles emanate and to which all circles approximate. Goodness is that *Archetypal Idea* which is the source from which the 'good' of all ages, past, present and future, emerges. Just as there is a difference between Beauty and the Beautiful, similarly there is a distincition between Goodness and the Good. The Beautiful is only an approximation to Beauty. The Beautiful objects of the past, the present and the future cannot exhaust Beauty which is absolute and unchanging. An object is beautiful only to the extent to which it approximates to Beauty. The moment it moves away from the point of approximation that very moment it ceases to be beautiful.

The *Archetype* is the ray of the Unmanifest in the realm of manifestation. The Unmanifest never becomes manifest. It only sends out its ray even as the Sun sends its millions of rays to illumine its solar system. The *Archetype* represents the fundamental note which the Unmanifest strikes for the Song of the Manifest which will unfold itself in the process of Time. While the song will combine many notes as it develops, it will sound musical only to the extent to which these notes approximate themselves to the fundamental Note. The *Archetype* is not the Unmanifest—it is manifestation in the purest form because it contains the first touch of the Unmanifest. The *Vibhutis* of the Lord, about which the Tenth Discourse speaks, are indeed the *Archetypes* which through the passage of Time wul give birth to myriads of forms on planes, physical and super-physical.

While it is easy to understand the Lord being the Goodness of the Good, it is extremely difficult to regard Him as the 'gambling of the cheat'. How can the Lord be associated with any concept of gambling? We have to remember that the Lord does not say that He is the cheat—He tells Arjuna that He is the gambling of the cheat. The cheat or the deceitful is evidently an expert in the act of gambling. He is an adept in throwing dice, and because of this expertness he is able to bid stakes which are very high. The ordinary gambler plays with low stakes, but the cheat is characterized by high stakes which would take away the breath of an ordinary man. The bidding of high stakes demands extraordinary courage—it displays a capacity for taking enormous risks. When the Lord says that He is the gambling of the cheat, He evidently means He is that Supreme Courage which is the root of all risks and adventures that are seen in the life of human beings. Perhaps no one approximates to this *Archetypal* Gambling more truly than a Mystic who, in his communion with the Unborn and the Unmanifest, plays high stakes in the game of life. Surely no stakes are higher than those of the Mystic, for he stakes himself as he plays the game of life with utmost joy. To stake oneself is to surrender all that one has and one is. The Mystic is such a perfect 'gambler' that he never loses the game. Even though he bids high staking himself, his gain is enormous. He stakes the finite but receives in turn the Infinite. With supreme courage, he risks all, but through risking his very life, he reaches staggering heights of illumined living. The Lord is indeed the gambling of the cheat, for the Mystic and the devotee, who are nearest to Him, are those who can gamble away their lives, and, find themselves in possession of Life Eternal.

The Lord says to Arjuna that 'of secrets I am the silence'. Surely there is no greater secret than silence. The secrets that are conveyed through signs, gestures and words are no secrets at all. They are only knowledge communicated through the language of allegories and symbols. The utilization of a strange language does not transform knowledge into a secret. The veils of allegory and symbol do not indicate the existence of a secret. The secret does not require secrecy to guard it and protect it from the gaze of the profane. The esoteric is not one over which a veil of secrecy has been cast. The secret lies in the open for all to see—and yet only few see it. The secret of life is not to be found behind closed doors. The secret of nature does not need a wall to protect it. True secret is never communicated—not even through symbols and allegories. The secret has to be discovered, and the discovery comes in the moment of utter silence. The silence in which not only one's breathing can be heard—but even the slightest movement of thought—in such silence, and, there alone, can the secret be discovered. The Unborn is ever the Silent, and so it is the Unborn that holds in its bosom all the secrets of life and death.

To bring this description of *Vibhutis* to a close, Sri Krishna says that there is no end to 'My divine manifestations. What has been declared by Me is only illustrative of My infinite glory'. How can the centre be exhausted? Even though millions of circles are drawn, there are millions more that abide in the Centre. The Unmanifest is an inexhaustible Source of manifestation. How can the glories of the Unmanifest be described in full? One can say about the Unmanifest in the words of a Sanskrit poet that:

> I feel as if I have gazed upon the beauty of thy face from my birth, yet my eyes are hungry still.

If one could have the intimations of the Unmanifest while

gazing on the face of the Manifest, one would live in a condition of ecstasy, of everlasting joy. In communing with the Unmanifest, one communes with the Seed of all existence; and does not the seed contain the whole tree? To commune with the Being of all things is to comprehend the secret of Becoming, because the becoming is rooted in being. One can become only what one is. Sri Krishna says:

> ...whatsoever is the seed of all existence that am I, O Arjuna; nor is there anything, moving or unmoving, that can exist without Me.

Here Sri Krishna differentiates the 'Me' from existence—the 'Me' is the source of all existence, but itself remains Non-existent. It is Non-existence which is the creator of existence—it is from Nothing that all things emanate. One is reminded of the Upanishadic story where the father instructs the son in understanding the great Mystery of Life. He asks the son to bring the fruit of a nearby tree. When the son brings it, he asks him to break it and to tell him what it contains. The son shows the countless seeds that are contained in the fruit. The father asks the son to take one of those tiny seeds and break it. The son does as he was asked. The father asks the son as to what has he found inside the tiny seed. The son replies: 'Nothing.' And the father points out to the son that it is the Nothing which is the begetter of the Mighty Tree. Non-existence as the Ground of all existence: Nothing as the Source of all things—this is what the *Gita* indicates. The meaning of existence is to be found in Non-existence—the significance of all things lies in No-thing. *Brahman* is not existence. It is only when all existences, physical and super-physical, are negated that one can commune with it.

. If the *Vibhutis* of the Lord are the *Archetyes* then the question is: can one perceive them here and now, or has one to develop certain psychic powers to comprehend them? A glimpse of the *Archetype* can come to man here and now. For the *Archetype* is ever present in all manifest things. Its presence, however, can be seen by discovering the point of Approximation which is intangibly and imperceptibly present in all manifested things. There is a beauty that resides in all things.

But there is, however, one angle, and only one, with reference to each object and person from where alone this Beauty can be perceived. To discover this angle is to know the point of approximation. It is this which is the Intangible in the most tangible of things. The discovery of this angle demands a Poise—for it is in the graceful poise of the seer that the grace and beauty of the Lord's Glory can be perceived.

CHAPTER XI

THE PSYCHIC AND THE SPIRITUAL

THE ELEVENTH DISCOURSE has been aptly described as dealing with the Transfiguration of the Lord, for here the Lord reveals to Arjuna His Universal Form. While the Tenth Discourse speaks of Uniqueness that resides in every speck of matter, the Eleventh Discourse tells us of the Universality that extends from the physical to the super-physical realms. Uniqueness is the intangible in manifestation. The perception of the intangible requires a sensitivity of mind and heart. It does not demand the possession of super-physical powers. The intangible is here and now—one has not to go anywhere in search of it. The perception of the intangible is the way indicated by mystics of all ages and of all lands. But there is another category of perception which is represented by Occultism. This deals not with the Intangible but with the Invisible. In fact, perceptions are of three kinds: they are the Perceived, the Unperceivable, and the Unperceived. The Perceived are those that are cognized by the senses; the Unperceivable belong to extra-sensory realms, and the Unperceived are those that can be perceived, but we do not perceive them due to an insensitivity of mind and heart. The first category belongs to Commonsense perception; the second is covered by Science, physical as well as super-physical, and the third is the province of Mysticism. It has to be remembered that Occultism is the extension of scientific method into realms that are super-physical. It is concerned with the knowledge of the Invisible even as Mysticism is concerned with the perception of the Intangible. The perception of the Intangible needs a deepening of consciousness, whereas the knowledge of the Invisible requires an extension of consciousness.

In the Eleventh Discourse Sri Krishna reveals to Arjuna His

Invisible Forms. Arjuna says to the Lord:

> O Supreme Lord, it is even as Thou describest Thyself; O best of beings, I desire to see Thy divine form.

Arjuna wants to see the divine form of the Lord. In dealing with the subject of the *vibhutis*, we saw how they represent the intimations of the Formless in Form through the element of Intangibility. But Arjuna now wants to see the extensions of the Form or the Universality of the Lord's Form. As Dr Radhakrishnan says: 'Arjuna wishes to see the Universal Form—the visible embodiment of the Unseen Divine.' He has understood the Mystery of the Seen, he now wants to perceive the Majesty of the Unseen. The Eleventh Discourse verily deals with the Unseen, for Sri Krishna in reply to Arjuna's request says:

> Behold, O Partha, My forms, a hundred-fold, a thousand-fold, various in kind, divine, of various colours and shapes.

It is not with the *vibhutis* in Form but shapes, colours and extended varieties of Form with which the Eleventh Discourse is chiefly concerned. In the Tenth Discourse we saw how the One is revealed in the Many through that factor of intangibility which is so elusive and yet so real in all manifested things. Here in the Eleventh Discourse we are concerned not with the One in all, but all in the One. In order to see the One in all, one has to commune with the Timeless Moment, but to see all in One, it is the vast expanse of Time and Space that needs to be explored. The all in One is indeed an extension of the One in Time and Space, even as the One in all is the merging of the expanse of Time and Space in the pin-point of the Timeless and the Spaceless. For the cognizing of the Timeless Moment what is needed is the breaking down of the limitations of the mind, because it is the mind which is the creator of Time. But for exploring the vast expanse of Time and Space what is needed is the extension of the sensory perception into realms that are extra-sensory. It is because of this that Sri Krishna tells Arjuna:

> ...thou canst not behold Me with this human eye: I will bestow on thee the supernatural eye.

Divyam dadami te chakshuh—the bestowing of the supernatural eye, that is what Sri Krishna considers necessary if Arjuna is to see the Invisible and Unseen. The vision that is vouchsafed to Arjuna in the Eleventh Discourse is not a spiritual vision, it is verily a supernatural vision. In such super-physical manifestation one of the factors that is visible is the extension of physical characteristics. Describing this manifestation, Sanjaya says:

> Of many mouths and eyes, of many visions of marvel, of many divine ornaments, of many divine uplifted weapons. . . . If the light of a thousand suns were to blaze forth all at once in the sky, that might resemble the splendour of that exalted Being.

In the above verse we see an extension of the physical characteristics in such expressions as 'many mouths' and 'many eyes'. In the *Purusha-sukta, Purusha* is described as having 'thousand arms and thousand eyes'. When one deals with the phenomena of extension, one finds always a quantitative description. As has been stated above, Occultism is an extension of the scientific method into the super-physical realm. Science is always concerned with parts, because it splits up an event or an object into its constituent units in order to understand it. Needless to say, the scientific approach, whether physical or super-physical, is a structural approach. This is evident from the following verse where Sanjaya describes what Arjuna saw:

> There Pandava beheld the whole universe, divided into manifold parts, gathered together in one, in the body of the God of gods.

The universe of manifold parts, gathered together in one—this is what the scientist does at the physical level—the putting together in a synthesis the manifold parts dissected by analysis. The whole universe which Arjuna beheld was a totality made up of the different parts. The entire description of what Arjuna saw with his supernatural eyes bears testimony to the fact that Sri Krishna was displaying an Occult phenomenon for the instruction of His disciple. Arjuna says:

> With mouths, eyes, arms, breasts multitudinous,
> I see Thee everywhere, of endless forms.

What strikes Arjuna in this vision is the endless forms. And these forms differ from the physical at the quantitative level rather than at the qualitative. In the Science of the Invisible, which Occultism fundamentally is, the basis of study is the structure of the invisible planes and the organisms that inhabit them. In this study one has to employ the use of psychic powers as the invisible planes are outside the purview of sensorial perception. With the help of these powers a variety of occult phenomena can be understood. The psychic powers so used are of different categories such as clairvoyance and clairaudience, psychometry and mental telepathy, pre-cognition and retro-cognition. Now in the Eleventh Discourse which deals with occult phenomena, for the perception of which Arjuna has been endowed with supernatural eyes, there is an emphasis on one grade of these phenomena. This is Pre-cognition. We have to remember that the *Gita* has for its background the battle of Kurukshetra. In this battle, Arjuna has thrown away the arms and Sri Krishna is persuading him to fight. In the Eleventh Discourse Sri Krishna gives, as it were, the preview of what is going to happen so as to induce Arjuna to take up the arms and engage himself in battle. That there is a preview of things to happen is evidenced from the following verses of the *Gita* in which Arjuna relates what he sees. Arjuna says:

> The sons of Dhritarāshtra, and with them
> The multitude of all these kings of earth,
> Bhishma and Drona, Suta's (mighty) son,
> And all the noblest warriors of our hosts,
> Into Thy gaping mouths they hurrying rush,
> Tremendous-toothed and terrible to see;
> Some caught within the gaps between Thy teeth
> Are seen, their heads to powder crushed and ground.
> As river-floods impetuously rush,
> Hurling their waters into ocean's lap,
> So fling themselves into Thy flaming mouths,
> In haste, these mighty men, these lords of earth.
> As moths with quickened speed do headlong fly
> Into a flaming light, to fall destroyed,
> So also these, in haste precipitate,
> Enter within Thy mouths destroyed to fall.

One may wonder, what after all is this description about?

Why is the Cosmic Form of the Lord so fearsome? The Lord is evidently revealing a particular destructive phase which would gradually descend as a physical happening—the outcome of the Kurukshetra war. After all physical events have their background in the non-physical. Before anger bursts out at the physical level, there is an upsurge of anger at the emotional and mental levels. The physical is really the working out of what has taken place at the non-physical level. An event like the Kurukshetra war has naturally its counterpart in the non-physical. If one could see the happenings at the non-physical levels, one could predict the nature of physical events. Just as an agriculturist on seeing the movement of the clouds can predict as to whether there will or will not be rain, similarly, one who has super-physical perception can predict the nature of the coming events by watching mental and emotional clouds. Once again as the farmer cannot do anything about those clouds—he cannot prevent their gathering—similarly, the man of super-physical perception cannot stop the coming in of the mental and emotional clouds. He can predict what would happen at the physical level when those clouds have gathered. He can say how the mental and the emotional clouds would descend at the physical level. This is the whole process of pre-cognition which forms part of man's psychic perception. In the Eleventh Discourse Arjuna is enabled to have this perception because of the 'supernatural eyes' with which he has been endowed. He sees through his vision the happenings of the Kurukshetra war on the super-physical planes. It is a frightening vision because he sees Bhishma and Drona and other rulers rushing headlong into the jaws of death. Time is indeed a relative term. That which constitutes the future from the physical scale of observation may be present or even past from the super-physical scale of observation. Even at the physical level, scales of observation give an indication of the relativity of the time-process. Scientists tell us that there are stars in the firmament from where light takes hundreds of thousands of years to reach the earth. If we could imagine a star, not very distant, from where light may take 5000 years to reach the earth, then by transporting ourselves to that star, we would find the battle of Kurukshetra still being fought on the plains of North India. The event which is in the past from the scale of observation which the earth provides, appears to be in the present form the scale of observation which the above-mentioned star represents. If however we consider the scale of observation represented by a far distant star then from that observational angle, the battle of Kurukshetra would seem to be an event still lying in the wombs of the future. If a visitor from the earth could go to that star he would be able to establish himself as a prophet describing the events that have yet to come! Pre-cognition has fundamentally to do with scales of observation. Through psychic powers one is able to change one's scale of observation. Arjuna could not do this at will—but Sri Krishna enabled him to look at events from a different scale of observation. And what he describes in the Eleventh Discourse is indeed what he saw from this changed scale of observation. The fact of a changed scale of observation is evident from what Sri Krishna says to Arjuna in this Discourse. He says:

> Time am I, laying desolate the world,
> Made manifest on earth to slay mankind!
> Not one of all these warriors ranged for strife,
> Even without thee, will escape from death.
>
> Drona and Bhishma and Jayadratha,
> Karna, and all the other warriors here
> Are slain by me. Destroy them fearlessly.
> Fight, thou shalt crush thy rivals in the field.

Sri Krishna says that Bhishma, Drona, Jayadratha, Karna and others have already been slain by Him—and yet He asks Arjuna to slay them! If they have been slain, how can Arjuna slay them again? And if they have been slain why ask Arjuna to engage in battle? Sri Krishna here gives to Arjuna a vision from a different scale of observation. From that observational angle these various warriors have already been killed. What has happened at the super-physical level has to be worked out at the physical level. In the natural course of events this is bound to happen, and that is why Sri Krishna tells Arjuna that 'not one of all these warriors ranged for strife, even without thee, will escape from death'. In other words, the Lord tells Arjuna that even if he refrained from fight, the destruction of these warriors could not be prevented. And so Arjuna is asked to complete at the physical level what has already been completed at the super-physical level of existence. The Lord says:

> By Me they are already overcome, be thou the outward cause, O Arjuna.

Arjuna has only to become a *nimmitta* or the outer cause—he has to become a physical instrument of the super-physical force which was working itself out and reaching the physical level. But to be a *nimmitta* is not easy. When Arjuna is vouchsafed a super-physical vision of war and destruction, he is naturally filled with a sense of overwhelming fear. This sense of fear is bound to influence his physical action, for how can he get rid of fear at the physical level when mentally and emotionally he is seized by that fear? Human personality does not lend itself to compartmentalization—what affects one part of the personality affects all the other parts as well. That Arjuna was overtaken by fear is obvious from what he says after having had the Cosmic Vision of the Lord. He says:

> I have seen That which none hath seen before,
> My heart is glad, yet faileth me for fear.

Arjuna's heart fails out of fear—the fear generated by what he had seen. A spiritual vision can never be frightening—but a super-physical vision can be awful and fearsome specially when it represents mental and emotional ramifications of war, destruction and devastation. If we could know the super-physical counterpart of our angry behaviour, we would probably be afraid of ourselves! There is a time-lag between the happenings at the mental-emotional levels and those at the physical. Once the mental-emotional force is let loose it will work itself out at the physical. But in so working itself out the force loses much of its ferocity—that is why the ugliest physical behaviour pales into insignificance before the ugliness at the psychic level. It is good that we do not normally have psychic faculties as otherwise we would hate our fellow beings all the more because of what we are likely to see in the super-physical counterpart of their undesirable physical behaviour. The vision which Arjuna saw had such a shattering effect upon him that Sanjaya describes his condition to the blind King thus :

> Having heard these words of Kesava, Arjuna, the wearer of the diadem, with joined palms, quaking, spake again to Krishna, stammering with fear, and bending low.

Arjuna was stammering with fear because he was completely unnerved by what he saw. He was the force of destruction in all its fury. It is not that the occult vision is always so fearsome and destructive. Here in the present context the fearsomeness of the vision is due to the fact that the Lord is giving to His disciple a preview of the destruction. In other words, it is the theme of war with which Sri Krishna is concerned and that is why He gives to Arjuna a vision of destruction and devastation. Here the Cosmic Form has taken the shape of the Lord of Destruction. It is the Dance of Destruction that is revealed to Arjuna's gaze. There is no wonder then that he asks Sri Krishna to appear before him in His normal form. He says:

> Diademed, mace and discus in Thy hand,
> Again I fain would see Thee as before:
> Put on again Thy four-armed shape, O Lord,
> O thousand-armed: of forms innumerate.

Arjuna wants to see the usual form of the Lord—instead of the thousand-armed, he would rather see the Lord with four arms. He wanted to see the gentle form of the friend and not the awful form of the Mighty Lord. To the untrained eye the occult vision is shattering. It causes confusion because of the bewildering nature of the super-physical forms which are but the extensions of the physical. Arjuna's eye was utterly untrained to perceive such colossal forms. Realizing this Sri Krishna tells him :

> Be not bewildered, be thou not afraid
> Because thou hast beheld this awful Form:
> Cast fear away, and let thy heart rejoice;
> Behold again Mine own familiar shape.

The *Gita* says that the Lord consoled the 'terrified' Arjuna by again 'assuming a gentle form'. It is interesting to note that Arjuna had no feeling of fear while listening to the *vibhutis* of the Lord. In the *vibhutis*, his attention was drawn more to the intangible and the formless than to the form and shape of things. This is the characteristic of the mystic vision. In occultism, however, one deals with forms and structures, shapes and colours of things invisible. It has to be remembered that occultism is concerned with a shift in one's scale of observation. When one speaks of the occult view one refers to an act of observation from a different angle. A change in the scale of observation is a change of degree, not of kind. The angle of observation may be differently inclined—but a difference in angle is only a difference of degree. In any scale of observation there is the duality of the observer and observed. The observer may change his position—nevertheless, the duality of the perceiver and the perceived is maintained. In a mystic vision, however, this very duality of the observer and the observed completely vanishes. The Mystery of the Intangible is revealed only in the moment of a complete fusion of the observer and the observed. The Majesty of the Invisible, however, is seen by shifting the scale of observation. The Tenth and the Eleventh Discourses of the *Bhagavad Gita* deal with the Mystic and the Occult Visions respectively—one speaks of the Intangible through the various *vibhutis,* the other describes the Invisible through 'forms innumerate.'

When Sri Krishna assumes His familiar form, Arjuna declares with joy and relief :

> Beholding again Thy gentle human Form, O Janardana, I am now collected, and am restored to my own nature.

As stated above in a spiritual vision there is always a calmness and a collectedness. The very vision produces this for there is a quiet gentleness that flows through everything spiritual. In spirituality there is no outer demonstration, nor an emphasis on form. What Arjuna saw in the Cosmic Vision was a majesty of forms. It was thus a psychic or super-physical vision, and not spiritual.

Sri Krishna tells Arjuna at the end of the Discourse that :

> In the form in which thou hast seen Me now, I cannot be seen either by the Vedas or by austerities or by gifts or by sacrifices.

It has to be noticed that when the Cosmic Vision was revealed to Arjuna, he saw it and yet could not see it! He was too frightened to see it, much less to understand its significance. It is true that one can develop psychic powers by the study and practice of Vedas, or by austerities or by sacrifices. The development of psychic powers would give an added perceptive faculty—but that is not enough. To see something is not merely to perceive it, but to observe it. How can there be observation when one is overpowered with a sense of fear? And fear there is bound to be when the development of psychic faculties has not taken place in the right background. This background is not given either by the Vedas or by austerities or by sacrifices. Such a background is given by a mystic experience. Occultism without a background of mysticism is very often fraught with dangers. Occultism reveals the patterns of construction and destruction. The patterns by themselves make no meaning; they are devoid of significance. It is the Purpose which gives meaning to Patterns. And the Purpose is comprehended in that moment where the observer is merged in the observed—where the perceiver has become the perceived. Call that moment by whatever name you like—some know it as mysticism, others call it devotion. It is with this note of mysticism that this Eleventh Discourse dealing with occultism ends. The last but one verse in this Chapter says :

> . . . by unswerving devotion to Me, O Arjuna, I can be thus known, truly seen and entered into, O Parantapa.

But what is Devotion? It is this which forms the subject-matter of the Twelfth Discourse, for, it speaks of the Yoga of Devotion.

CHAPTER XII

THE ONE WITHOUT A HOME

IN THE RELIGIOUS practices both in the East as well as in the West there is a distinct place given to Bhakti or Devotion. It is most interesting to see how Sri Sankaracharya, a great intellectual genius, who touched such heights of philosophical thinking as has not been conceived of by philosophers in Western or Eastern lands, found it necessary to express his deepest experiences in hymns that are surcharged with a devotional spirit of the profoundest nature. He scaled the Everest of Knowledge but stood there speechless with the complete surrender of a devotee. Sri Sankaracharya says in his Hymn to Hari as follows :

> Him, the resplendent Lord, who is speedily realizable even in this world by those who strive to seek Him by means of faith, devotion, meditation, self-control and other expedients, but Who is hard to realize, even through hundreds of lives for those who are devoid of these expedients—that Hari, the destroyer of the darkness of the world, I praise.

This great teacher affirms that Reality can be found by Devotion and Faith, and not by other means. Yet the philosopher-mystic of India, Sri Sankaracharya, upheld with relentless logic the supremacy of Wisdom. For him *Gnana Yoga* was supreme as is evidenced from his commentary on the *Bhagavad Gita* and other scriptures. The question is : If *Gnana Yoga* is supreme, why has he indicated *Bhakti* or Devotion as the most potent instrument for spiritual realization? The question is: What after all is Devotion? Sometimes it is said that Devotion is the shortest, and the easiest path to Reality.

It has to be realized that Knowledge, Devotion and Action are not three distinct and separate paths having no relationship with each other. On the contrary, they together make the Whole. It does not matter which is man's starting point—he may start with knowledge or with devotion or with action, but he must encompass them all ere he becomes a *Yukta* or an Integrated Individual. It is not the words that matter—it is the content of the word which is of supreme significance. For example, one may start with *Bhakti* or Devotion but devotion in its initial stages will have mental images as its object of worship. The actual image may be in stone but the mind of the devotee clothes it with the attributes woven by his thought-emotion process. There is no doubt that in the preliminary stages the Deity is created by the Devotee in his own image. He projects into the image of his God all his likes and dislikes. The various cults of *Bhakti* that developed in India roundabout the Vaishnavite thought had one subject for their devotions and that was the physical form of Sri Krishna. In this worship the physical form was not regarded as a symbol, but as the reality itself. The symbol was mistaken for the Substance and from that confusion arose many forms of worship that were undesirable. These devotees projected into Sri Krishna all their likes and dislikes. This is the initial stage of devotion where the devotee fills the image with the material his mind has gathered—it does not matter what the nature of this image is : it may be of stone or of word or of concepts: In this stage of devotion there stands between the Devotee and the Deity a screen of mind's projections.

This is the conceptual stage of devotion and may be described as knowledge in devotion. True devotion comes only when this stage is transcended so that the devotee stands not in front of the Known but the Great Unknown. It is only when the devotee is face to face with the Unknown that a complete surrender comes into existence in his life, naturally and spontaneously. But to face the Unknown the mind must be divested of the known. This happens on the Path of Devotion when the image of the Deity is emptied of all the conceptual and emotional content that the devotee has put into it. Thus the devotee too must tread the path of knowledge before he can come to the experience of Pure Devotion.

There are many in the world to whom the appeal is not of Knowledge nor of Devotion, but of Action. It is action that brings out the best in them. But even the man of action must tread first the path of knowledge. What is this factor of knowledge that the man of action must understand? Along the path of action, long before action arises, it is the actor that struts about enjoying the display of himself. Needless to say, the presence of the Actor corrupts all actions, however noble they may seem in their patterns. The motive of action is the actor—and the action can be pure only when all motive drop away. In other words, it is only when the actor disappears that true action comes into existence. In order that the actor may disappear, one must know how the actor projects himself, perceptibly and imperceptibly, in all forms and patterns of action. To the man of action this indeed is the path of knowledge. A dedicated or a consecrated action is that in which the action is performed not by the actor—it is an action in which 'something mysterious' acts through the actor. The actor is only a *nimmitta*, an instrument. He is like a well-tuned instrument capable of responding to the gentlest touch of the Master. The instrument must surrender itself to the Master-Musician if it is to serve as an instrument at all. But when can it so surrender? Only when it is freed from its own notes and therefore is ready to play any note that the Master may strike. This freedom from one's own notes is similar to divesting the image of all the contents which the devotee has put into it. Thus for the devotee as well as for the man of action, the treading of the path of knowledge is a prime necessity as it is for the man of knowledge to come to the ecstacy of devotion so as to transform his knowledge into wisdom and thereby show forth non-attachment in action. From knowledge to devotion and then from devotion to action are the ascending and the descending streams of man's spiritual life. Knowledge, Devotion and Action—these three constitute the wholeness of spiritual life. In the *Gita*, Sri Krishna after dealing with Action and Knowledge comes to Devotion as He unfolds His teaching in the Twelfth Discourse.

The first question that Arjuna asks of his Master is: 'Which is greater—worship of Thee or the worship of the Imperishable and the Unmanifested?' Throughout the pages of this book we have maintained that the 'Me' in the *Bhagavad Gita* refers to the Unmanifest. Now here in this inquiry of Arjuna there is introduced for the first time, as it were, a distinction between the 'Me' and the Unmanifest. For understanding the meaning of this distinction, one must bear in mind the background of the Tenth and the Eleventh Discourses. It is in the context of these two Discourses that the meaning of the Twelfth Discourse can be comprehended. The two earlier Discourses deal with the manifested nature of Reality—the *vibhutis* or the Glories of the Lord speak of the Presence of Reality in the realm which is visible and tangible. This Glorious Presence reveals Itself through 'something' intangible which constitutes the living quality of all things. In the Cosmic Form of the Lord there was given to Arjuna a peep into the worlds Invisible and Unseen. Thus both these Discourses dealt with the manifested aspect of the universe. Nevertheless, the Lord says that only a fragment of Himself is revealed in manifestation. Thus the ultimate Reality can be comprehended in a two-fold manner—one, the fragment that is manifested, and second, that which remains Unmanifest. This distinction of the Manifest and the Unmanifest with reference to the 'ME' becomes evident as we read the Tenth and the Eleventh Discourses. It is in this background that the teaching of the Twelfth Discourse should be examined. To the above-mentioned inquiry of Arjuna, Sri Krishna says :

> The difficulty of those whose minds are set on the Unmanifested is greater, for the goal of the Unmanifested is hard to reach by the embodied beings.

Sri Krishna explains to Arjuna that those who worship 'Me' in the manifest and those who worship 'Me' in the Unmanifest both come to 'Me'—but the path of the Unmanifest is difficult for the embodied beings to tread. As we saw in the earlier part of this Chapter, the first stage of devotion is always through images. Thus devotion has its beginning in the Manifested. One must pass through the Manifest in order to reach the Unmanifest. To set one's mind on the Unmanifest is extremely difficult because the Unmanifest is beyond the reach of the Mind. What the mind calls the Unmanifest is only abstract thinking as contrasted with concrete thinking. Mathematical thinking is abstract, dealing as it does with symbols—but still the abstract is not the Unmanifest. Mind dealing in objects and the Mind dealing in symbols—these represent concrete and abstract thinking respectively. From the concrete to the abstract is the path that the mind takes in its growth and evolution. In concrete thinking one deals with Forms; while in abstract thinking one deals with the Names of things. *Nama* and *Rupa*, Name and Form—these constitute the whole world of the Mind. The Formless and the Nameless lie outside the frontiers of the Mind. Sri Krishna says that the difficulty of those whose minds are set on the Unmanifest is very great—because the mind trying to understand the Unmanifest can never find what it seeks. Sri Krishna does not say that the Unmanifest cannot be comprehended—what He indicates is the difficulty for those who seek IT by the processes of the Mind.

It is interesting to note that in this Discourse, Sri Krishna gives various stages of Devotion. True devotion is a state where all mentation has ceased. But one cannot arrive at this state all at once. One has to transcend the mind with the help of the mind. The various stages of devotion are to the end of transcending the mind. From the concrete to the abstract and thence to the Unmanifest is this process leading from Mind to Super-mind.

Sri Krishna tells Arjuna : '. . . into "Me" let thy reason enter; then without doubt thou shalt abide in "Me" hereafter'. To let reason enter refers to that category of knowledge which is called Knowledge by being Reason always remains outside; it never enters. To ask reason to enter is to demand a transcending of the whole process of reasoning. If one could do that then surely one would abide forever in the Supreme. Sri Krishna does not ask Arjuna to give up reasoning: he is not asking him to resort to pre-logical thinking. He is not indicating a condition which is below the mind. Reasoning there must be, but instead of reason remaining outside, it must make an entry into the House of Reality. This is indeed asking the mind to become mindless—this is demanding of reason that it transform itself into intuition.

But how to come to this condition where reason instead of examining a thing from outside, enters it and knows it from within? Sri Krishna says :

> If, however, thou art unable to fix thy thought steadily on Me, then seek to reach Me by the practice of concentration, O Arjuna.

Mind becoming mindless is verily the highest state of meditation because here the Manifest becomes the symbol of the Unmanifest. But before one can arrive at this state there has to be a process of concentration, or more truly effortless attention. Where attention demands an effort there the mind is caught up in distractions. And what is it that distracts the mind? The mind is pulled and distracted by motives, conscious as well as unconscious. Unless there is effortless attention there cannot happen the miracle of reason entering. The entering of reason is reason divested of its reasoning effort. The dropping away of the effort is possible only when the mind is freed from the pull of distractions.

But Sri Krishna tells Arjuna that if he cannot come to this condition of effortless attention then 'be as one whose supreme aim is My service; even performing actions for My sake, thou shalt attain perfection'. Effortless Attention is possible only when all motives have dropped away. Motives, it must be remembered, exist not only at the conscious level but also at the unconscious level. Sri Krishna tells Arjuna that he should perform actions for 'My' sake. In all our actions it is the 'I' that is prominent, but as the mind develops, this 'I' remains under disguise. The functioning of the 'I' in an open manner would be regarded as too uncivilized! And yet the 'I' must function, and so it operates in the form of unconscious motives. Needless to say, the unconscious motives are very powerful and exercise a strong influence on the working of the conscious mind. Sri Krishna asks Arjuna to turn to these unconscious motives and eliminate them so that he can come to Effortless Attention which will result in the mind becoming mindless—the highest state of devotion.

But the Lord being very considerate to His disciple says that if even this is not possible then start with the elimination of conscious motives, for He tells Arjuna :

> If thou art not able to do even this, then taking refuge in My disciplined activity, renounce the fruit of action, with the self-subdued.

The renouncing of the fruit of action is indeed a conscious effort. The anticipation of fruit is the motive which operates at the conscious level of the mind. Most men engage in action because of the reward that they expect—the reward may be material or it may be so-called spiritual. Before coming to the state of Pure Devotion man must begin with the elimination of conscious motives, for, so long as motives remain, the devotee must needs get distracted—he cannot experience Effortless Attention where alone the Vision of the Deity, clear and direct is possible.

Thus in the whole problem of Devotion, Sri Krishna gives, as it were, various stages to Arjuna so that he may come to the Supreme Vision. The elimination of conscious motives by renouncing the fruit of action; the breaking up of the unconscious motives by the performance of action in His Name; the bringing of the mind to a condition of Effortless Attention where into the Lord the reason enters enabling the devotee to abide in the Lord for ever—these are the stages of the Path of Devotion revealed by Sri Krishna to His friend and disciple. Dr Radhakrishnan says in the *Bhagavad Gita*:

> Devotion, meditation and concentration are more difficult than renunciation of the fruits of action.

It is because of this that Sri Krishna suggests as the first step to devotion the renunciation of the fruits of action—in other words the freeing of the mind from its conscious motives. When this is done the aspirant can deal with the unconscious motives and proceed from there to Effortless Attention so as to come to the Presence of God, leaving behind all the images of God which his mind had created.

In the Twelfth Discourse, Sri Krishna describes the characteristics of a true devotee—the one who lives in the Presence of God and not one who merely plays about with images. He says that the devotee is 'forgiving'. To describe forgiveness as one of the first characteristics of the devotee seems strange. What is forgiveness and who can forgive? The common phrase 'Forgive and Forget' has a great deal of meaning in it. Forgiveness is not possible without the capacity to forget. And to forget is to wipe away all traces of memory. It is memory that distracts, being one of the greatest obstacles to Effortless Attention. The devotee or the mystic having rendered his mind mindless is forever free from the traces of memory and, therefore, is able to show forth the supreme virtue of Forgiveness. He is always characterized by a generosity of heart, for, 'he beareth no ill-will to any being' and is 'friendly and compassionate' to all. Real friendliness is possible only in the background of forgiveness. The mind that remembers too much can never forgive and therefore must ever remain a stranger to friendliness. Talking about the man of devotion, Sri Krishna says :

> He from whom the world does not shrink and who does not shrink from the world—who is free from elation and danger, from fear and agitation, he is dear to Me.

From whom does the world shrink? It shrinks from those who are cruel and aggressive—those who are never relaxed but always resistant. But a devotee does not wish to establish anything nor does he want to convert anybody and so is perfectly relaxed. But while the world does not shrink from him, he too does not shrink from the world. In order to pull out some one who has fallen into the mire, he too enters the mire, unconcerned whether his clothes will get soiled or remain clean. There are no centres of resistance in him and so is able to move freely. He is accessible to all for he has constructed no self-enclosing wall about him. He lives in the open, receiving what life brings. Sri Krishna says further in describing the characteristics of the devotee thus :

> He who has no expectation, is pure, efficient, unconcerned and untroubled, renouncing every undertaking, he my devotee, is dear to Me.

It is expectation which brings concern and trouble in the life of an individual. The mind that expects looks all the time to the future for the fulfilment of the past that has remained incomplete. But a man of complete action has no concern about the future—in his actions, the beginning and the end are simultaneously present. The *Gita* uses a peculiar phrase while describing the man of devotion—it says that he is one who does not begin anything. What does this mean? A beginning has always an end and the two are separated by an interval of time. It is in this interval of time that hope and expectation, fear and anxiety come into existence. To act but not to begin anything is to be free from these decaying processes of time. Pure action is one in which there is no distinction between the beginning and the end. The man of no beginning has stepped out of the time-process. As he begins nothing he is for ever established in the Timeless.

The *Gita* says that the man of devotion renounces good as well as evil. Good and evil are the opposites of the mind. The mind that thinks of Good brings into existence the Evil. The great Chinese philosopher, Lao-Tze says :

> When all the world understand beauty to be beautiful—
> then ugliness exists,
> When all understand goodness to be good—then evil exists.
> Thus existence suggests non-existence.

The man of devotion does not renounce Goodness—but he renounces good, for good is the opposite of evil. To understand Goodness as good is to mistake the part for the Whole. Being rooted in the Vision of the Whole, the devotee is free from the pairs of opposites comprising good and evil, true and false, beautiful and ugly.

Summing up the qualities of the man of devotion, Sri Krishna says :

> He who holds equal blame and praise, who is silent, content with anything that comes, who has no fixed abode and is firm in mind, full of devotion, that man is dear to me.

The man of devotion has no fixed abode—he is *Aniketa,* one without a home. Such a man is entirely uncommitted. To have a home is to have a commitment. Here the home is to be understood not in its physical sense, but in its psychological aspect. A man without psychological commitment is a man who is completely free, his mind not tethered anywhere. He upholds nothing and so he has not to defend anything. He is content with anything that comes and yet he is of firm mind. To receive life as it comes is not to show a tendency of mental drift. The man who drifts is carried away by the current, but one who receives life as it comes floats with the current and yet is a witness to it. He who is carried away by the current cannot receive life that comes the next moment. One who is a witness in the midst of participation is truly firm and yet is content to receive what life gives. This is the quality of the man of devotion. Devotion is not sentimentality; it is sensitiveness. Devotion is not an addiction to a code; it is a free movement having no centres of attachment whatsoever. It is of such a man of devotion that Lao-Tze speaks when he says :

He looks not at self, therefore he sees clearly,
He asserts not himself, therefore he shines,
He boasts not of self, therefore he has merit,
He glorifies not himself, therefore he endures.

It is the man of faith who alone endures—all others perish. The man of faith has given up the known and is not afraid to face the Unknown. Devotion has meaning only with reference to the Unknown. The man who has thrown away all securities that the world can offer, he alone knows the true security of the Unknown. To endure in the midst of constant flux is to see the Permanent in the fleeting. It is to this Eternal Vision that the *Gita* takes us as it now speaks of the Field and the Knower of the Field.

CHAPTER XIII

THE SILENT WATCHER

THE *Bhagavad Gita,* in the form in which it has come down to us, is a narration of the happenings on the battlefied of Kurukshetra by Sanjaya to the blind king, Dhritarashtra. The introduction of the character of Sanjaya in the *Bhagavad Gita* is most significant, for he represents a clear and impersonal perception of things and events. Sri Krishna in His entire teaching of the *Gita* lays a special emphasis on the objective perception of the events of life. Right action, according to the *Gita,* is possible only in the background of Right Perception. Now a true objective perception is that from which all subjective projections have been eliminated. All subjective projections distort the objects of perception. And so in Right Perception it is not enough that we see the object; it is also necessary that we see clearly the perceiving instrument which is the subject. If the perceiving instrument has a bias, if it is coloured, then the whole act of perception is vitiated. True knowledge implies a knowledge not only of the object known but also of the knower. Without an understanding of the knower, all acts of knowledge are incomplete, and therefore devoid of validity. But how is one to know the knower of knowledge? It is most interesting to note that the knower is all the time present in the process of knowing. The knower can be found out by the way knowledge is being acquired. In other words, it is in the process of thinking that the thinker is all the time present. It is not the conclusion that matters—what matters is : How the conclusion was arrived at? It is not the collection of data that matters—what matters is: How much of the selectivity of the perceiver's mind was present in the process of collecting the data? Human mind can always find in a situation what it wants to find, for, it sees in it what it has put into it! And so in the whole problem of Knowledge, three things are most fundamental : the Knower, the Known and the Process of Knowing. It is true that in knowledge there are two components : the Knower and the object Known; but in order to know the Knower one has to examine the process of knowing because it is in that process that he is reflected. With reference to knowledge, the *Gita* unmistakably emphasizes both these components : the Subject and the Object, for, in the Thirteenth Discourse, Sri Krishna says :

> Knowledge as to the Field and the Knower of the Field, that in My opinion is True Knowledge.

Kshetra and *Kshetragna* are the two topics discussed in this Discourse—they refer to the Field and the Knower of the field. The Field is the object of knowledge—the external world, while the *Kshetragna* is the knower of knowledge. From a metaphysical standpoint, *Kshetra* and *Kshetragna* are the *Prikriti* and the *Purusha* respectively. In the Thirteenth Discourse, Sri Krishna instructs Arjuna about this deeply metaphysical subject which is the basis of all philosophy whether of the East or the West. He says:

> Hear briefly from Me what the Field is, of what nature, what its modifications are, whence it is, what he—The Knower of the Field is, and what his powers are.

Thus the whole range of the subject of *Purusha* and *Prikriti* has been indicated in this verse. Describing the Field, the *Gita* says:

> The great Elements, Individuality, Reason and also the Unmanifested, the Ten Senses and the Mind and the five pastures of the senses.

This is indeed a complete picture of the whole Field in which numerous modifications take place from moment to moment. The Field is the Five Elements of Earth, Water, Fire, Air and Ether—they are the elements to which all component things of physical matter can be reduced. The Field is also the Ten Senses—the five senses of cognition and the five senses of action. In terms of Hindu psychology, Mind is also regarded as one of the senses—in fact, it is the King of Senses, whose seal of interpretation is essential for transforming sense reports into knowledge. The Five Pastures of the senses are *Shabda, Sparsha, Rupa, Rasa* and *Gandha*—Sound, Touch, Form, Taste and Smell respectively. The *Gita* says that Reason too belongs to the Field, because reason is the abstract and logical thinking of the mind. The Individuality or the Ego is also a part of the Field. As Dr Radhakrishnan says: 'The ego is an artificial construction obtained by abstraction from conscious experience.' The ego or the sense of individuality is indeed that factor of continuity which the mind projects into the phenomenon of eternal flux. While describing the Field, the *Gita* tells us that the Unmanifested is also a part of the Field. If the Field is to be understood as the Manifested how can the Unmanifested form a part of it? We have seen earlier that the *Gita* speaks of two kinds of Unmanifest—one lower and the other higher. We have called these two as the Subjective and the Transcendental. The Subjective is the invisible or the unseen. And so according to the *Gita* the Field does not cover merely the visible aspect of manifestation—it spreads over the invisible realms also. Thus the Unmanifested as Subjective truly belongs to the *Kshetra*. As mentioned above this description of the Field is very comprehensive as it takes both the visible as well as the invisible into account. But the knowledge of the Field does not mean merely defining its range, it also means the cognizance of the modifications that take place in this Field. Once again Sri Krishna gives in this Discourse a long and comprehensive list of modifications that take place in the Field. Sri Krishna describes these modifications as:

> Desire, aversion, pleasure and pain, aggregation, intelligence, firmness.

The principal modifications according to the above verse are *Ichchha, Dvesha, Sanghata, Chetana* and *Dhriti*. These five have some relationship with the modifications described by Patanjali in his *Yoga Sutras*. For *Chetana* is akin to *Avidya* or Ignorance; *Sanghata* is *Asmita* or Aggregateness; *Ichchha* and *Dvesha* are the *Raga* and *Dvesha* or Attachment and Aversion; and *Dhriti* refers to *Abhinivesha* or Continuity. Within these principal modifications of a five-fold nature there are numberless transformations that take place both of positive as well as negative categories. Sri Krishna makes reference to these transformations which are ultimately attributable to the above five-fold modifications that take place in the Field.

After describing the Field and the modifications that arise in it, Sri Krishna speaks of the *Kshetragna,* the Knower of the Field. We have to realize that the *Gita* indicates a two-fold nature of the Ultimate Reality. This is Transcendence and Immanence. According to the principle of 'As Above: So Below', the aspects of Transcendence and Immanence are seen in the Individual also, for the Individual is the reflection of the Cosmos. In the *Mahabharata* it is stated that when the self is associated with the modes of nature, then it is called *Kshetragna;* when it is released from the modes of nature then it is called the *Paramatman* or the Supreme Self. Because of the two-fold nature of the Supreme, its description always contains paradoxical characteristics—for how can Something be both transcendent as well as immanent? In the language of the mind there is no place for the simultaneous existence of both. How can He, who is without and within, far away and near, unmoving and moving, undivided and yet divided, be described except in terms that are mutually exclusive? Sri Krishna says in the *Gita* that the Supreme is 'said to be neither existent nor non-existent'. Describing the nature of the Supreme, Sri Krishna says:

> He appears to have the qualities of all the senses and yet is without any of the senses, unattached and yet supporting all, free from the gunas and yet enjoying them. He is without and within all beings. He is unmoving as also moving. He is too subtle to be known. He is far away and yet He is near. He is undivided and yet is He divided among beings.

As the *Gita* says in the above verse: 'He is too subtle to be known'. In fact the term used by Sri Krishna is that He is imperceptible because of His subtlety. The Supreme as immanent is so intangible that He is missed except by one who has extraordinary sensitivity. How can He who is unattached be at the same time the Support of All? Support without attachment is something unthinkable. How can one who is impersonal be at the same time most intimate? The highest truth is known and expressed only through paradoxes. But the paradox cannot be solved by the mind—any effort to do so is self-defeating. In Zen Buddhism the Master poses koans after koans before the disciple. All these koans are statements containing paradoxes. The more the disciple tries to solve them, the more ridiculous he becomes. A paradox can be resolved—it can never be solved. But the resolution of the paradox is never by the mind. It is where the mind is quiet that the resolution of the paradox comes —it dawns upon the consciousness illumining its range with a new light.

In the *Bhagavad Gita,* the words *Kshetra* and *Kshetragna* have been used with reference to different levels of manifestation and expression. These terms seem to be flexible as applying to the *Logos* and the *Mulaprikriti,* or to Monad and its Field, or to Ego and its realm of activity. Truly speaking *Kshetra* and *Kshetragna* denote Expression and Experience respectively. The *Gita* says:

> Matter or Nature is called the cause of the generation of causes and effects; Spirit is called the cause of the experience of pleasure and pain.

As Sri Krishna says in the previous verse 'modifications are all matter-born'. Since all modifications are matter-born, matter is indeed the field of causes and effects. These modifications refer to the configuration of matter, for, matter is the field of expression. The *Gita,* however, says that 'Spirit is called the cause of the experience of pain and pleasure'. Here Spirit is obviously used in the sense of Ego. This will become clear as we turn to the next verse of this Discourse which says:

> Spirit seated in Matter tasteth the qualities born of Matter; attachment to the qualities is the cause of his births in good and evil wombs.

The above verse speaks of the Spirit being born in good or evil wombs. Now the *Gita* has stated again and again that the Spirit is unborn—it is birthless and deathless. Thus, in the above verse Spirit or *Purusha* is used in a different sense—it is an entity which is subject to birth and death. One can conclude that the Spirit is used here as Ego. The Ego is the sense of 'I' which is born of the mind. It is this which the Buddhists describe as *Skandha*. The mind out of its experiences abstracts an entity which it calls the Ego. It is this which is the cause of the experience of pain and pleasure. It is this which is born in 'good and evil wombs' according to its attachments.

But apart from the Spirit and *Gita* speaks of the Supreme Spirit or the Highest *Purusha*. This may be called the Monad who indeed is the Supreme Spirit with reference to the individual. About this Supreme Spirit, the *Gita* says, it is the Witness or *Upadrashta*, the Permitter or *Anumanta*, the Supporter or *Bharta*, the Enjoyer or *Bhokta*. This four-fold relationship of the Supreme Spirit with reference to manifestation is most significant. At the lowest level it is known as *Bhokta* for the individual declares: 'I enjoy'. At a higher level it is seen as *Bharta* where the duality of Spirit and Matter is reorganized—the duality of the supporter and the supported. Then comes the relationship of *Anumanta*—the spirit permitting the body to do certain things so that there is a tacit understanding between the two. And lastly comes that relationship where the Spirit is the *Upadrashta* or the witness—the Silent Watcher. In the Voice of the Silence, H. P. Blavatsky gives a simile of the Three Halls while dealing with the Pilgrimage of the Soul. These Three Halls are those of Ignorance, Knowledge and Wisdom. She says that only as the Soul emerges from the Three Halls that he is ready to enter the Vale of Bliss. This simile is comparable to the various levels of relationship between the Spirit and the Body as given in the above verse of the *Gita*. The *Bhokta*, the *Bharta* and the *Anumanta* are the conditions of the Halls of Ignorance, Knowledge and wisdom respectively. The experience of the Vale of Bliss comes only when there arises the relationship of *Upadrashta* or the Witness. The four-fold relationship naturally refers to the relationship of *Kshetra* and *Kshetragna*. When the relationship of *Upadrashta* or Witness is known then does the individual know the Supreme who is the *Maheswara*. The *Gita* says that a man may come to this realization either by devotion or by knowledge or by action. The following verse makes it clear:

> Some by meditation behold Self in self by Self; others by Sānkhya, and still others by the Yoga of action.

In the above verse meditation obviously refers to Devotion just as *Sānkhya* refers to the Path of Knowledge. The vision of the *Maheswara*, the Supreme Lord comes to one who sees 'the unperishing within the perishing'—it is a perception of the Permanent in the midst of the fleeting. The *Gita* says:

> Seeing indeed the same Lord equally dwelling everywhere, he doth not destroy Self by self, and thus treadeth the highest Path.

What is really meant by destroying the Self by the self? The destruction of the Self is the clouding of the vision. This happens when the mind raises a cloud of dust through its own agitations. When the individual sees the same Lord equally dwelling everywhere, it implies that his mind has come to a steadiness. And it is the man of steady mind who treads the highest Path. Here a question may arise: Does the Lord dwell equally everywhere? Does he not dwell more in the saint than in the sinner? In man resides the nature of *Brahman*—the *Atman* and the *Brahman* are identical in nature. If this be so the quality of the *Brahman* resides equally everywhere. Between man and man there may be and there are differences of expressions—but there can be no difference as to essence or quality which is shared equally by all. He who can thus see the quality of things in the midst of quantitative divergences—he truly is the treader of the highest Path. The *Gita* makes this clear in the following verse:

> When he perceiveth the diversified existence of beings as rooted in One, and also spreading forth from it, then he reacheth the Eternal.

To see the Being and the Becoming in their true relationship is indeed to have an approach of the Timeless in Time. The Becoming is a frustrating process when viewed away from the Being. The Becoming is the tree which issues forth from the roots of the Being. To follow the line of thought introduced in this Discourse, one may say that the Becoming is the Field while the Being is the Knower of that Field. The Being is all the time present in the process of Becoming—but its presence is so subtle that one misses it. The *Gita* says:

> As the one Sun illumineth this whole world, so the Lord of the Field illumineth the whole Field, O Bharata.

The Being illumines the whole field of Becoming. He who can see the light of the Being in the darkness of the Becoming is truly a wise man. Rooted in the experience of Being he goes forth into the diversified expressions of the Becoming. The Becoming is in the process of time, but the restrictive influence of time drops away when there comes into it the touch of the Timeless which the Being fundamentally is. The *Bhagavad Gita* tells us:

> They who by the eye of Wisdom perceive this difference between the Field and the Knower of the Field, and the liberation of beings from Matter, they go to the Supreme.

To perceive the difference between the Field and its Knower is once again to see the Imperishable in the midst of the Perishable. And it is this perception which truly constitutes 'liberation of beings from Matter.' This liberation is possible for all, here and now, but for this man must grow in sensitivity, because it is only to the sensitive perception that the vision of the intangible is vouchsafed. The Path of deepening awareness, which sensitivity most assuredly is, has been described by the *Gita* under Practical Yoga. The last five discourses of the *Bhagavad Gita* lead us on to the Path of Practical Yoga.

CHAPTER XIV

THE UNCONDITIONED PERCEPTION

PATANJALI, the great compiler of the *Yoga* system defines *Yoga* as the cessation of mind's modifications. The mind that is subject to modifications, due to outer or inner stimuli, is a disturbed and distracted mind. For the cessation of mind's modifications one does not have to retire into a forest or a cave. Such retirement may perhaps stop modifications of the mind that arise due to outer stimuli. But even there the modifications caused by inner stimuli will remain. The problem of mind's modifications is very complex indeed, as the mind operates not merely on the surface but also at varying depths. Unless the conscious, the sub-conscious and the unconscious layers of the mind are taken into account, one cannot effectively deal with this problem of modifications. Patanjali says that mind's modifications arise due to five-fold factors. These are, according to him *Pramāna, Viparyāya, Vikalpa, Nidrā* and *Smriti*. They may be translated as Logical thinking, Impulsive thinking, Imagination, Sleep and Memory respectively. Logical thinking and Impulsive thinking belong to conscious mind; Imagination refers to the sub-conscious mind because of the factor of association implied in it; Sleep and Memory indicate the operational activities of the personal unconscious. Thus in this five-fold description of the causes of mind's modifications, Patanjali has covered the conscious, the sub-conscious and the unconscious layers of the mind. In *Yoga* one has to deal with this entire mind as otherwise cessation of modifications cannot be achieved. Needless to say mind's modifications arise because of the conditioning factors that impinge upon one's consciousness. It is the conditioned mind that is subject to constant modifications. Therefore the cause of modifications is to be sought in these conditioning factors. What is it that conditions the mind? How does it get conditioned? What is the process by which it can be de-conditioned? These are practical and fundamental problems with which both *Yoga* and Depth Psychology are concerned. The ***Bhagavad Gita*** throws immense light on this problem of vital importance to man. Sri Krishna tells Arjuna:

> The three modes (*gunas*), goodness (*sattva*), passion (*rajas*) and dullness (*tamas*), born of nature bind down in the body, O Mighty Armed, the imperishable dweller in the body.

Thus according to the above verse the three modes, *Sattva, Rajas* and *Tamas*—Goodness, Passion and Dullness—are the conditioning factors of the mind. They are verily the attributes of the human mind. The *Sattva*, the *Rajas* and the *Tamas* are also translated as Harmony, Mobility and Inertia respectively. Since these are the conditioning factors of the mind, in *Yoga* the aspirant seeks out those practices by which the mind can be completely de-conditioned. The term used by the *Gita* for a de-conditioned state is *Trigunātit*—the state in which the three *gunas* or the modes are transcended. The *Gita* gives a clear description of the three *gunas* and their effects on the mind which has been conditioned due to their functioning. Each *guna* or attribute produces in the mind an attachment or addictment because of which the very act of perception becomes distorted. Sri Krishna says:

> Of these goodness (*sattva*) being pure, causes illumination and health. It binds, O Blameless One, by attachment to happiness and by attachment to knowledge.

Sattva is a condition of harmony or goodness. But the goodness of the mind has always a sense of 'I' in it. The goodness of the mind is a synthesis abstracted from the functioning of the two opposites. It is an artificial product drawn from the similarities and dissimilarities of two opposing states. It represents a subtle way of mind's continuity. The conflict of opposites is a threat to the mind's sense of security—and yet it cannot do without opposites for, they constitute its field of movement. While it retains the opposites, it also wants from time to time a truce between these opposites. It is this truce which is *Sattva* where the opposites have for the time being been kept in check. *Sattva* shows a balance of opposites, not a transcending of opposites. The balance of opposites is always very delicate and so gets easily unbalanced. It is a synthesis which in turn gives birth to a thesis which generates an anti-thesis, resulting once again in a conflict between the two. The *Gita* says *Sattva* binds by attachment to happiness and by attachment to knowledge. Knowledge is the realm of thought even as happiness is the realm of emotions. Thought and emotions constitute the two opposing poles of the mind. The synthesis of the mind is now in terms of thought, and now in terms of emotion. Thus in *Sattva* there is a conditioning arising out of its attachment to a thought-synthesis or an emotional synthesis—its addiction to knowledge or happiness. *Sattva* contains an artificial product of the mind, very attractive to look at but having no fragrance in it. Thus the virtues of the mind are like artificial flowers. *Sattva* may indeed be described as mind's virtuosity. There is a semblance of goodness in it, but it is a goodness where opposites have been temporarily balanced—they have not been transcended.

Describing the second attribute of *Rajas,* Sri Krishna says:

> Mobility, passion-natured, know thou is the source of addiction and thirst for life, O Kaunteya, that bindeth the dweller in the body by attachment to action.

If *Sattva* is a balance of the opposites, *Rajas* is the conflict of the opposites. It is rooted in the desire to become something. The mind desires to move away from what it is to what it would like to be. It is this movement which is the cause of incessant conflict. The becoming is an endless process and it is this which is the basis of mind's activity. Activity is thus a conditioning factor of the mind. The third attribute of the mind is *Tamas* or Dullness or Inertia. Speaking about this the *Gita* says:

> But dullness (*tamas*), know thou, is born of ignorance and deludes all embodied beings. It binds, O Bharata, by heedlessness, indolence and sloth.

In Tamas or Inertia there is a confusion of opposites, for in it there is no clarity of perception. For defining the opposites the mind needs to be active. But in *Tamas* no such defining is possible as the mind is given to sloth and indolence. The mind that is caught up in inertia prefers drift to decision. It wants a continuity of habit at all levels of its expression. The confusion of opposites, the conflict of opposites, and the balance of opposites—these three constitute the qualities of the three *gunas*—*Tamas, Rajas* and *Sattva*. The man of inertia or *Tamas* develops an attitude of indifference born of insensitivity. Sometimes indifference is mistaken for impersonality—but there is nothing in common between the two. Impersonality is born of sensitivity. The person of sensitivity is hesitant lest he smother the growth of the other individual by his interference. But indifference, however, is a condition where the person is not even aware of the other individual! He may be aware of him physically but not in his subtler forms of expression. *Sattva, Rajas* and *Tamas* cause a conditioning of the mind by their conclusions, their conflicts and their habits.

In the description of these three attributes of *Sattva, Rajas* and *Tamas*, the *Bhagavad Gita* has given an indication of the three fundamental psychological tendencies. The three attributes are present in all human beings, but the difference in psychological tendencies is to be seen by the predominance of one or the other factor. In certain parts of our nature we are given to *Tamas*, in certain others to *Rajas* and still in some others to *Sattva*. In man's psychological growth he moves from the confusion of opposites to the balance of opposites through a conflict between the opposites which the mind has defined. In the *Gita* Sri Krishna gives a detailed description of the functioning of these three *gunas* and shows what are the characteristics of the person's behaviour when one or the other of the three *gunas* predominates. About *Sattva* or Goodness He says:

> When the light of knowledge streams forth in all the gates of the body, then it may be known that goodness has increased.

We have seen that *Sattva* indicates a balance of opposites. When this harmony of mind is established there is naturally an increase of goodness. The very fact that the *Gita* uses the word 'increase of goodness' shows that here we are dealing in things that are measurable. But how can goodness be measured? Obviously what the *Gita* means here is the pattern of goodness —not the quality of goodness. The quality of goodness is immeasurable—it does not lend itself to mathematical calculation of 'more' or 'less'. But the pattern of goodness can be measured. The *Gita* says that when harmony of mind is established then there is a change in the whole pattern of goodness. The pattern of goodness is the accepted code of morality, and the goodness which is the result of the balancing of opposites cannot go beyond the moral plane. Dr Radhakrishnan in his *Bhagavad Gita* says:

> Even *sattvika* goodness is imperfect since this goodness has for its condition the struggle with its opposite. The moment the struggle ceases, and the goodness becomes absolute, it ceases to be goodness and goes beyond ethical compulsion.

When we speak of the balancing of opposites we have to realize that we are still in the field of the opposites. In order to balance the opposites, a certain amount of effort is necessary. In the condition of *Sattva,* the opposites are separated by an interval of time and space. If such an interval did not exist there would be no point in establishing a balance. In all patterns of morality there is to be seen this balancing of opposites and this demands the use of one's energy to a very large extent. Moral effort is very exacting for it takes away all the energy one has. *Sattva* condition is no doubt necessary—but one has to rise beyond it so that one transcends the plane of moral opposites and comes to the peace and quiet of spiritual experience. As Dr Radhakrishnan says: 'By means of *Sattva* we overcome *Rajas* and *Tamas,* and then get beyond *Sattva* itself.' The good man must indeed become a saint—for the saint is a *trigunātit,* he has verily transcended the three *gunas.*

The *Gita* tells us that 'greed, activity, restlessness, envious desires'—these predominate when there is a prevalence of the attribute of *Rajas* in one's nature. We have seen that *Rajas* denotes a conflict of opposites. The impelling power of this conflict is the desire to become something or somebody. This impelling motive is described as 'greed, restlessness and envious desires'. Activity is no doubt necessary, but the question is:

What is the impelling power of that activity?

Describing the condition where *Tamas* prevails, Sri Krishna says: 'Darkness, stagnation, indolence and delusion' are to be seen in the life of an individual given to *tamasic* characteristics. No doubt stability is essential for existence, but the question is: What is it that sustains this stability? Is it stagnation and indolence, or is it the stability born of deep silence? The non-activity of a dull mind is not to be mistaken for the tranquility of a sensitive mind.

There is no doubt that the *Gita* asks the aspirant to transcend all the three *gunas* including the *sattva* if he is to arrive at a pure, unconditioned state of spiritual illumination. For example, Sri Krishna says:

> When the embodied soul meets with death when goodness or *sattva* prevails, then it attains to the pure worlds of those who know the Highest.

Commenting on this verse, Dr Radhakrishnan says that these persons 'do not obtain release but birth in *brahmaloka*. *Nistraigunya* or the transcendence of the three *gunas* is the condition of release'. Thus the *sattvika* or the 'good' people have a period of life in heaven at the end of which there arise for them a compulsion for rebirth. One is released from the necessity of birth and death only when one transcends the operative field of the three *gunas*. Spiritual life verily knows no compulsion: it is the moral life which is subject to compulsions. The whole question of the transcending of the three *gunas* has been very briefly and yet clearly put by Sri Krishna in the following verse:

> When the seer perceives no agent other than the modes, and knows also that which is beyond the modes, he attains to My being.

To perceive no agent other than the modes is indeed to see clearly. It is a perception from which the subjective factors have been eliminated. When one sees the *gunas* working among the *gunas* then is it possible for the seer to see that which is beyond the *gunas*. The difficulty with most of us is that we get entangled in the working of the *gunas*. We identify ourselves with the inertia, the activity and the balance which constitute the three states of expressional behaviour. To perceive no agent other than the modes is to dissociate oneself from the functioning of these modes. If one could observe oneself in the habits, in the conflicts and in the conclusions to which one clings then would one see the modes functioning among the modes. And in this observation one would also perceive the true nature of oneself as above and beyond the modes.

Arjuna here asks certain pertinent questions regarding the *gunas* and the transcending of them. The questions are:

> By what marks is he, O Lord, who has risen above the three modes characterized? What is his way of life? How does he go beyond the three modes?

The characteristics given by Sri Krishna in answer to these questions are similar to those given by Him with reference to the man of Steady Intelligence in the Second Discourse and also similar to those given in the Twelfth Discourse while speaking about the man of Devotion. Whether we move along the path of Knowledge, or the path of Devotion, or the path of Action, the characteristics of the Perfect Man are the same. Here in this Discourse, Sri Krishna says:

> He, O Arjuna, who does not abhor *Sattva*, *Rajas* and *Tamas* when they arise, nor longs for them when they cease.

What does abhorrence of *Sattva, Rajas* and *Tamas* mean? The *gunas* are the nature of matter. In their functioning the emphasis shifts from one to the other. When the three *gunas* are present in the same proportion then there is no manifestation at all. Manifestation pre-supposes the prevalence of *Tamas* or *Rajas* or *Sattva*. In the very act of manifestation these three modes arise in varying proportions. The eternal flux of life is reflected in the changing relationships of these three *gunas*. To receive life as it comes is to allow the *gunas* to function according to their nature without any interference from the actor himself. In life there is a rhythm of flux and reflux—to allow this rhythm to work itself out is to be above the three *gunas*. This idea has been clearly expressed in the following verse of the *Gita*:

> He who is seated like one unconcerned and unperturbed by the modes, who stands apart, without wavering, knowing that it is only the modes that act.

The above is the description of a man who has transcended the three *gunas*. Such a man is for ever unconcerned and unperturbed. Such a man is *Udasin*—uncommitted, and therefore is unwavering. To stand apart and look at the modes functioning within oneself is indeed a supremely spiritual state. To look at one's habits and yet to be separate from them; to see one's activities and yet to regard oneself as not the actor of those activities; to perceive one's virtues and accomplishments and yet to lay no claim over them—this is the characteristic of one who has freed himself from all conditioning. Of such a man the *Gita* says:

> Same in honour and ignominy, same to friend and foe, abandoning all undertakings—he is said to have crossed over the qualities of the mind.

The unconditioned man abandons all undertakings—this is a very strange description of a spiritual man. To abandon all undertakings is not to be idle, nor does it mean running away from activities. In an undertaking there is always an end or a purpose in view. But the man who is free from all conditioning has no end or purpose to fulfil. The purpose of life can never be away from living itself. He who lives in order to fulfil some purpose does not live at all. In living the beginning and the end are present simultaneously. The man who has transcended the three *gunas* lives for no set purpose, and therefore he lives most purposefully. The great Chinese philosopher, Lao-Tze says:

> In movement the child knows not whither it is bound; at rest it is not conscious of doing anything—but unconsciously adapts itself to the exigencies of its environment. This is the art of preserving life.

To live unconsciously is to live naturally. There is no effort in it nor is there a striving towards the fulfilment of any purpose. To allow the modes to function according to their nature and yet not get entangled in their functioning—this is the supreme state where the opposites are transcended, not merely balanced. To be aware of the functioning of the *Tamas*, the *Rajas* and the *Sattva*, and yet not interfere with them—this indeed is freedom from all conditioning. In such a state the mind of man is rendered pure and innocent capable of responding to the gentlest touch of the Supreme and the Transcendental.

CHAPTER XV

THE MUTABLE, THE IMMUTABLE AND THE INDESTRUCTIBLE

IN THE religious and mythological lore of the Hindus there are two divine personalities that have evoked from tens of thousands of people throughout the ages love and adoration which have been most spontaneous and absolutely natural. These divine personalities are Sri Ramachandra and Sri Krishna. Sri Ramachaandra has been described as the *Maryādā Purushottama*—meaning thereby the restrained Incarnation of Divinity. Sri Krishna, however, has been described as the *Purna Purushottama*—meaning thereby the fullness of Divine Incarnation. The two personalities differ completely from each other. In one, there is the predominance of morality and rectitude; in the other, the predominance of ecstacy and unconventionality. Sri Ramachandra represents a Perfection along the traditions of Occultism; Sri Krishna represents a Perfection along the path of Mysticism. In these two divine personalities one sees the glorious expression of Supreme Divinity along these two fundamental lines—the lines of Occultism and Mysticism. In the *Bhagavad Gita,* under the *Viswarupa-Darshana* and the *Vibhutis,* both these aspects have been considered. Apart from these two, the *Gita* speaks of Reality in its theree-fold categories; these are the *Kshara,* the *Akshara,* and the *Purushottama* which may be translated as the Mutable, the Immutable and the Supreme or the Transcendental. The Mutable is represented by the changing forms, both physical as well as super-physical. The Immutable may be described as the *Archetypal.* The Supreme is obviously the Transcendental. The Mutable and the Immutable are the Immanent even as the Supreme is the One that transcends all manifestation. The *Kshara* and the *Akshara*—the Mutable and the Immutable belong to the world of Forms—one, changing and, the other, unchanging. But the Transcendental is beyond all Forms. The *Gita* says:

> There are two Purushas in this world, the changeful and the changeless; the changeful is all beings, the unchanging is called Kutastha. The highest Purusha is verily Another, declared as the Supreme Self, He who pervading all, sustaineth the three worlds, the Indestructible Lord.

The Mutable, the Immutable and the Indestructible—these three have been described as *Purushas* in the *Bhagavad Gita*. Here, for the Immutable, the word used is *Kutastha*. While this word means rock-seated, it also means 'veiled in mystery' or 'seated inside *Maya*'. The Immutable is indeed the *Archetypal* for the latter is unchanging. It is truly seated in *Maya*, for, it is the projection of the Divine Mind. But while the Immutable is unchanging, it is not indestructible, because with the dissolution of the Universe, the *Archetypes* too are dissolved. The Logos must create in His Universe fresh *Archetypes* to serve as the Ultimate Goal for all created things. And so destructibility is to be seen with regard to both the mutable and the immutable. But there is the highest *Purusha* who is Indestructible. He is the Supreme, who pervades all the manifested things.

In the Fifteenth Discourse, the *Gita* speaks of the Tree of Life—the tree which has its roots above, and branches below. We seek for the roots of life in the material universe. We try to explain the phenomenon of evolution through struggle for existence. But the eternal law of life is: Function precedes the organ. The explanation of life is not to be found by dissecting the organ. It is the impulse from above which brings into existence forms below. Plato was indeed referring to this Tree of Life when he said:

> As regards the most lordly part of our soul, we must conceive of it this wise: we declare that God has given to each of us, as his demon, that kind of soul which is housed in the top of our body, and which raises us—seeing that we are not an earthly but a heavenly plant—up from earth towards our kindred heaven.

The meaning and the significance of life are to be found not by digging into the earth but by ascending into the heavens.

Speaking about Life, the *Gita* says:

> Nor here may be discerned its form, nor its end, nor its origin, nor its rooting place.

It is neither in the mutable nor in the immutable that the meaning of existence can be found. It is the Indestructible, the Supreme, that alone holds the key to the understanding of life.

But how does one go to that Indestructible state? The *Gita* tells us:

> Without pride and delusion, victorious over the vice of attachment, dwelling constantly in the Self, desire pacified, liberated from the pairs of opposites, known as pleasure and pain, they go, undeluded, to that indestructible state.

In the *Gita* one comes across a recurrence of certain fundamental ideas. These are not in the nature of repetitions—they constitute an effort on the part of Sri Krishna to present some of the vital truths from as many standpoints as possible. In the above verse once again there is an emphasis on being liberated from the pairs of opposites. Going beyond the pairs of opposites indicates a transcending of the frontiers of the mind. One cannot deny the existence of opposites—but they can either be in conflict with each other, or they can be like light and shade, giving by their co-existence, an exquisite beauty to the landscape. Without light and shade the landscape would appear flat and devoid of perspective. Similarly in the landscape of life too a co-existence of light and shade gives a perspective to existence. It is in light and shade that the position as well as the depth become clearly defined. It is these—position and depth—that constitute the fundamental basis of any perspective. But normally the light and shade of life are in opposition to each other. This is because of the operational activities of the mind. To transform opposition into co-existence is to divest the mind of all its content. But co-existence is not two things just lying in juxtaposition—there is a mysterious fusion even in the midst of a definable duality. To be without pride and without delusion—this is, according to the *Gita*, the way to the Indestructible state. Pride comes with knowledge and delusion is the result of ignorance. Neither knowledge nor ignorance—that is what constitutes the innocence of the mind. With knowledge comes the agressiveness of the mind, and with ignorance comes the dullness of the mind. It is innocence which gives a negativity to the mind, and in that negative or sensitive condition man comes to the Indestructible state.

The *Gita* says: '. . . having gone thither they return not.' The experience of the Indestructible state is such that after that a man can never be the same again. Even though the experience may last for a split-second, it leaves a permanent impress upon one's consciousness. As that priceless manual of spiritual life *Light On the Path* says:

> The silence may last a moment of time, or it may last a thousand years. But it will end. Yet you will carry its strength with you.

There can be no return for the man who has had a real spiritual experience. To come to the Indestructible state is to render oneself incorruptible. This state is time-less and so cannot be measured with the yardstick of time. One thing is certain: when from the experience of the time-less man comes to the regions of time he brings with him a new quality and a new fragrance. He gives to his daily living a new dimension brought from the region of the Indestructible.

The Imperishable is all the time present in the very heart of the perishable. Even though we have eyes, we do not see it; even though we have ears, we do not hear it. The *Gita* says:

> A fragment of My own self, transformed in the world of life into a living Spirit, draweth round itself the senses of which the mind is the sixth.

Thus it is the fragment of the Divine which is the sustaining force of all forms; for IT gathers round it the senses and the mind which bring into existence the whole world of *Nama* and *Rupa*—of Name and Form. But most of us see the form and miss the presence of that Divine Fragment, and yet without Its presence the forms would be dead. The *Gita* says that the Fragment transforms Itself into a living spirit. Thus the living quality of all things is derived from the presence of this Fragment. The *Gita* says it is the *Vimudhah*—the dull—who do not perceive this Fragment which is the life-giving force of all creation. Sri Krishna tells Arjuna that

> ... though struggling, the unintelligent perceive Him not, their selves untrained.

The *Gita* indicates clearly the sensitivity of consciousness which alone can bring this Great Vision to man. Here for insensitivity the *Gita* uses the word *Achetasah*—the unawakened condition—the mind in which awareness is not born. Sri Krishna says that one may struggle as long as one likes—but through such struggle one does not come to the Spiritual Vision. What is needed is not struggle or effort—what is of importance is awareness or sensitivity. The man of sensitivity can realize the truth of the statement contained in the following verse:

> That splendour issuing from the sun that enlighteneth the whole world, that which is in the moon, and in the fire, that splendour know as from Me.

The fire, the moon and the sun represent the physical, the emotional and mental states. The *Gita* says that all the splendour of these three worlds emanate from that Indestructible state. In worlds, visible and invisible, there resides the Supreme Splendour which can be cognized only by the awakened, by one who is extraordinarily sensitive. To be aware of His Presence in the material things of life is to discover a new dimension of living, nay, it is to find the Secret of Happiness itself. Sri Krishna says:

> Becoming the fire of life in the bodies of living creatures and mingling with the upward and downward breaths, I digest the four kinds of foods.

Even the digesting of food can be left to Him provided the enjoyer of food has that sensitivity and awareness of which the *Gita* speaks in this Discourse. Usually we eat not merely to assuage physical hunger, but to satisfy the hunger of the mind. But how can mind's hunger be assuaged by physical food? Since this cannot happen the enjoyer of food eats without discrimination, thinking, that with a larger quantity of food swallowed there will be a greater satisfaction accruing to the mind. The result is—the mind remains unsatisfied and the body is overloaded with food. Such overloading naturally produces a diseased condition. But if one eats only when the *Vaiswānar* has been awakened then there can be no condition of disease at all. To feed the *Vaiswānar,* and not the palate nor the mind is to be aware and sensitive even in the ordinary act of eating. He who does this is *Yukta,* for he neither indulges nor does he deny.

In this Discourse, Sri Krishna instructs Arjuna to transcend the *Kshara* or the Material, as also the *Akshara* or the *Archetypal,* and come to the vision of the Transcendental—the *Purushottama.* In the Eighteenth verse of this Chapter the *Gita* says:

> As I transcend the Mutable and am higher even than the Immutable, I am proclaimed as the Supreme Person in the world and in the Veda.

But the vision of the Supreme can come only to one who is 'undeluded'. To be deluded is to see through the glass, darkly. Such perception is through the veils cast by the projections of the mind. He who is caught up in these delusions knows not what is good and what is evil. The *Gita* therefore turns in the Sixteenth Discourse to this age-old problem—the Problem of Good and Evil.

CHAPTER XVI

THE GOOD AND THE EVIL

FROM the remotest ages, man has been in search of a solution to the baffling problem of Good and Evil. Philosophers of all lands have dealt with this problem—each according to his light. Seers and sages of all times have indicated a way to the solution of this complex problem affecting the life of people in their everyday avocations. Yet man is still in search of an effective solution to this problem of problems. Why is this so? Have not the answers of sages and philosophers been satisfactory? The difficulty with most of us is that we want a ready made answer to the probems of life. But life is intensely dynamic. How can there be set-answers to the problems that arise in the course of one's living? Each situation demands an approach which is appropriate to it. The approach of yesterday becomes irrelevant in the situation of today. Life is like a river in which fresh waters come every moment. And so life has to be understood and approached from moment to moment, since each moment has its own uniqueness. While one may have rules for general guidance, they have to be held very tentatively. These rules of guidance must be regarded as only fingers pointing the way. They are like signposts indicating the road—they have not to be mistaken for destination. But very often man regards the signpost as the destination and settles down there. What the philosophers and the sages have indicated are of the nature of signposts. They have their value in as much as they show the way. One may or may not tread the way—but once man decides to travel along that path, he must be ready to meet all exigencies. The signpost cannot describe what may or may not turn up on the way. If the pilgrim does not have the presence of mind or the pliability of thinking needed for meeting the varying situations, he is bound to feel frustrated on the way.

What after all is the problem of Good and Evil? Can any one say with a finality that 'this is good' and 'that is evil'? Can life be divided into clear-cut compartments, calling some 'Good' and describing others as 'Evil'. Good and evil are indeed relative—what is good for one man is not necessarily good for the other. What is good for a particular situation may not be good in another situation. Thus the determination of good and evil depends upon the relative position of the man who seeks a solution to the complex problem of Good and Evil. The whole problem of good and evil is fundamentally a problem of choice. In the complex patterns of life one does not always know what to choose and what not to choose. Yet man's happiness and sorrow depend upon the choice that he makes. The question of choice becomes all the more difficult because nothing is good or evil by itself. As the Adept Teacher, known in certain Occult schools as Master K. H. wrote to A. P. Sinnet:

> Evil has no existence *per se*... Nature is destitute of goodness or malice... The real evil proceeds from human intelligence and its origin rests entirely with the reasoning man who dissociated himself from Nature.

According to the above statement it is the reasoning mind of man that has created the problem of good and evil. It is the mind of man that imparts goodness or badness to the activities of nature, and this happens because man dissociates himself from Nature. What is this dissociation from Nature? There is a Will of Nature in terms of which life is organized and sustained throughout the universe. But man through the operations of his mind brings an element of Individual Will to bear upon his problem of life. Thus man through his mind brings into existence a conflict of Two Wills. It is the Individual Will pitted against the Cosmic Will which constitutes man's dissociation from Nature. Nature's forces impinge upon all forms of manifestation. However, these forces are neither good nor evil by themselves. They receive their character of being good or bad through the impress which the human mind puts on them. In the Occult literature of the world these forces are broadly divided into two and are called the Forces of Light and the

Forces of Darkness. They are sometimes known as White Magic and Black Magic. The *Bhagavad Gita* describes them as the *Daivi Sampatti* and the *Asuri Sampatti*. A conflict between these two forces is a subject dealt with in all mythologies. In the Hindu Mythology this assumes the form of wars between the *devas* and the *asuras*—those who are the children of light and those who are the sons of darkness. In the Sixteenth Discourse there is a description of these two properties—the Divine and the Demoniacal. Needless to say they represent the Forces of Good and the Forces of Evil respectively. The *Gita* says:

> Fearlessness, purity of mind, wise apportionment of knowledge and concentration, charity, self-control and sacrifice, study of the scriptures, austerity, uprightness, non-violence, truth, freedom from anger, renunciation, tranquility, aversion to fault-finding, compassion to living beings, freedom from covetousness, gentleness, modesty, steadiness, vigour, forgiveness, fortitude, freedom from envy and pride—these O Arjuna, are the endowments of him who is born with the divine nature.

If one analyses the above list of divine properties, one would immediately notice that all of them refer to a condition of mind. The Forces of Light are not objective in character. It is the mind of man that gives to the forces of nature their character. The Forces of nature by themselves are neutral. When they pass through a mind that is serene and tranquil then they assume a character of goodness; but the same forces when they pass through a mind that is impure and selfish, then they become dark and evil in their character. In the above list two properties are very significant, one is, 'aversion to fault-finding' This may be translated as 'absence of crookedness' in one's nature. It is the crooked who are given to fault-finding. If there is any crookedness in one's nature then one is sure to become an agent of evil forces. This fault-finding comes from envy and pride to which reference is made in the above list. The man of pride is conscious of his achievements and the man of envy is conscious of his lack of achievements. These two are the opposite states of the mind and both generate the trait of fault-finding. To have a consciousness of one's accomplishments or lack of them produces in one either a superiority complex or an inferiority complex. A sense of superiority as also a sense of inferiority, generates this tendency of fault-finding. Another significant property given in the above list is Modesty. The man of divine properties, of *Daivi Sampad,* is one who is characterized by his modesty or humility. The truly spiritual man is ever humble. It is the man of knowledge who is conceited—the man of wisdom is always full of humility. The man of knowledge is proud of what he thinks he knows; the man of wisdom is humble for he knows that he knows nothing.

Similar to the above list, the *Gita* gives also a list of those who have a Demoniac nature. It says:

> Ostentation, arrogance, conceit, anger as also harshness and ignorance, these, O Partha, are the endowments of him who is born with demoniac nature.

Here the word 'born' is to be interpreted as one who possesses, for no one is born-of divine or demoniac nature. These endowments are of the mind and therefore belong to one's own personal heredity. They constitute one's psychological heredity as against biological or social. In the above verse, the interesting trait is 'ostentation'. A desire to display anything, whether power or position or pelf, is indicative of a shallow mind. It signifies psychological immaturity. Why does one display anything? A display arises out of a sense of insecurity. He who feels utterly insignificant by himself seeks to show one's significance through the display of power, position, wealth or so-called spiritual virtues. The *Gita* also says that 'harshness' is indicative of demoniacal nature. When a person is conscious of his achievements he is sure to develop a trait of harshness and cruelty. In this harshness too there is a display of one's power. We become harsh towards our inferiors because we want them to realize that we have unlimited power in our hands—power to crush and destroy them. It is interesting to note that throughout the list of demoniacal powers, the *Gita* shows the presence of a sense of 'I'. In fact it is this sense of 'I' which imparts to the force a character of darkness. White and Black Magic are to be characterized by the absence or the presence of this sense of 'I'. The nature of the demoniacal properties is brought out clearly in the following verses of the *Bhagavad Gita*:

> This today by me hath been won, that purpose I shall gain; this wealth is mine already, and also this shall be mine in future. I have slain this enemy, and others also I shall slay, I am ruler, I am enjoyer, I am perfect, I am powerful, I am happy. I am wealthy, well-born; who else is there that is like unto me. I will sacrifice, I will give alms, I will rejoice.

Throughout this enumeration there is the sense of 'I' constantly present. These the *Gita* describes as 'deluded by unwisdom.' It is the consciousness of 'I' which is the basis of *Asuri Sampad* or Black Magic. The *Gita* says:

> The demoniacal men know neither right activity nor right abstinence; nor purity, nor even propriety, nor truth is in them.

Even abstinence has to be right—for a mere pattern of abstinence does not make it right. There can be ostentation in activity as well as in abstinence. There can be a show of indulgence as also a show of denial. Self-mortification is also a form of exhibitionism. To shine out either with pomp or with self-denial is to seek self-gratification. The *Gita* describes such people as 'intoxicated with pride' and as possessing 'sanctimonious hypocrisy'. They want to appear holy, but their holiness is utterly hypocritical. Describing further the men of demoniacal nature, Sri Krishna says:

> Self-glorified, obstinate, filled with the pride and intoxication of wealth, they perform lip-sacrifices for ostentation, contrary to scriptural ordinance.

'Performing lip-sacrifices for ostentation'—this is indeed an apt description of these men of hypocritical behaviour. There is no sincerity in what they do. Their patterns of behaviour may seem noble—but the content of that behaviour is dark and unholy. Thus the *Gita* all the time sets the standard of rightness not on the pattern but on the motive of behaviour. It is motive that determines whether a person is an agent of the White or the Dark Powers. It must be remembered that it is not the Power that is either White or Dark—it is the mind that is pure or impure. If the mind has the slightest impurity then through it the individual can become an agent of undesirable influences.

He will become a focal point of discord and disharmony, of division and disintegration. The *Gita* says that the man of demoniacal properties has his mind 'bewildered by numerous thoughts, enmeshed in the womb of delusion'. The man who is pulled along many distractions is bound to be deluded; and how can the deluded know what right choice is in the midst of the complex situations of life?

The *Bhagavad Gita* says:

> The gateway to hell leading to the ruin of the soul is three-fold—Lust, Hate and Greed. Therefore, these three, one should abandon.

Lust, hate and greed—these three are the corrupting factors of mind. The mind that is corrupted by them becomes an instrument of destruction and discord. Why have these three been described as the gateway of hell? What is lust? It is an attachment to form—it is the mistaking of the symbol for the substance. It is an effort on the part of man to possess the intangible by clinging to the tangible. As the intangible can never be possessed by holding on to the tangible, the man of lust is for ever frustrated. He is caught up in an insatiable craving: the more he clings to the tangible in the hope of possessing the intangible, the more is he consumed by craving. The opposite of Lust is obviously Hate, for if in lust there is attachment, in hate there is repulsion. In fact, lust and hate are a married couple—they cannot be divorced. Where lust is, hate is bound to appear. In the denying of forms there is imperceptibly present the element of lust. Lust and hate are thus the opposites of the mind; they represent the positive and the negative poles. But what is Greed?

Both lust and hate are motivated by possession—but their possessive activities are directed towards specific objects. Thus possessive activities of the positive and the negative kinds are present in lust and hate. Greed, however, has a different basis for its existence. Greed is possession itself—not just possessive activity. In fact it is Greed that gives birth to lust as well as hate. Greed is the motivating factor behind all activities which are either lustful or hateful. In other words, lust and hate are the expressions of greed. If greed is the source, lust and hate are the patterns of expression and activity born of that source.

The *Gita* says Lust, Hate and Greed are the gates to hell—they are most assuredly the gateways to decay and degeneration. It is possession in all its aspects which is the begetter of sorrow. Man wants to possess because he thinks that is the way to security. His possessive activities are reflected in lust and hate and they are rooted in greed. But how can life be possessed? All efforts at possessing life are self-defeating. How can the mind which is caught up in possession ever know what is good and what is evil? A possessive mind is dull and stagnant, it is heavy with inertia. It is corrupt and impure, because it clings to its possessions and the possessions cling to it. Such a mind has lost its innocence. It is only the innocent mind that can know what is good—not good as opposed to evil, but good in its absolute sense. To be able to see the absolute in the relative is to commune with the intangible even when dealing with the tangible things of life. The *Gita* sums up the whole problem of Good and Evil in the following verse of the Sixteenth Discourse:

> Therefore let the scripture be thy authority for determining what should be done and what should not be done. Knowing what is declared by the rules of the scripture, thou shouldst do thy work in this world.

This appears to be a strange advice given by Sri Krishna to Arjuna. In fact this instruction seems quite contrary to the whole spirit of the *Gita*. Is life a static thing so that all answers to life's problems can be found in the scriptures? What is meant by the authority of the scriptures? Have the scriptures to be followed blindly? If not, what is the role of the scriptures? In one of the Sanskrit books, the *Pancha-tantra,* there is a verse which says:

> How can scriptures help him who has no intelligence of his own? The looking-glass is of no use to the person without eyes.

The scriptures are like a mirror. But one can use a mirror only if one has eyes. To the person without sight the mirror is of no value. As was pointed out earlier in this chapter, what the philosophers and the sages have said are like guideposts and the scriptures are verily the pointers showing the way. These pointers have been put by those who have trodden the spiritual path and have therefore a certain validity born of their experience. When commencing a journey it is most advisable to read the signposts. To ignore them is to act immaturely. Not to cling to signposts but at the same time not to reject them is the soundest advice that can be given to the spiritual pilgrim. It is this advice which is contained in the above verse of the *Gita*.

For a man without intelligence scriptures are of no avail. Therefore the *Gita* says in the Second Discourse that one must take refuge in *Buddhi* or Intelligence. The scriptures contain observations of those who have walked along the spiritual path. But the observations of another have no value whatsoever if there are no observations of one's own. The scriptures are certain landmarks established by those who have gone ahead. The landmarks are both the starting points as also the points of departure. To use the authority of the scripture is to regard the scripture as a point of departure even as a signpost is a point of departure. But when can one make a signpost as a point of departure? Only when one is able to read it intelligently. In order to read the signposts of life, which the scriptures are, one must have the intelligence to read what is written there. In other words, the mind must be alert and yet at the same time open to find out what is indicated on the signpost.

Thus to the problem of Good and Evil the *Gita* brings a contribution which is unique and yet simple. According to it, it is not the mind that can understand this vast and complex problem of life. The mind deals with things that are static; it cuts up the movement of life into still pictures to examine and find out as to what life contains. But how can still pictures give an understanding of life's dynamism? For this what is needed is *Buddhi* or Intelligence. But the illumination of *Buddhi* can come only when the mind is alert and yet utterly negative. The last two Discourses of the *Gita* deal with this practical aspect of life, namely, the way to the illumination of the mind by the living touch of *Buddhi* or Intelligence. The problems created by the Mind cannot be solved by the Mind—into the consciousness of man must descend the Light of *Buddhi* if he is to come to the comprehension of the Great Dual Principles—Good and

Evil, Right and Wrong, Pain and Pleasure. How can the Mind that functions on the plane of duality know the meaning of duality? For this there has to take place the transcending of the Mind. The closing Discourses of the *Bhagavad Gita* verily lead us to this great miracle—the Miracle of Transcendence.

CHAPTER XVII

THE THREE INSTRUMENTS

THE STORY of evolution consists not merely of changes in forms, structures and patterns, but also of the unfoldment of different layers of consciousness. In fact, in evolution, consciousness is primary, structures and forms are only the derivatives. When a shift in consciousness takes place, there arises the need for new forms and structures. The meaning of evolution can never be found by merely studying the structures and their transformations. It is in the shift of consciousness that one can find the meaning and significance of evolution. From the standpoint of consciousness, there are three major landmarks to be seen in the march of evolution. They are Instinct, Intellect and Intuition. The sub-human creatures and the early races of humanity have their centre of consciousness focussed at the instinctual level. They are guided by instincts in all their activities. In times of difficulty they trust their instincts for showing them the right path. A complete faith in instinctual guidance is what characterizes the behaviour of primitive men. With the development of mind the human individual moves away more and more from the instinctual path. In instinctual guidance he sees a denial of his own freedom. He thus relies more and more on his intellectual capacities. The growth of humanity witnesses this shift of consciousness from Instinct to Intellect. With the functioning of intellect the element of faith disappears and its place is taken by belief. Belief operates on the plane of the known and the intellect is proud of what it knows. It believes that there is nothing that it cannot know. It relies completely on its own powers. This is a necessary phase for without it man cannot develop a sense of independence. With the help of intellect he is able to explore the field of his own capacities.

But sooner or later he realizes that in his growth and development the intellect cannot take him very far. He begins to be aware of the limitations of intellect. It is at this stage that a new shift in consciousness takes place and that is from Intellect to Intuition. With the dawn of Intuition there comes once again into the life of the human individual an element of faith. But faith at the level of intuition is completely different from the faith at the level of instincts. The Instinctual Faith is the Faith of the Ignorant, but the Intuitional Faith is the Faith of the Innocent. The *Bhagavad Gita* begins the Seventeenth Discourse with a discussion of the different categories of faith. Sri Krishna says:

> Threefold is by nature the inborn faith of the embodied—the good, the passionate and the dull.... The Faith of each is shaped to his own nature, O Bharata, the man consists of his faith; that which his faith is, he is verily that.

To say that the faith of each is shaped to his own nature is to indicate that the basis of faith changes according to the growth of the individual. Further, the *Gita* says in the above verse that it is faith that makes the character of man. Man's growth is determined by the category of faith that he espouses. Sri Krishna speaks here of the Faith of the Dull, the Faith of the Passionate and the Faith of the Good. Now the faith of the Dull is obviously the Faith of the Ignorant. The Dull are those whose minds have not awakened—they suffer from mental inertia and lethargy. Their faith has a basis of fear in it. The *Gita* says these men worship the spirits and ghosts. This is indicative of fear which is born of ignorance. The Passionate or those moved by *Rajas* are active and restless for they are moved by intellect. The intellect is very often clever and unscrupulous. There is no wonder that the Passionate worship the demons. The Faith of the Passionate is faith in themselves—in the power of the intellect, in the cleverness of the mind. Sri Krishna says that the Good worship the gods—they are the worshippers of the beneficent forces. They have a Faith—but it is the Faith of the innocent. For, is not innocence the very basis of goodness? They are innocent because they are freed from the pride of mind's knowledge. Thus the three categories of faith described above refer to man's instinctual, intellectual and intuitive living. The fundamental problem of humanity today is to move from Intellect to Intuition—from Mind to Super-mind. How is this movement to be initiated?

In the Seventeenth Discourse, Sri Krishna draws the attention of Arjuna to three instruments which if used properly would lead him to the life of true faith—the Faith of the Good or the Innocent. The Three Instruments are *Yagna, Tapa* and *Dana*—Sacrifice, Austerity and Charity. Sacrifice is obviously a dedicated service or a discriminative action. It is a life of awareness—but it is an awareness with choice. The *Gita* speaks of the three kinds of food. Those who are to perform sacrifice or those who wish to move along the path of discriminative action must be careful regarding the food that they eat. Discrimination should most assuredly begin with the food, for food has much to do with the condition of the mind. How can one engage oneself in discriminative action if the food one takes is of the wrong kind? The food which increases the dullness of body and mind is to be discarded, for it would be an obstacle to right action. Similarly, the food which is hot and stimulating is likely to make both the body and the mind restless. How can the one who is restless ever engage himself in discriminative action? The food that promotes vitality and cheerfulness is obviously the best for by taking this food the body would remain supple and capable of quiet activity. The Discriminative Action is the first step on the path leading from Intellect to Intuition. To be watchful of one's daily activity, lest it be corrupted by inertia on the one hand and dissipative restlessness on the other is indeed the starting point of one's spiritual journey. To watch one's activity is verily to perform sacrifice. But what should be the basis of this sacrifice? The *Gita* says that the sacrifice which 'is empty of faith' is of the *tamasic* category—it is based on inertia. It is an action that is performed out of habit and therefore utterly mechanical. Surely mechanical action cannot be described as discriminative activity. The *Gita* further says that the sacrifice that is performed for the sake of display and reward is of the *rajasic* kind—it is truly passionate in nature. Its basis is the desire to become something as a result of the sacrifice performed. This too cannot claim to be called discriminative activity. What is then discriminative action—what is that action which can be called sacrificial action? In the *Gita* the word sacrifice has a different connotation from the one that is associated with Vedic sacrifices. Dr Radhakrishnan in his *Bhagavad Gita* says:

> The *Yagna* of the *Gita* is not the same as the ceremonial sacrifice of the Veda. It is sacrificial action in general by which man dedicates his wealth and deeds to the service of the One Life in all. People with such a sacrificial spirit will accept even death gladly, though unjustly meted out to them, so that the world may grow through their sacrifice. Savitri tells Yama that good people maintain the world through their suffering and sacrifice.

Thus the question is: What is sacrificial action? What indeed is discriminative activity? In a sacrifice that which is offered is of primary importance. Therefore a sacrificial action is true only when man offers himself. So long as the 'self' has not been offered the action is not sacrificial. But what does the offering of the 'self' mean? It means the dropping away of all expectation of reward. The sense of 'I' continues in action through reward—it does not matter whether the reward expected is material or so-called spiritual. True sacrificial action is that which is performed out of a sense of duty. But what after all is duty? Duty indicates what is due to the other man. Thus duty must have a quality of appropriateness in it. That which is dutiful is always appropriate. If duty implies something due to the other person then surely we cannot know what is due unless we have eliminated our subjective biases and prejudices from our perception. Thus in a sacrificial action all subjective biases must be burnt away. To be constantly aware of the subjective factors that are being projected into one's activities is to perform a sacrifice which is good or *sattvic*. Thus according to the *Gita* sacrificial or discriminative action is the first step in the journey towards Life Eternal.

If the first step on the Path is Right Activity, the second step, according to the *Gita* is Right Austerity. While activity deals with the body, austerity deals with the emotion—or more truly, it deals with the emotional content of life. Here again the *Gita* speaks of the three kinds of austerities—the austerities that purify the body, those that purify the speech and those that purify the thought. The *Gita* says:

> The worship of the gods, of the twice-born, of teachers and of the wise, purity, uprightness, continence and non-violence—this is said to be the austerity of the body.

In other words, Reverence, Purity, Uprightness, Continence and Non-violence are the five principles of bodily austerities. The main emphasis in the above principles is on refraining from dissipating one's energies. To preserve one's energies and to direct them into right channels is the objective of bodily austerity. The last four in the above verse speak of the preservation of energy while the first four dealing with worship refer to the direction of one's energy along right lines. Conservation of energy and proper direction of the conserved energy—this is what is indicated in the austerity of the body. It has to be remembered that while Sacrifice or *Yagna* has concern with Discrimination, Austerity or *Tapa* refers to Desirelessness. The question of Desirelessness has been dealt with by the *Gita* in its comprehensive nature covering thought, speech and action. These three are the means of communication that the individual has with reference to the environment in which he lives. Desirelessness, however, is possible only when a man has passed through the first stage of sacrifice or Discrimination. We have stated above that the Path from Intellect to Intuition has been indicated by the *Gita* in the last two Discourses. It is obvious that intellect cannot transform itself into intuition. But when the intellect is divested of all its contents then the empty vessel so created is filled with the waters of Intuition. It is indeed the emptying of the contents which has been suggested by the *Gita* through the three instruments of *Yagna, Tapa* and *Dana*—Activity, Austerity and Charity. In *Yagna* one has to discard unholy oblations and this is to be done by being watchful of one's activity lest nothing corrupt may creep in to contaminate the offering put into the sacrificial deed. *Tapa* or Austerity is a further process of discarding—it is the putting away of the non-essentials of life. The austerities of body, speech and thought are indeed to that end. But while in austerities one discards the non-essentials, in Charity one must renounce even the essentials, because Charity of non-essentials is no charity at all. Thus through *Yagna, Tapa* and *Dana* there goes on a process of increasing negativity till the mind is emptied of all its contents. *Yagna* is a discriminative process where the essentials and the non-essentials are sorted out. *Tapa* is the process of discarding the non-essentials. *Dana* is verily the process where even the essentials are discarded so that the spiritual aspirant is stripped of everything, ready to be clothed in the pure garment of innocence.

We have seen that the austerity of the body is concerned with the conservation of energy. This signifies the body giving up all non-essentials in the use of energy. It is in non-essentials that the energy is dissipated. The bodily austerity therefore consists in giving up all activities that are non-essential. The *Gita* then talks of the austerity of speech. Referring to this it says:

> Speech causing no annoyance, truthful, pleasant, and beneficial, and the regular recitation of the scriptures—this is said to be the austerity of speech.

Speech that causes no annoyance—this is indeed the core of the austerity of speech. When does the speech annoy the other? When the utterance of words is done from centres of reaction then it is that speech offends the other person. The centre of reaction may be flattery or it may be condemnation—but whatever comes from that centre proves annoying to any one who has the least sensitivity. The *Gita* says that for the speech to be non-annoying, it must be true, it must be pleasant and it must be beneficial. Here the true and the pleasant refer to the manner of speech while the beneficial refers to the motive of speech. It is of the highest importance that the motive of all speech must be to prove beneficial to others. But that is not enough, because the motive of beneficence should be expressed in a language that is true and pleasant. In fact, that which is truly beneficial can never be expressed in a language that is untruthful or in words that are unpleasant. Thus the austerity of speech instructs the spiritual aspirant to guard his speech and to remove from it all non-essentials. If the non-essentials are removed from speech then surely much of our chattering will cease. There is a poem in the English language which says:

> If your lips would keep from slips
> Five things observe with care;
> Of what you speak, to whom you speak,
> And how, and when, and where.

This is indeed a sound advice for one who wishes to practice the austerity of speech. The speech which has a truly beneficial motive and which is expressed in pleasant and truthful manner can never cause annoyance to any one. One who does this will never repent for what he has said—for there will not arise any cause for repentence. From the austerity of speech, the *Gita* turns to the austerity of mind, for mind too must discard what is non-essential. The *Gita* says:

> Tranquility of mind, gentleness, silence, self-control, purity of thought—this is called the austerity of the mind.

It is interesting to note that the *Gita* speaks of silence with reference to mind and not with reference to speech. Very often one practices silence of words but the mind continues with its chatterings. Such silence is of no avail. In fact, in the background of a chattering mind the silence of words is dangerous, for, when it is broken the words that emanate are likely to be unpleasant, causing much annoyance to those who hear them. Here in the above five-fold characteristics of the austerity of the mind there are shown the increasing depths of the mind. Tranquility represents the quiet of the conscious mind. When the agitations of the conscious mind cease then there comes a gentleness which has its charm and grace. The conscious mind always resists—for, through resistance it seeks self-preservation. But when the conscious resistence has ceased then the mind becomes very gentle. In that gentleness there comes a silence which belongs to a deeper layer of the mind. When the conscious mind is bereft of resistance then the unconscious too becomes quiet, for it is the resistence of the conscious mind that gives vitality to the unconscious. When both the conscious and the unconscious are quiet then there is true self-control. Self-control as to mind is verily a condition of absolute freedom. It is only the free mind that is truly controlled. It can move anywhere and everywhere without being tied or tethered. It is the free mind that is pure in the true sense of the term. Purity of mind indicates a state of innocence. Thus the austerity of body, speech and thought leads the spiritual aspirant further on the Path. However, the *Gita* tells us that:

> Austerity which is practised with the object of gaining respect, honour and worship, and for ostentation is said to be *rajasic* or passionate.

Austerity is to the end of desirelessness and so if there is any desire for respect, honour or worship, or a desire to show oneself of, then such austerity is devoid of meaning. The *Gita* also says that where self-torture exists in the acts of austerity there austerity is bereft of significance. All austerities, whether of body or of speech or of thought, must have a naturalness about them. The non-essentials of life must drop away without any effort, because austerity which demands an effort has in it corruption and contamination.

If *Yagna* or Sacrifice represents an act of Discrimination, if *Tapa* or Austerity signifies Desirelessness, *Dana* or Charity has verily its roots in Good Conduct. In fact charity is identical with good conduct. But what is charity? Is it merely the giving of alms? Is it the giving away of one's superfluities? The superfluous is non-essential—in giving it away there is no charity involved. True charity is the giving away of the essentials of life. Describing the true character of Charity, the *Gita* says:

> That gift which is made to one from whom no return is expected, with the feeling that it is one's duty to give, and which is given in proper place and time and to a worthy person—that gift is held to be good.

In the above verse it is said that in making a charity both the objective as well as the subjective factors should be taken into account. The objective factors are the place and the time—the *desha* and the *kala,* and the subjective factor is the person or the *Patra* to whom the gift is made. Such a person must be worthy to receive charity. What does the worthiness of the person mean? It really means that the charity must fulfil the need of the person to whom the gift is made. To take into consideration the need of the other person is to eliminate completely the factor of personal likes and dislikes. It is only when the personality is put aside that true charity can come into existence. The giving up of the personal factor is indeed the discarding of the essentials of life, for, surely to man there is nothing more essential than his own self. The *Gita* says that the gift which is made:

> ...with the hope of a return or with the expectation of a future gain or when it hurts to give

then it is not true charity. The charity that is made grudgingly is devoid of charitableness. There must be a grace about all charitable acts. That which is not graceful is not charitable at all. That is why the *Gita* says that when charity is made with contempt, then it is unworthy to be called charity. If the person who makes charity has a sense of superiority then such charity has no goodness in it. In fact true charity is always anonymous. If even the slightest touch of 'I' comes into the act of charity then charity loses all its grace. If the person who receives is made to feel small or inferior then the gift itself is polluted.

The *Gita* says that *Aum Tat Sat* is the great symbol of the *Brahman* and it is this *mantra* which must become the basis of all sacrifice, all austerity and all charity. What does this mean? To utter these three words is indeed to experience three states of consciousness. *Aum* stands for the Waking state, *Tat* for the Dream state, and *Sat* for the Deep Sleep state. They represent deepening conditions of awareness. In sacrifice the mind must come to a waking state so that the essentials and the non-essentials are sorted out through Discrimination. In austerity the mind must come to a dream state where through Desirelessness the non-essentials are discarded. In Charity the mind must come to a deep sleep where through the discarding of the self man shows forth Good Conduct in the truest sense of the term. The reciting of the *mantra*, *Aum Tat Sat*, must result in this deepening of consciousness—if it does not happen then the repetition is only mechanical, devoid of spirit. He alone is real or Brahman alone is real—these are not mere empty words. The purpose of sacrifice, austerity and charity is to bring the spiritual pilgrim to the realization of this Supreme Fact. But the realization can come only when the non-essentials and even the essentials are discarded—when the Self is emptied of self. When this happens then man is no longer in conflict—his individual will has found its fulfilment in the Cosmic Will. In the Eighteenth and the final Discourse, the *Bhagavad Gita* brings us to that Spiritual Climax when the merging of the Individual Will with the Cosmic Will takes place—where the dew drop merges in the sea—and in thus losing itself it discovers Itself. Indeed, when the dew drop slips into the sea a great miracle takes place: the miracle of the sea entering the dew drop; the Microcosm becoming the Macrocosm. It is the discovery of the *Brahman* in the very heart of the *Atman*.

CHAPTER XVIII

THE IDENTITY OF TWO WILLS

PERHAPS nowhere has philosophy reached such stupendous heights as it has done in Hindu *Vedanta*. There is no doubt that *Vedanta* has been one of the most courageous plunges into the Great Unknown of Life from where it has brought the most revolutionary of spiritual truths, namely, the identity of the *Atman* and the *Brahman*. In man resides the nature of God—that indeed is its cardinal doctrine. If God resides in man then it is in the heart of man that He can be found. Along with the *Upanishads* and the *Brahma Sutras*, the *Bhagavad Gita* is a book of *Vedanta*. But its approach to the vast and fascinating subject of the *Brahman* and the *Atman* is very simple. This is probably the reason why the *Gita* has been, throughout the ages, the most popular book on *Vedanta*. The *Gita* has brought inspiration and illumination to millions of people all over the world by its simple and direct message of spiritual life. It has not asked the spiritual aspirant to renounce the world; on the contrary, it has emphasized the fact of man coming to spiritual realization in the midst of a work-a-day world. The teachings of the *Gita* are based on the day-to-day psychological struggles of man, for, it is with mind and its problems that it has been fundamentally concerned. From the confused and the distracted mind of Arjuna as evidenced in the First Discourse, the *Gita* takes us to the illumined and enlightened mind of this great disciple as seen in the Eighteenth Discourse of this Soul-stirring Gospel. From Mind to Super-Mind is the journey outlined by the *Gita* in a clear and an unambiguous manner. The *Gita* has again and again stressed one point, namely, the veils of the mind should be put away before the Spiritual Vision could be vouchsafed to man. The unconditioned consciousness, the utter sensitivity of the mind—this indeed is the instrument suggested by the *Gita* for the realization of the Supreme Truth of Life. One is reminded here of what a Sufi has said on this subject of spiritual realization. He tells us that:

> Three veils must be removed from before the pilgrim's heart ere the door of Happiness is opened to him. First, that, should the dominion of both worlds be offered to him as an eternal gift, he should not rejoice, since whosoever rejoiceth on account of any created thing is still covetous, and the covetous man is debarred from the knowledge of God. The second veil is this, that, should he possess the dominion of both worlds, and should it be taken from him, he should not sorrow for his impoverishment, for this is the sign of wrath, and he who is in wrath is tormented. The third is that he should not be beguiled by any praise or favour, for whosoever is beguiled is of mean spirit, and such a one is veiled from the Truth.

The Three Veils of the Sufi are reminicent of the Three Attributes about which the *Gita* speaks again and again. The Sufi emphasizes the fact that a spiritual pilgrim must transcend both joy and sorrow—but this is not enough, as he should remove even the veil of beguilement so that he becomes truly incorruptible. The corruptible must put on incorruptibility—this is verily the central theme of the message given by Sri Krishna to Arjuna. The corrupting influences of the mind are the Three *Gunas* or Attributes. A person who rises beyond these Three *Gunas* is a spiritually integrated individual. Such a man is not afraid to act because his action is devoid of any binding quality. The Eighteenth Discourse deals with this whole subject of Mind's attributes in a comprehensive manner. It speaks of Three Kinds of Knowledge and Three Kinds of Action. It deals with the subject of Three Kinds of Doers and Three Kinds of Understanding. It applies the topic of the Three Attributes to the problems of happiness as also to the question of Mind's Steadiness. The Practical *Yoga* of the *Gita* is concerned with the transcending of the Three Attributes of the mind. It is with reference to this that the *Gita* begins the Last Discourse with a discussion of Renunciation and Relinquishment, with *Sanyāsa* and *Tyāga* respectively.

Arjuna wishes to understand a distinction between the two, and so Sri Krishna says:

> The wise understand by renunciation, the giving up of desire-prompted actions; the abandonment of the fruits of all actions, the learned declare to be relinquishment.

Thus in *Sanyāsa* there is the giving up of certain actions while in *Tyāga* it is the fruit of actions that is relinquished. It is true that in abandoning the fruits of actions, certain types of action would automatically drop away, so that in *Tyāga* while there is no question of abandoning actions as such, there are certain kinds of actions the continuance of which is rendered meaningless when the fruit of actions is discarded. Sri Krishna discusses the whole subject of relinquishment mainly in three sections. They are (1) the relinquishment of fruit, (2) the relinquishment of the idea that the self is the actor, and (3) the recognition that it is the Supreme who is the author of all actions. The *Gita* says that he who renounces the performance of duty is given to *tāmasic* tendencies. It is to cover up his own indolence that such a person talks of renunciation. Not to perform one's own duty out of inertia and laziness and to call it renunciation is to show forth utter delusion of mind. Similarly, to give up the performance of duty because it is painful is to be a victim to *rajasic* tendencies. In fact in such renunciation there is a motive of seeking security for oneself. The *Gita* says that the really wise man is he who has 'no aversion to disagreeable action and no attachment to agreeable action.' The real quality of *Tyāga* consists in doing what needs to be done without aversion or attachment.

But the question may arise: can any action be done with sincerity and enthusiasm if both aversion and attachment are to be avoided? Will not an action done without aversion and attachment contain a factor of indifference on the part of the actor? An action done with real interest is completely free from indifference as well as interference. Usually when we are not indifferent, we are given to interference so that we disturb the pattern of things, and are unwilling to accept things as they are, Curiously enough, when we are asked to accept things as they are, we become indifferent to those things. Pure interest in that mid-point where both indifference and interference are eliminated. Indifference is the expression of *tamas* while interference is the reflection of *rajas*. Thus actions done with indifference belong to the category of dullness even as actions performed with interference have to be classed as passionate. There is a third category of action which is *sattvic* in which there is no indifference nor is there interference, but there is a subtle insolence born of self-righteousness. *Light on the Path* says 'The self-righteous man makes for himself a bed of mire'. Thus his actions are naturally rooted in mire. The mind all the time moves between the two opposite poles of Unrighteousness and Self-righteousness. The Pure Interest of the child-state is to be seen neither in indifference nor in interference nor in insolence born of self-righteousness. It is the man of Pure Interest who has given up the fruit of action. There is neither aversion nor attachment in his actions, since he is free from all motives. As the *Gita* says: 'It is indeed impossible for any embodied being to abstain from action altogether.' It is not action that binds: it is the fruit of action that results in bondage. The mind that looks forward to fruits of actions is caught up in the time-process, for, the fruit of action is in the future, while the performance of action is in the present. Once again the anticipation of fruit is determined by the memory of past experiences. Thus the mind that looks to fruits of action is for ever distracted in the present. His actions are incomplete—he moves from one incomplete action to another incomplete action. Man's bondage is due to the pull of incomplete experiences. The completion of experience does not depend upon the prolongation of an event—it depends upon the cessation of the thought-process with reference to that event.

The *Gita* says all actions arise from five-fold factors. They are *Adhisthanam* or Motive, literally the seat of action, *Karta* or Actor, *Karanam* or Instruments, *Cheshta* or Patterns of Behaviour, and *Daivam* or the Unpredictable element. Here actions are to be understood as those that bind, those that are the cause of misery and unhappiness.

The five factors quoted above are indeed the constituents of all actions. The seat of all action is indeed the motive, because it is out of the roots of motive that all actions arise. In all actions there is the *Karta* or the Actor—the sense of 'I' that is present in all that a man does. There are also the organs of action, *Karanam*. These are the expressional media, whether of thought or speech or sensorial responses. Apart from the media of expressions there are also the patterns of action described in the *Gita* as *Cheshta*. About this the *Gita* says that there is a variety of patterns—in fact, there is a countless variety. One of the constituents of action is *Daivam* or the Unpredictable factor. It may be described as man's destiny or *Karma*. This factor is indeed man's psychological heredity. In all his actions it is this heredity which dogs his footsteps. This is from one standpoint the unconscious factor behind all actions. We have stated above that motive is the seat of all actions. The motive has to be differentiated from impulse. Animals and primitive humanity act from impulse. The impulses change from moment to moment, but motive has an element of continuity in it. It is the 'I' which gives continuity to motive. This is indeed the source from which all actions emanate.

Regarding these five constituents of action, the *Gita* says that:

> Whatever action a man performeth by his body, speech and mind, whether right or the reverse, these five are the cause thereof.

In terms of the *Gita*, action is not merely a bodily activity—it includes whatever is done through the medium of speech and thought as well. In actions of all categories these five constituents are to be seen. In Pure Action even though the five constituents are present, they assume a new significance. The *Adhisthana* of Pure Action is motivelessness and its *Daivam* becomes the Universal Unconscious instead of the Personal Unconscious which is the operational base of psychological heredity. With regard to Pure Action even the *Karta* or the Actor undergoes a change, for he is the 'I' from which all 'I-ness' has disappeared. In case of Pure Action, the instruments of action are rendered very sensitive and the patterns of action too become rich in variety. Thus the five constituents of action are present everywhere even though their levels of functioning differ in accordance with the categories of action. In the following verse of the *Gita*, a distinction between Pure and Impure action is perceptible. The verse says:

> . . . the man of perverse mind who, on account of his untrained understanding looks upon himself as the actor, he does not see truly.

The man of untrained understanding is one whose vision is clouded. He is the one whose mind is unillumined—the mind in which the ray of Intuition has not come. Such a person regards himself as the sole agent of all actions hardly realizing that he is conditioned and fettered by *Daivam*—his personal unconscious. It is the man who sees the conditioning factors of his own psyche who is released from himself—he retains his identity but it is devoid of 'I-ness'—his Self is emptied of the self. This is made clear in the following verse of the *Gita* which says:

> He who is free from self-sense, whose understanding is not sullied, though he slay these people, he slays not, nor is he bound.

It is the self-sense which sullies one's understanding—the clouding of vision takes place because of the sense of 'I'. The *Gita* here classifies all actions in terms of their incentives and in terms of their components. Sri Krishna says:

> Knowledge, the object of knowledge and the knowing subject are the threefold incentives to action: the instrument, the action and the agent are the threefold components of action.

Here in the above verse the subject, the object and the relationship between the two have been indicated both with reference to action as also with reference to knowledge. The incentive to action comes invariably from knowledge. But knowledge itself is a composite process arising from the relationship of the knower and the known. Knowledge is indeed the background of action. It is of highest importance that one must find out whether this background is pure or polluted. This can be done by finding out the relationship between the knower and the known—in other words by inquiring into the very process of knowing. There is also a triplicity of action which is the actor, the thing acted upon and the instrument through which the action is performed. The instrument is indeed the means by which any act is executed. Now the means is most important because the end lies in the means itself. Wrong means can never lead to right ends as the end is not away from the means. Now to discover the 'I' that remains concealed in disguise in the nooks and corners of our existence one may either inquire into the process of knowing or one may examine the nature of the means employed. The man of knowledge may be inclined to make his search through the process of knowing, whereas the man of action may feel impelled to find out the 'I' through the means that he uses in the execution of his work.

In the Eighteenth Discourse, the *Gita* examines in detail the fields of knowledge as also the fields of action. Each is divided into its three-fold categories of *Tamas, Rajas* and *Sattva.* About knowledge it says:

> That by which the seer sees one indestructible Being in all beings, inseparate in the separated, know thou that knowledge as good.

To see Unity in Diversity is indeed that category of knowledge which can be classed as 'good' or *sattvic.* Similarly, as the *Gita* says that knowledge which sees only the diversity and not the unity behind it is *rajasic* or passionate. But the knowledge that can be classed as *tamasic* is the one where the part is mistaken for the whole. It may be asked that since the *Gita* speaks of transcending the three *Gunas* or the Attributes, what is that knowledge which is beyond the *sattvic*? Can there be anything beyond seeing Unity in Diversity? The Transcendental Knowledge, the knowledge that is beyond the *sattvic,* is verily seeing the Unique in the Universal. The Unique, the Universal, the Particular and the Partial may be regarded as the four categories of knowledge. The last three are *sattvic, rajasic* and *tamasic* respectively, while the first is transcendental.

The *Gita* gives a similar classification for action—actions which have *sattvic, rajasic* and *tamasic* contents respectively. It says:

> An action which is ordained, which is performed without attachment, without love or hate by one undesirous of fruit, that is said to be good.

Here the action is performed as a duty where no attachment

either of a positive or a negative kind exists. Such good action is performed by one who has no desire for fruits. Sri Krishna says that the action which requires 'great effort' or which involves strain, due to an eye towards the fulfilment of some desired result, may be classed as passionate. Here the implication is that good action must be natural, effortless and without any strain. Whenever there is any conscious effort for the fulfilment of an end there strain and stress inevitably arise, because conscious effort is always with a motive. The *Gita* says that when an action is undertaken without regard 'to capacity and to consequences' then such an action is dull or *tamasic.* This indicates that the person who performs action has not taken into account the subjective and the objective implications of what he is attempting to do. Capacity refers to subjective implications while consequences relate to objective implications. Without knowing whether one possesses the necessary capacity and without knowing what would be the consequences of one's actions, when one indulges in action then surely it is dull or *tamasic.* Here also a question may arise as to whether there is any action which transcends the category of good or *sattvic.* The *Gita* says that the *sattvic* action is one that is ordained and is therefore performed as a duty. Now there is a category of action which transcends the plane of duty. It is action that emerges from Love. There is a difference between an act of love and an act of law; between an act of grace and an act of obligation. When an action is performed in a state of love mysteriously enough there is no actor present in that act. In a loving action the duality of the subject and the object vanishes. It is this which can truly be called the Transcendental action.

It has to be remembered that the Three Attributes of the *Gita* are verily the varying conditions of the mind. From *tamas* to *rajas*, and from *rajas* to *sattva* there is a movement in depth or a movement towards a deepening of awareness. These three attributes are comparable to the *Jagrat*, the *Svapna* and the *Sushupti*—the Waking, the Dream and the Deep Sleep—states of consciousness. The *Turiya* or the Transcendental state is not of the mind. It represents a state which may be described as the Super-Mind. Nowhere has the *Gita* given a description of the Super-Mind because such description can never be given.

A description is immediately transformed by the mind into an image or into a concept. Super-Mind is beyond all conceptual understanding. The *Gita,* therefore, ends with the injunction that all the *gunas* or the attributes must be transcended—what happens after that is a matter of experience, not of description.

The *Gita* speaks here of three kinds of doers—the *sattvic,* the *rajasic* and the *tamasic.* The first category of actor is described thus:

> Liberated from attachment, not egoistic, endued with firmness and confidence, unchanged by success or failure—that actor is called good.

The man of *sattvic* qualities is resolute and enthusiastic—in failure he is resolute and in success he is enthusiastic. This is because there is in him an element of self-effacement. Conditions of selfhood differ at varying levels of consciousness. At the level of *tamas* there is only the Unawakened Selfhood, at the level of *rajas* there is the Assertive Selfhood and at the level of *sattva,* there is to be seen the Mellowed Selfhood. In this last stage the 'I' has mellowed down and has become gentle and soft. This is what is known as 'liberated from attachment.' The doer who is of the *rajasic* type is according to the *Gita* a man who is swayed by passion. He is a man of strong likes and dislikes and is therefore moved by joy and sorrow. There is more movement than steadiness to be seen in the make-up of the *rajasic* type of doer. That is why he displays an aggressive selfhood. The *tamasic* actor is described by the *Gita* as one who is *Prakritah* or vulgar. He is unrefined and uncultured. Being dull and indolent he is always procrastinating. The term used in the *Gita* for this is *Dirghasutri* meaning who weaves a long yarn for not doing something—one who is ready with excuses for the postponement of a work that needs to be done. Because of the unawakened selfhood, he is heavy with inertia. There is a category of doer who transcends even the state of *sattva.* He transcends the condition even of mellowed selfhood—he is the one from whom selfhood has disappeared completely and totally—he has identity without 'I-ness', he is unique and yet not isolated.

The *Gita* deals with the question of Understanding in a very clear manner in the Eighteenth Discourse. It gives the three main grades of understanding—or rather three grades of significance. To the dull mind there can be no clear understanding whatsoever. It imparts to all things that it perceives a deluded significance. It is a perception that is rooted in habit, and therefore habitual thinking is its main characteristics. It is unable to distinguish between right and wrong. To the mind that is *rajasic* or passionate, there comes an understanding which is of a different order. The passionate mind is caught up in an incessant movement of thought. Whatever it sees is coloured by this movement. It projects its own likes and dislikes and from this arrives at a mistaken view of men and things. It gives to all situations a projected significance. The rope being mistaken for a snake is illustrative of the understanding that belongs to the *rajasic* or the passionate mind. The *sattvic* mind however is sharp and alert. The alertness of the *sattvic* mind is clearly indicated in the following verse of the *Gita*:

> The understanding which knows action and non-action, what ought to be done and what ought not to be done, what is to be feared and what is not to be feared, what binds and what does not bind the soul—that understanding, O Partha, is good.

The alert mind is that which is able to perceive the opposites in a clear and distinct manner. A clarity of perception is obviously the characteristic of the alert mind. The main function of the mind is to define with utmost clarity the problem or the situation that it faces. Such a definition indicates the perception of opposites with reference to the given problem or situation. When the mind has defined the opposites, its function is over, for, it has reached the position of its highest possibilities. For the comprehension of truth there has to be both the positivity as well as the negativity of the mind. The positive mind formulates the problem while the negative mind solves it. Any effort to solve a problem with a positive mind is bound to result in utter frustration. The mind can only formulate a problem; it cannot solve it. The solution of a problem has to be done by the negative mind. Dr Maxwell Maltz, an eminent plastic surgeon, has written a remarkable book entitled *Psycho-cybernetics*. In this book he states that while the conscious mind must clearly formulate the problem, it must, after such formulation, hand over the problem to the Unconscious because, according to him, it is the Unconscious that can bring about a solution of the problem that has been defined by the conscious mind. The Unconscious cannot solve a problem which has not been clearly defined. The clear definition is the function of the conscious mind. It is only the conscious mind in its alertness that can define and formulate a problem. In the *Gita* we are given an indication of an alert mind which can clearly define action and non-action as also what ought to be done and what ought not to be done. In other words, the *sattvic* or the good mind has a clear perception of the opposites. Into such a clearly perceiving mind the solution comes—it arrives from those realms which are outside the frontiers of the mind. It is the Super-Mind or the Universal Unconscious which indicates the solution of a problem which has been well-defined by the *sattvic* mind. The Dull mind sees the opposites one after the other and therefore does not see them as opposites at all. The Passionate mind is unable to clearly define the opposites—its perception of the opposites is blurred and indistinct. The Good or the *sattvic* mind, however, is able to see the opposites all at once and that too clearly and distinctly.

In this background of the three grades of understanding, the subject of the Steadiness of the mind discussed in this Discourse of the *Gita* becomes all the more clear. The steadiness of mind has various layers. If these layers are not understood then one may have a confused understanding of men and things. There is the steadiness of the Indolent Mind, there is also the steadiness of the Identifying Mind, and lastly, there is the steadiness of the Attentive Mind. These three grades of steadiness naturally refer to the Dull, the Passionate and the Good mind respectively. The steadiness of the Indolent mind is no steadiness at all—it is verily a stagnant condition of the mind. A stagnant pool of water appears very steady, but it is so heavy with silt and mud that it is unable to move. Its steadiness therefore arises out of its inability to move. The *Gita* tells us that this steadiness has a nature of dullness in it, for it says:

That steadiness by which a fool does not give up sleep, fear, grief,

> depression and arrogance, that, O Partha, is of the nature of dullness.

Thus it is a steadiness born of well-established habit. The steadiness of the dull mind is rooted in inertia. It is a passive state of consciousness. There is, however, a steadiness that belongs to the *rajasic* or the passionate condition of the mind. It is the steadiness of an Identifying mind. When the mind identifies itself with something, then through that identification certain steadiness is born. However, this steadiness is short-lived. It gets constantly disturbed due to the incessant flux of life. Identification has always within it a pull from that which is outside the charmed circle of identification. When identification is very strong and intense this pull is imperceptible and the mind appears to be steady. But this steadiness is very superficial, for, the intensity of identification wears off in no time and when this happens once again the conflict of the opposites rages in all its ferocity. The *Gita* speaks of the steadiness of the passionate mind thus:

> The steadiness by which one holds fast to duty, pleasure and wealth desiring the fruit in consequence thereof—that, O Partha, is the nature of passion.

The ambitious man has a singleness of purpose due to which he keeps his mind firmly occupied, without any distraction, on gaining the object of his ambition. It is a steadiness born of complete identification with the desired object. The successful businessman has a remarkable steadiness of mind—but this steadiness gets easily disturbed because its source is outside and not within one's own being. Not being able to control the flux of life this steadiness is most unsteady. It is the steadiness of an occupied mind. Once the occupation ceases the mind gets disturbed and restless. So long as the mind needs some occupation to keep it steady, so long it must remain unsteady. There is, however, a higher grade of steadiness which is described by the *Gita* as the steadiness of the good or the *sattvic*. Speaking about this the *Gita* says:

> The unwavering steadiness by which, through attention, one holds the movements of the mind, the life-breaths and the senses, that O Partha, is of the nature of goodness.

This is verily the steadiness of the Attentive mind. The *Gita* speaks of the 'holding of the movements of the mind through attention'. Commenting upon the word *dhritih* meaning steadiness appearing in the above verse, Dr S. Radhakrishnan says:

> Steadiness of attention which makes us aware of much that our ordinary vision is not able to observe. Its power is proportional to our detachment from regrets over the past and the anxieties for the future.

The steadiness of attention is possible only when the mind is not distracted. As Dr Radhakrishnan says, this is possible only when there are no regrets over the past and no anxieties of the future. In other words the consciousness in the condition of attention must function in the present—not the chronological present but the psychological present. It is interesting to note that the steadiness of the dull mind is rooted in the past—in habits and tendencies brought forward from the past; the steadiness of the passionate mind is rooted in the future—the ambitions and the successes that one wishes to gain being in the future—but the steadiness of the good mind exists in the present. It has been freed from the habits of the past and from the conflicts that rage due to the allurement of the future. Such are the steadiness of the Indolent mind, the steadiness of the Identified mind and the steadiness of the Attentive mind.

It has to be remembered that steadiness pre-supposes a balance—a balance of the opposites. The balance of the dull is due to the unawareness of the opposites; the balance of the passionate is due to an identification with one of the opposites; the balance of the good is however due to a reconciliation between the opposites—due to a synthesis established between the thesis and the antithesis. There is a state beyond steadiness—and that is the state of Silence. When the mind comes to a totality of attention then there descends upon it a silence which is not of the mind but which arrives from the Land of the Unknown. This Silence is like a grace which comes when the mind is freed from the pulls of the past and the future.

The problem of steadiness naturally brings us to the question of Happiness to which the *Gita* turns in the Eighteenth Discourse. We have to remember that the Dull, the Passionate and the Good are not so much classifications of people as they are states of consciousness. It would be wrong to think that there are some people who are born dull, some others born passionate, and a few born good. The dull, the passionate and the good are the conditions of the mind. As is the state of the mind so is the nature of one's happiness. To the dull mind living in a world of make-believe is happiness. He builds castles-in-the-air and lives in an utterly deluded world. He is comparable to a man who having taken certain drugs lives in an artificial state of bliss. The *Gita* describes the happiness of those of dull mind in the following words:

> That pleasure which both at first and afterwards is delusive of the self, arising from sleep, indolence and negligence—that is declared to be of the nature of dullness.

When the mind moves from the state of dullness to a condition of conflict and restlessness then the concept of happiness too changes. To the *rajasic* nature of the mind, happiness consists in sensations and excitements—the more of these the greater is the feeling of happiness for such an individual. But all sensations and excitements, while they give pleasant feeling in the beginning, render the enjoyer of that happiness tired and exhausted. Sensationalism is nerve-racking and so the person who is given to it experiences nervous breakdown and mental unbalance. The more one gives to sensationalism, the more grows the craving for it. That is why the *Gita,* while describing this state of happiness says that at first it is like nectar, but in the end it becomes a venom. But what about the happiness that comes to the *sattvic* state of mind? The *Gita* says:

> That happiness which is like poison at first and like nectar at the end, which springs from a clear understanding of the Self is said to be of the nature of goodness.

What is meant by happiness being poison at first? It really means that in that state of happiness there is no consciousness that one is happy. When the sense of happiness is unconscious then it results in a condition of bliss. Bliss is not of the mind but in the supreme state of unconsciousness, the experience of bliss comes. One is detached from that which appears to be poison. The man of *sattvic* quality is detached in the midst of favourable conditions of life and so in the end he is supremely happy. It is happiness born of detachment.

But the practical question is: How can one come to this state of Supreme Happiness—the happiness that endures, not the one that decays in the process of time. Here the *Gita* introduces a subject of great significance for the spiritual aspirant. It talks of *Svabhava* and *Svadharma*, of Being and Becoming. The *Svabhava* is the Being of man—his original, uncontaminated nature. *Svadharma* is the Becoming that emanates from the Being—it is the true vocation of man. Thus the Nature of Man and the Vocation of Man are the two subjects to which the *Gita* draws our attention as it proceeds with the problem of man's happiness. The *Gita* tells us that:

> Man reacheth perfection by being intent on his own duty.

Thus Perfection is along the path of *Svadharma*, but before one can tread the path of Perfection, one must discover one's own true nature—one's own *Svabhava*. But how is one to discover one's own true nature? This is possible only when one is liberated from one's acquired nature. The Becoming that has its roots in the acquired nature is self-defeating and frustrating. The field of Time in which all becoming proceeds seems to most of us unending because there is no naturalness in our becoming. The Becoming that emanates from the acquired nature demands tremendous effort from the individual who treads the path of Perfection. But perfection must be like the blooming of a flower. Poet Rabindranath Tagore says that 'He who opens the flower does it gently'. The blooming of the flower happens very gently, almost imperceptibly. Perfection must also be so natural, gentle and imperceptible. But a gentle movement towards Perfection is possible only when one is liberated from one's acquired nature so that rooted in one's original nature one can journey to the end of time without any feeling of frustration or tiredness. Liberation must precede Perfection, for how can he who is entangled in the demands of his false nature ever know what perfection is? It is to this original nature of man that the *Gita* has given the name *Svabhava*. We shall see later in this Chapter what are those processes by which man can be released from his acquired nature. Let us first see what the *Gita* has to say regarding the question of *Svadharma* or the true Vocation of Man.

There is a fourfold classification of Vocations that the *Gita* has given. These are the *Brahmana*, the *Kshatriya*, the *Vaishya* and the *Shudra*. They are the Teacher, the Protector, the Nourisher, and the Worker respectively. This is a functional classification of man, but behind it one can see the comprehension of the psychological aptitudes of man. The fourfold classification has both a social as well as an individual significance. In its social setting it indicates an ideology of social integration. It lays down fundamental principles of true democracy. As Dr Radhakrishnan says:

> Society is a functional organization and all functions which are essential for the health of society are to be regarded as socially equal. Individuals of varying capacities are bound together in a living organic social system. Democracy is not an attempt at uniformity, which is impossible, but an integrated variety.

In the fourfold classification we get a clear picture of an integrated variety. But here in the *Gita* we are not so much concerned with the social context of the fourfold classification as with the individual. In this classification is to be seen not only social integration but individual integration as well. In fact without individual integration social integration is impossible. What is individual integration in terms of this fourfold classification? Man's individual nature has four fundamental components—they are the Physical, the Vital, the Emotional and the Intellectual, leaving out the spiritual for the time-being. All the fourfold components should be integrated as otherwise man will remain in conflict within himself. Now the Physical component has reference to the classification known as the *shudra*. Man must be *shudra* in his physical aspect meaning thereby that he must be active physically, able to do manual work. If he regards manual work as something derogatory then he is sure to bring that bias in his social relationship as well. He will regard the *shudras* as functionaries in society, as inferior. He will begin to give to the differences of functions certain status and distinction. It is when distinctions are imparted to differences that social unrest and disintegration arise. In order to abolish these distinctions man must be able to function as a *shudra* in the physical counterpart of his personality. To be able to do all physical jobs with efficiency and without any sense of shame or degradation is necessary for one's integration. Similarly, in the vital part of one's being one must be able to function as a *vaishya*. The *vaishya* is a nourisher: man in his vital nature must be a nourisher too. He must be a centre of vitality and healing wherever he goes. The nursing of the sick, the feeding of the poor, the tending of the weak and the crippled—these must be natural to man. One of the old Hindu customs was that a householder cannot eat before he has offered a fivefold sacrifice. This meant making offerings of food to gods, to ancestors, to animals, to fellow-human beings and to the disembodied spirits. This indicated the individual discharging the functions of a *vaishya* in his individual capacity and relationship. But man must be a *kshatriya* too in his individual life and this has reference to his emotional nature. The *kshatriya* is a protector of people. In ancient India the ruler was regarded as the father and the mother to his subjects. The *Gita* describes the following as the characteristics of the *kshatriyas*:

> Heroism, vigour, steadiness, resourcefulness, not fleeing even in a battle, generosity and the quality of being a protector—these are the duties of a *kshatriya* born of his nature.

Heroism, generosity and readiness to protect others—these are indeed qualities of emotional maturity. To be able to give protection to the needy is verily the duty of a true *kshatriya*. This requires not merely heroism but resourcefulness and generosity. It is the emotionally sensitive who alone can render true assistance. The spirit of the *kshatriya* has been beautifully expressed by H. P. Blavatsky in her *Voice of the Silence* thus:

> Let thy soul lend its ear to every cry of pain like as the lotus bares its heart to drink the morning sun. Let not the fierce sun dry one tear of pain before thyself hast wiped it from the sufferer's eye.

How is this possible unless there is extraordinary sensitivity in one's emotional nature? It is the task of the *kshatriya* to show forth 'a valiant defence of those who are unjustly attacked'. He is not an aggressor—he is a protector, the defender of the Realm of God. There is still another part of man's psyche and that is the mental or the intellectual. This corresponds to the *Brahmin* nature in man. Man must be not only a Worker, Nourisher and Defender but also a Teacher. The qualities of the Teacher are given clearly in the following verse of the *Gita*:

> Serenity, self-control, austerity, purity, forbearance and uprightness, wisdom, knowledge and faith—these are the duties of the Brahmin, born of his nature.

Man must have intellectual pursuits, for he does not live by bread alone. The intellectual pursuits cover a wide range—it includes not only science, religion and philosophy but also arts and various cultural pursuits. A Sanskrit verse says that a man devoid of literary pursuits, of musical and artistic interests is one who is no better than an animal. A *Brahmin* is known for his wide range of interests. In the old *Gurukuls* of India, the disciple learnt from the teacher various sciences, philosophies and arts. The teacher of old India was not merely versed in religion. He covered the whole range of human interest and imparted to his disciples that catholicity of outlook which is the hall-mark of a true *Brahmin*. Thus the fourfold classification has as much to do with the integration of the individual man as it has to do with the integration of society. It is the man who is at the same time a *Shudra*, a *Vaishya*, a *Kshatriya* and a *Brahmin* who is truly integrated. In his social relationship he will be able to keep differences at a functional level without imparting into them distinctions which are a cause of social unrest and conflict.

But it may be asked: Does man have only the physical, vital, emotional and intellectual components in his psyche? What about the spiritual nature of man? The spiritual transcends the fourfold classification. In ancient India apart from the fourfold classification there was one that transcended this classification. It was known as *Sanyasa*. The *Sanyasi* did not belong to any of the fourfold classification; he was not governed by their rules and their codes of social morality. He was a law unto himself. The truly spiritual man is indeed a law unto himself. It has to be remembered that it was not the *Brahmin* who was the spiritual preceptor. The spiritual preceptor had to be more than a *Brahmin*—he had to be a sage. The *Brahmin* dealt with the wide variety of intellectual pursuits, but it was the sage who imparted spiritual instruction. Thus the spiritual counterpart is above and beyond the fourfold classification. It is only the integrated man who can come to this spiritual experience, and the integrated man is one who has harmonized his physical, vital, emotional and intellectual components of his being.

It is necessary to note that while a truly integrated man is at once a *Shudra*, a *Vaishya*, a *Kshatriya* and a *Brahmin*, he has also within him a predominance of any one of these four characteristics. The predominant note of his character is his natural mode of expression. It is through this natural mode of expression that a man can discover his true and original nature. This original nature is his *svabhava* out of which emanates his *svadharma* or his natural duty. The *Gita* says that 'man reacheth perfection by each being intent on his own duty'. The Path of Perfection lies along the line of the performance of one's own duty. Sri Krishna tells Arjuna:

> Better is one's own duty, though destitute of merits, than the well-executed duty of another. He who doeth the duty laid down by his own nature incurreth no sin.

Here the *Gita* explains clearly as to what is meant by one's own duty. It tells us that it is the duty 'laid down by one's own nature'. In the next verse this is further explained by the term *sahajam* meaning spontaneous or natural. The fourfold classification represents modes of expression. If these modes do not emanate from one's original nature then they are mere imitations, devoid of grace and charm. To discover one's original nature is to come to the highest state of consciousness. But how is one to come to it? Dr Radhakrishnan writing about this in his *Bhagavad Gita* says:

> The highest state is here (in the *Gita*) described, not positively as entering into the Lord, but negatively as freedom from *kama*.

In order to discover the original nature, it is the negative path that has to be taken. It is the path in which the acquired nature is being continually negated. In the negation of the acquired nature, one comes to the supreme discovery of one's own original nature. In terms of the *Gita* the acquired nature is the *Para-dharma.* To become aware of the *Para-dharma* which one has ignorantly adopted is to move in the direction of discovering the *svadharma.* The *Gita* says it is by renunciation that one comes to the supreme state. The discovery of one's own original nature is truly a supreme state, because the *Brahman* and the *Atman* are identical in nature. To discover the *Atman* is therefore to discover the *Brahman.*

Now the process of negation suggested by the *Gita* is, casting aside 'egoism and violence; arrogance and lust; anger and possessiveness.' Anger, arrogance and violence show increasing stages of resistance while possessiveness, lust and egoism show increasing stages of identification. It is the process of acceptance and rejection which is indicated here in the six characteristics which have to be negated ere one can come to the Supreme State. The acquired nature of man is built out of this process of Acceptance and Rejection. From the field of relationship in which man grows he accepts certain things and rejects others, and so within this sphere of acceptance and rejection he builds up the entire structure of his acquired nature. If he must negate his acquired nature in order to discover his true and original nature, then he must examine this process of acceptance and rejection. How does he accept certain things and reject others—and why does he do so? The How and the Why of this process would reveal to him the secret by which his acquired nature is built up. Needless to say behind this process lies the operational activities of the mind—for it is the mind that accepts and the mind that rejects. To examine the movement of the mind with reference to this process is therefore of utmost importance. But how is this movement to be examined? It is in the observation of the mind and its activities that this process of acceptance and rejection can be understood. The question is: What is exactly meant by observing the mind?

To observe the mind is to see the whole range of thought, not merely the conscious but also the unconscious. The unconscious range can be seen only from what comes into the realm of the conscious—but when the conscious mind stops its resistance, the unconscious becomes an open book. So to observe the whole range of thought means to see the conscious thought and also whatever the unconscious sends up in a condition of non-resistance established by the conscious mind. The first thing to observe in the operations of the mind would be the Nature of Thought. What kind of thoughts come into the mind?—this is essential for any detailed observation of the mind. We are hardly conscious of what goes on in the mind. There is an incessant stream of visitors making a call on the mind during all hours of the day and the night. Some of these visitors stay on, others leave after a courtesy call. It is necessary to keep a register of all these 'callers' so that one may know what type of company the mind has, both casual as well as intimate. From the Nature of Thought one must move on to the Drift of Thought in this process of observation. Just as there are visitors that call on the mind, the mind too goes on its own friendly calls. It is true that it goes only to its intimate friends—nevertheless it is necessary to know the mind's circle of friends. This can be found out by looking into the drift of the mind. Let the mind be given an occupation and left alone to deal with it. We will find invariably that the mind slips away from its occupation and goes on a visit to some intimate friend or the other. This drift gives an indication of what is going on at the subconscious level even when the conscious mind is occupied with something. The third field of observation would be to watch the Impulses of Thought. Most of us experience sudden outbursts of thought and feeling. For no reason whatsoever we feel greatly elated and then again for no reason whatsoever we feel suddenly depressed. These swings of elation and depression give a very useful indication of what goes on in the mind. How and when do such swings of emotion come? Have they to do with physical conditions, or do they arise from certain unconscious habits of the mind? There are sights that depress us and there are sights that fill us with enthusiasm. Why does this happen? This inquiry into the Impulses of thought immediately brings us to the question of the Association of thought. One must carefully study one's own associations of thought. Behind these associations lies the long history of mind's activities and entanglements. By examining the free association of thought one can delve into this history of the mind—its antecedents, its successes and failures, its vested interests. There is much that comes up in dreams which can be deciphered only through this process of association, and dreams are a very useful agency for investigating the contents of the mind. The Association of thought reveals the existence of a Conflict of thought in the operational field of the mind. In the very process of association one can see the resistance of the mind to certain evocations of thought. Such resistance is obviously caused by mind's identification with certain other evocations of thought. Thus the mind gets entangled in conflict, which sometimes takes acute proportions. It is necessary to become aware of this conflict—its habitual patterns and its modified patterns too. All conflicts have as their basis the desire to become something—it is a desire to move away from what is to what one would like to be.

The conflict, in other words, is between the Actual and the Ideal—the ideal being the end product of the entire process of becoming. Thus conflicts lead us to the problem of ideals and aspirations. All ideals contain positive as well as negative contents—it is these which may be called the Acceptance and the Rejection by the mind. The positive content of the ideal is mind's acceptance, and the negative content of the mind is mind's rejection. Thus our inquiry into mind's operations brings us to a state when we must probe into the very structure and the significance of ideals, both negative as well as positive. This probe, however, is possible only when the earlier processes of mind's observation have been gone through, namely, the Nature of Thought, the Drift of Thought, the Impulses of Thought, the Association of Thought and the Conflicts of Thought. It is in the background of this inquiry that it is possible to go into the question of the Rejection of Thought and the Acceptance of Thought. This entire inquiry into the processes of the mind enables us to see how we have built up an acquired nature due to which we are caught up in *Para-dharma* and have lost sight of the *Svadharma*. To become aware of the acquired nature is to start the process of being free from it. The basis of acquired nature is security, for it is from the fear of insecurity that man establishes newer and newer adjustments to outer environment, be the environment physical or psychological. Man is afraid that if he does not adjust to changed conditions, he would be wiped off. So he builds up an acquired nature which he hopes will stand him in good stead under the impact of changed circumstances. It is true that adjustments are always necessary—they can be made by distorting one's nature or by intelligently manipulating the circumstances so as to give new facilities to the original nature to express itself. Most of us want to settle down in new habits instead of keeping an intelligent watch over the changed and the changing circumstances of life. It is in the formation of new habits that the acquired nature comes into existence. However, when the process of becoming is undertaken with an acquired nature there is always struggle and frustration in store for such an individual.

To discover one's original nature is to be initiated into a new dimension of living. This discovery is a revolutionary event in the journey of life. In the moment of this discovery man is given a new name—from then onwards it is this name which becomes his true name. He leaves behind his old name, never to be uttered again; and with the casting away of the old name, all associations and memories of the past are also obliterated. Among the Hindus there is a custom that when one puts on the robes of a *sanyasi*, he takes a new name—or rather his *Guru* gives him a new name. Whatever happened prior to the giving of this new name is wiped out from memory. In fact the wiping away of the old memories and the assuming of a new name are a simultaneous process. The giving of the new name is indeed the grace of the *Guru*. The new name is the nucleus of spiritual life formed within the consciousness of the disciple. It is the establishment of this nucleus which truly is the descent of the grace from the Unknown and the Transcendental. The *Guru* or the Master is not the physical body—he is the Transcendental Consciousness. The grace from the Transcendental Consciousness is like the flash of lightning which for a split second breaks through even the thickest cloud and illumines the path of the pilgrim. Call this intuition or what you will. When this Grace descends all doubts are dispelled and the aspirant knows clearly what is the path that lies before him. Sri Krishna tells Arjuna in the *Bhagavad Gita*:

> Though ever performing all actions, taking refuge in Me, by My grace he obtaineth the eternal indestructible abode.

It is said in an Occult manual that the disciple cannot seek the Master, it is the Master who seeks the disciple. Since the Master is the Transcendental Consciousness, how can the limited consciousness of the mind through its efforts know that which is beyond its reach? The effort of the mind can go up to a particular point, but at that point it must stop realizing the limitations of mind's conscious efforts. In that pause of the mind where the known has dropped away the Grace of the Unknown descends. But the condition for the descent of the Grace is that the disciple must take refuge in the Me or the Unknown. So long as the mind clings to the known, it must remain confined to its own sphere. When the known drops away and the mind is stripped of everything that it had acquired through the ages, then, and only then, does come to man the Grace from on High, the ineffable Light from the Land of the Unknown. It is in that Light that man discovers his true and original nature, he is endowed with a new Name. When man comes into his own estate then does he not only know his own true name but the true name of all things in the universe. Knowing this he calls all things by their true names. Nature responds to his call, for nature recognizes only the real names, not the acquired ones. From now onwards man and nature become collaborators in the great scheme of things. This is indeed the destiny of all men. The *Gita* says:

> Thinking of Me, thou shalt overcome all obstacles by My grace; but if from egoism thou wilt not listen, thou shalt be destroyed utterly.

The Grace of the Unknown is there for all of us to have—but it is egoism that stands in the way. The ego is the acquired nature of man. The ego is the sum total of mind's efforts. It contains the accumulated knowledge of the mind. One is very proud of this knowledge regarding it as the resolver of all problems. So long as knowledge speaks, the voice of Wisdom cannot be heard. But when the pride of knowledge drops away then there comes the Grace of Wisdom, the Gift of the Unknown, the Light ineffable from Beyond. Man can overcome all obstacles when this Grace descends because he fights no longer with merely his strength—to his strength is added the strength of the All-Powerful and the Almighty. Sri Krishna tells Arjuna:

> Flee unto Him for shelter with all thy being, O Bharata. By His grace shalt thou obtain supreme peace and eternal abode.

To seek shelter in the Unmanifest with all one's being—this is the injunction of Sri Krishna. The term used by the *Gita* is *Sarvabhaven*—with the entire being. The surrender to the Unknown has to be complete, without any reservation whatsoever. The love of Radha for Sri Krishna is a symbol of integral love on all planes of being, from the spiritual to the physical. This is illustrative of that total surrender about which the *Gita* speaks here. The mind must be stripped of everything ere the Grace of the Unknown can come. The mind must be divested of the nature that it has acquired for the purposes of its own security. The mind must become utterly nameless before the real name can be revealed to the spiritual pilgrim.

It has to be remembered that by total surrender the *Gita* does not espouse a blind faith. For even at this stage Sri Krishna tells Arjuna:

> Thus has wisdom more secret than all secrets been declared to thee by Me. Having reflected on it fully do as thou choosest.

There is no element of compulsion in the *Gita*. If surrender is with compulsion then it is no surrender at all. Compulsion indicates a conflict—it suggests that man would have taken a different course but has been compelled to take a particular one due to the force of circumstances. Total surrender comes only when all desires and aspirations of the mind drop away—they are not consciously discarded. The act of surrender is a plunge into the Unknown. He who can put his complete faith in the Unknown is truly saved, for it is the Unknown that looks after him. Sri Krishna tells Arjuna:

> Abandoning all duties, come unto Me alone for shelter; sorrow not, I will liberate thee from all sins.

To abandon all duties is to cast away all the acquired interests of the mind. The mind has its will which is born of the acquired nature. When man abandons the will of the mind, then it is that the Cosmic Will takes charge of him. In fact in the putting away of the Will of the Mind, man sees for the first time what the Will of his true nature is. The Will of man's original nature and the Will of the Cosmos are not two different things. Since the nature of the *Brahman* resides in the *Atman*, how can the *Atman* have a will that is contrary to the *Brahman*. Thus in the discovery of one's original nature, the conflict of wills completely disappears. Man's total surrender is not to something external; it is a surrender to oneself—to one's true and original nature. Thus the doctrine of surrender is not a doctrine of dependence—on the contrary, it is a doctrine of unrestricted freedom. This is indicated clearly in the following verse of the *Bhagavad Gita*—the last that Sri Krishna addresses to Arjuna:

> Has this been heard by thee, O son of Pritha, with one-pointed mind? O Arjuna, has thy distraction of thought caused by ignorance been dispelled?

At the end of the entire teaching of the *Gita*, Sri Krishna asks Arjuna: 'Have you listened to what I have said?' Even at this stage Sri Krishna does not lay down the law. He does not exercise any authority over Arjuna. The Master asks His disciple: 'Has thy distraction of thought caused by ignorance been dispelled?' This question is indicative of the fact that the teaching of the *Gita* was primarily concerned with the problem of mind's distractions. Arjuna's mind was distracted. But what was the cause of distraction? Sri Krishna says that it was ignorance that caused distraction to the mind of his friend and disciple. We may ask: Ignorance of what? Surely, the ignorance is the one that arises from the forgetting of one's true nature. As the Poet Wordsworth says: 'Our birth is but a sleep and a forgetting: The Soul that rises with us, our life's Star hath had elsewhere its setting, and cometh from afar.'

The answer that Arjuna gives to the inquiry of Sri Krishna is most significant. In fact it is with that answer that the *Gita* concludes. Arjuna says:

> Destroyed is my delusion. I have regained memory through Thy grace. I stand firm with all my doubts dispelled. I shall do Thy bidding.

Arjuna is at last willing to do as Sri Krishna desires. What has brought this complete transformation in him? It is the Grace of the Lord that has wrought this miracle and the Grace descended upon him even as he was listening with full attention to the wonderful teaching of the Lord. It was in the very act of listening that the doubts of Arjuna were dispelled. If only we could listen to the song of life then we too would come to a vision of indescribable beauty and splendour. To listen without any justification or condemnation is to cross over the threshhold of the mind and enter a realm of ineffable joy. To listen with attention is to be free from delusion. It is to see things in their right perspective. This is exactly what Arjuna says to the Lord: 'Destroyed is my delusion'. But what does the destruction of delusion mean? It indicates the 'regaining of memory'. Arjuna did not suffer from loss of memory. But it was the confusion of memory that had taken place. When does such confusion arise? When facts are overlaid with fiction; when the factual memory lies concealed behind psychological memory. It is listening with attention that cleared his memory so that he was able to see facts as facts. But such listening is possible only when the centres of psychological resistance are wiped away. It is for this that the message of the *Gita* lays stress on *Abhyasa* and *Vairagya*—on the observation of the mind in action. Mind can be truly observed only in action or in relationship. To watch one's thoughts and emotions in the mirror of relationship is verily to arrive at that state where listening with total attention becomes possible. To listen with attention is to receive life as it comes and in the receiving of life, without resistance or indulgence, that one is blessed with the Grace from on High—the Grace which drives away all doubts and brings to one the Great Vision of Life. When Arjuna says to the Lord 'I shall do Thy bidding' there has taken place the supreme event of the merging of the Individual Will with the Cosmic Will. The whole struggle of Arjuna arose because of the pull exercised by the will of the mind. But when in listening to Sri Krishna with attention, the mind became quiet; it was divested of its will; the regaining of memory took place, and the vision of Life Eternal came to him. It is in this vision that the perception of the identity of wills came to Arjuna. He said that 'My doubts have been dispelled'. He had so far thought that the Cosmic Will was different from his own will. This delusion persisted so long as mind was active with its own movement. The movement of the mind was comprehensively described by Sri Krishna under the categories of the *tamas*, *rajas* and the *sattva*. So long as Arjuna listened with *tamas* so long was he distracted by the death of the near and dear ones. When he listened with *rajas* he was depressed by a sense of discontinuity. When he listened with *sattva* he was confused by a false sense of duty. Thus death, discontinuity and duty were the three factors causing distraction to Arjuna. When he transcended the three *gunas* was he able to understand clearly. His doubts arising from a false sense of duty were dispelled. He realized that his will and the Will of the Cosmos were identical. When he told Sri Krishna 'I shall do Thy bidding,' he had come to the realization that there was no conflict between what his true and original nature desired and what the Cosmic Will had asked him to do.

The *Gita* closes with this great teaching of the Identity of Two Wills. Free Will and Determinism are merely the problems created by the mind. When one transcends the mind there is no such problem. What appears to the mind as Determinism is only due to its own likes and dislikes. When the two opposites of the mind drop away then there is left but one path only. It is the *Svadharma* revealed to man in the moment of discovering the *Svabhava*. When man discovers his own nature, then does he declare: *Nanyah Panthah Vidyate Ayanaya*—There is no other Path at all. It is in this realization that Arjuna declares *Karishye Vachanam Tava*—I shall do Thy bidding. He saw that Sri Krishna was indicating to him only his *Svadharma*. He had so far resisted moving along that path because he had not seen his own *Svabhava*. Once the perception of his true nature came to him, he spontaneously chose the Path that was indicated to him. His conflict was over; his doubts were dispelled. The *Brahman* was discovered in the very heart of the *Atman*.

While the teaching of the *Gita* concludes with this declaration of Arjuna, there still remains the final observation of Sanjaya who had listened to the dialogue of Sri Krishna and Arjuna with a great sense of wonder and joy. Sanjaya who was an impersonal observer and narrator of the great events of Kurukshetra, sums up the entire teaching of the *Gita* in but one verse—and that is the last verse of this great and universal scripture. Sanjaya says:

> Wherever there is Krishna, the Lord of *Yoga*, and Partha, the Archer, assured are there prosperity, victory, progress and righteousness.

In the Kurukshetra war Sri Krishna was only the Charioteer of Arjuna's chariot. He had declined to take up arms, and Arjuna had chosen to have Sri Krishna on his side in the capacity of his Charioteer. While Duryodhana decided to have Sri Krishna's army on his side, Arjuna had unhesitatingly asked for Sri Krishna even though the latter had declared His intention of not taking up arms. Duryodhana had thought that Arjuna had been unwise in not asking for the brave warriors of Sri Krishna's army to fight on his side. Yet the events proved that it was Arjuna who was wise. But what is the meaning of this choice, and what is the significance of the above verse recited by Sanjaya?

In the Mahabharata war Sri Krishna symbolizes Inaction even as Arjuna represents Action. When action is performed in the background of inaction there is bound to be success in one's undertaking. In the *Gita* Arjuna stands for the human Mind, alert and active. But Sri Krishna symbolizes the Super-Mind. When the mind is illumined by the Super-Mind or by *Buddhi* then is victory assured for the individual. If one could only make *Buddhi* the charioteer of one's life then there will be no going astray. But *Buddhi* can function as charioteer for the mind that is alert and active, and not for a mind that is dull and passive. The mind must do its legitimate function, then only can the illumination of *Buddhi* come. Most often we move about with passive and dull minds and yet expect the guidance of *Buddhi*. Sometimes we carry minds that are active and positive. The guidance of *Buddhi* can never come to such minds. For the illumination of *Buddhi*, the mind must be alert and yet negative. Arjuna represents such a mind. He was alert and capable of using arms; and yet he was humble enough to entrust his chariot to Sri Krishna. He did not want Sri Krishna to fight his battle. He was prepared to do the fighting—but while he was a dauntless fighter, he wanted the reins of his war-chariot to be in the hands of Sri Krishna. What the *Gita* says has been indicated in one of the Occult manuals which tells the neophyte: 'Though thou fightest, be not thou the warrior'. To fight and yet not to be a warrior seems paradoxical. It is with this paradox that the *Gita* is concerned, for it says: Let thy action be in the background of Inaction. When Vision or *Yoga* and Action or *Dhanuh* are combined, when Mind and Super-Mind function in perfect harmony, when Mind invites *Buddhi* to be its charioteer, then victory in the battle of life is assured. The Mind to become an instrument of the Super-Mind—this verily is the message of the *Bhagavad Gita.* To the mind-ridden civilization of ours, the *Gita* brings the inspiring message of the *Buddhi,* for it says that the problems created by the Mind can be solved only when the mind is illumined by *Buddhi.* Into the realm of human consciousness the *Gita* brings a new dimension of understanding—it is a dimension not of the Mind but of the Super-Mind. From Mind to Super-Mind—this is indeed the path indicated by the *Bhagavad Gita* to all those who aspire to reach the great Summit of Life. The *Gita* invites us to leave the valleys of our life and to become for ever the Dwellers on the Hills.

EPILOGUE

THE YOGA OF THE BHAGAVAD GITA

THE Bhagavad Gita is pre-eminently a book of Yoga. It is *Yoga Shastra* or the Science of Yoga. Each discourse of the Bhagavad Gita deals with one particular aspect of this great Science of sciences. However, some of the descriptions of Yoga mentioned in the book seem rather strange. The first discourse is known as *Vishada Yoga* or the Yoga of Despondency. One may ask, and rightly, how can there be a Yoga of Despondency? In the first discourse we find Arjuna in a state of complete dejection; he is in a mood of intense despondency, so much so, that even the great bow which he had weilded with matchless valour slips out of his hands. He, the great warrior of warriors, is unwilling to fight. But does this state have any relevance to Yoga? Surely dejection or despondency is associated more with the man of the world rather than with the man of Yoga. What then is the meaning of the phrase: Yoga of Despondency which appears in the very first discourse of the Bhagavad Gita?

As the Bhagavad Gita opens, we find Arjuna in a confused state of mind, unable to decide as to what should be done. He himself says that his mind is reeling, and this happens when his war-chariot is placed between the two armies. This has a deep psychological significance. It shows a difference between what one recognises as a possibility and what one sees as an actuality. When the war-chariot of Arjuna was placed between the two armies, then, for him, what was so far a possibility suddenly became an actuality. While the recognition of a possibility may create in one a feeling of uneasiness, it is the seeing of the actual which has a powerful impact causing a state of intense despondency. And Yoga begins only by seeing the actual, not by playing about with possibilities. So long as the actual is not seen, so long the path of Yoga does not open for the aspirant. To see the actualities of life is a shattering experience. One shudders to look at the actual, and, if, per chance, one gets a glimpse of it, one immediately covers it up with numerous explanations offered by the mind. These explanations and justifications of the mind always serve as shock-absorbers so that the full impact of the actual may not be felt. Coming on the battlefield of the Mahabharata War, Arjuna first hears the blowing of the conches. When he heard the tumultous sound of these conches he recognised the possibility of a grim war. But that was all. The recognition of this possibility did not disturb him so much as the viewing of the two armies from the position where his war-chariot was placed. The impact of such viewing was terrific as it unbalanced even a seasoned fighter as Arjuna. As one reads through the first discourse one finds that Sri Krishna did not do anything to soften the impact; in fact, he allowed the intensity of the impact to grow. And this is indeed the starting point of Yoga. Yoga must begin with the right perception of things which means seeing things as they are. It must begin from the point where the aspirant is able to see facts as facts without any super-imposition by the mind. If one starts on the path of Yoga without seeing the facts of life then one is sure to be frustrated sooner or later. If Yoga is to take the aspirant very far, then surely he must begin near; and there is nothing more near than the unalterable facts of life. But when one sees the facts of life, one gets dis-illusioned and therefore greatly disturbed. If the disturbance is covered over with explanations and justifications then the impact wears out. But if the disturbance is left uncovered then it grows into a state of staggering despondency. Unless one is deeply disturbed, the life of Yoga does not begin. Despondency is indeed the first step of Yoga. And so rightly has the first discourse of the Bhagavad Gita been described as *Vishada* Yoga or the Yoga of Despondency.

The Bhagavad Gita, through its eighteen discourses, does not suggest eighteen different types of Yoga. There is only one approach of Yoga which the Gita indicates, and it is this one approach which is discussed in eighteen different aspects. The eighteen discourses together constitute the Yoga of the Bhagavad Gita. And the starting point of this Yoga is the state of despondency or more truly the state of Discontent. There must arise first an intense discontent with oneself. Such discontent naturally creates a sense of uneasiness amounting to despondency. Without this there can be no starting point of Yoga. An intense discontent is indeed the preparation for Yoga, and we find, as we read the first discourse of the Gita, that Arjuna, because of his despondency or *Vishad*, comes properly prepared for his initiation into the Way of Yoga, discussed by Sri Krishna in the other discourses of the Bhagavad Gita. The question arises: Must discontent result in despondency? While discontent is a healthy state of mind, despondency is not. With a despondent frame of mind nothing can be clearly seen and therefore no right action can emerge. Can there be discontent without despondency? Why does discontent result in depression or despondency? This happens when the fact is not seen but what is seen is mind's super-imposition on that which is an unalterable fact. When discontent arises because of the perception of mind's super-impositions then one is bound to feel depressed and dejected. Arjuna's despondency arose in the background of what his mind had super-imposed, and that is why his discontent did not release in him the necessary energy to fight; on the contrary, it resulted in making him incapable of coming to any clear decision. If one desires to move on the path of Yoga then there has to be first a discontent without despondency. One has to see that the discontent is not sought to be softened by mind's explanations and justifications, nor is it allowed to create a condition of dejection or despondency. There has to be neither self-justification nor self-pity. The question is: How to avoid these two dangers as one journeys into the land of Yoga? To keep the flame of Discontent alive and yet not to allow it to flicker either towards self-justification or towards self-pity -- it is this with which the Yoga of the Bhagavad Gita begins.

As one comes to the Second Discourse of the Gita, one finds Arjuna utterly despondent, and it is to this disciple, in the throes of complete dejection, that Sri Krishna speaks and shows the Way of Yoga.

The description of Arjuna given in this discourse is *Vishidantam*, meaning despondent. To him Sri Krishna speaks with a smile telling him that grief for the inevitable is utterly meaningless. Sri Krishna indicates to Arjuna that his grief has arisen because he does not see the fact but only views that which his mind has super-imposed. He uses the word *Apariharya*, meaning the inevitable or the unalterable. Surely the only thing that is inevitable is the fact. To weep over something that is unalterable is devoid of meaning. But would not the seeing of the unalterable nature of facts amount to fatalism? Would it not indicate the adoption of a passive view of life? It would, if the motivating factors for such perception of the unalertable nature of facts are either self-justification or self-pity. Both these tendencies point to the inertia of the mind. The inert mind may have periodical spells of dis-satisfaction but then they subside under the influence of self-justification or self-pity. Thus the inert mind can never be aware of the unalterable facts of life. It may know despondency; but it never comes to the experience of Deep Discontent. Man begins obviously with a sense of dissatisfaction — but this may either degenerate into a condition of despondency or it may move in the direction of intense discontent. The man of despondency only seeks evasion and escape; it is the man of discontent who experiences the urgency of a problem. Obviously a problem can be solved only if there is an urgency. Self-justification and self-pity which are the begetters of despondency never allow a problem to come to a condition of urgency. Sri Krishna saw that Arjuna was dissatisfied with the situation in which he was placed. He did not strive to soften the impact which his disciple was facing; in fact he saw to it that the impact grew in greater intensity. But Arjuna was getting unnerved by the challenge that confronted him, and so he moved in the direction of self-justification and self-pity. The Bhagavad Gita uses such words as *Kashmalam* meaning dejection and *Hridaya-daurbalyam* meaning faint-heartedness to describe the condition of Arjuna. Sri Krishna asks him as to why he had become a victim to such unbecoming feelings. Arjuna admits that he suffers from *Karpanya-dosha*, indicating faint-heartedness or a sense of despondency. Arjuna had to be awakened from this condition of despondency where he was lost in self-justifying and self-pitying arguments. Arjuna must see the falseness of the stance he had taken; he must transform his dissatisfaction into a healthy discontent, for thus alone he would be in a position to meet the challenge with which he was faced. And it is this which Sri Krishna does by first pricking the bubble of his seemingly noble arguments.

Sri Krishna, being a great teacher, saw that Arjuna must be first shown the utter falseness if his arguments. For this it was necessary to meet him on the plane of intellectual understanding. And so he asks Arjuna to see the discrepency between what he says and what he does. He told Arjuna that while he was speaking like a learned man, his actions had no relationship with his lofty professions. Sri Krishna wanted Arjuna to see for himself the falseness in which he was caught. And so rightly has the Second Discourse of the Gita been described as *Sankhya Yoga*. One of the dictionary meanings of *Sankhya* is deliberation or reasoning. Arjuna's problem arose out of a confused and a distracted mind. How could such a mind reason with effectiveness? Sri Krishna saw that Arjuna's reasoning must first be put aright so that he can have an intellectual clarity with which to see the situation in which he was placed. There is a clarity that comes due to flawless reasoning but there is also a clarity which comes due to an intuitive insight. However, intuitive insight dawns upon human consciousness only when the full range of reason has been explored.

It is because of this that Sri Krishna first approaches the problem of Arjuna through reason and intellectual understanding. This is obviously the path of *Sankhya*. Arjuna had dwelt at length on death and destruction that would be caused by the fratricidal war. And so in the Second Discourse Sri Krishna discusses this problem of death and destruction. He appeals to Arjuna's sense of reasoning, and points out to him that in the ultimate analysis there is no death. The Lord tells his disciple that Soul never dies, because it is never born. And it is after all the soul that matters, for bodies come and go. Forms must die in order that newer forms may come into existence for the soul to express itself. It is true that the Soul is ever unborn, and yet seeks to express itself through forms that can respond to its impulses. And the impulses of the soul are such that they require newer and newer forms, for, no one form can ever contain its urges. Death of form is inevitable; nay, it is essential, for otherwise how can Soul express itself? Without destruction, nothing new can ever emerge. Sri Krishna describes the bodies as *Antavanta* meaning finite and therefore subject to end and destruction. He refers to soul as *Anashinah* and *Aprameya*, meaning indestructible and immeasurable. Sri Krishna wants Arjuna to understand this fact without any confusion of thought.

Arjuna belongs to the warrior class, and after all what is the duty of a true Kshatriya or a warrior? Obviously his duty is to destroy outmoded forms, those forms that stand in the way of the emergence of new expressional impulses of the Soul. The warrior must help in the destruction of such forms whether at the individual level or at the social level. How can Arjuna step back from this legitimate duty which devolves upon him as one belonging to the warrior class? Sri Krishna tells Arjuna that both from a philosophical as well as a social standpoint his vision seems to have become blurred. Perhaps his reluctance to perform his social duty arises because he has been unable to come to a clear philosophical or intellectual perception of things. If Arjuna realizes that forms must die in order that the expressional urges of the Soul may be free from all hindrances, then surely he would not relent from the duties that devolve upon him as a great Warrior among warriors. But if the warrior has to engage himself in the task of destroying outmoded forms, the forms that impede the smooth flow of life, how is he to do this work of benevolent destruction? If he is carried away by the wave of destruction then surely he will be cruel and merciless, and thus may destroy too much. But if he relents from the work of necessary destruction then he will not only be half-hearted in his work, he will leave the work of destruction half-finished which perhaps is worse than the destruction not begun. The true warrior such as Arjuna was has to be iconoclastic leaving no icon untouched which has within it the seeds of future disintegration and disorganisation.

It may be noted that in the fourfold classification in the Hindu social polity, there was a great element of psychological and spiritual truth. The *Shudra* was the Crafstman whose work was to fashion forms; the *Vaishya* was the Nourisher whose task it was to preserve and nourish forms; the *Kshatriya* was the Warrior whose duty was to destroy outmoded forms and to protect those that were needed for individual and social living; the ***Brahamin*** was the Inspirer who was entrusted with the task of calling down new Life Impulses which may become the content of new forms. This was the great rhythm of Life for the individual as well as the society. All concerned must maintain this rhythm, for upon its maintenance rested the welfare of all. Will Arjuna strive in the direction of maintaining this rhythm, or will he violate it? This was the question which Sri Krishna placed before his great disciple. An understanding both of the philosophy of the Soul as well as of social obligations demands that this rhythm of life be maintained. If the task of the warrior is to help in the destruction of outmoded forms, then surely Arjuna must re-orient himself to this inevitable rhythm of life. The question is not merely Arjuna agreeing to fight; the question is: How is he going to fight? Will he be carried vay by the wave of violence or will he fight with reluctance? Neither of these will help in maintaining this rhythm. Arjuna must show forth a quality of neither indulgence nor denial with reference to the social obligations that emanate from the philosophy of the indestructibility of the Soul and the inevitability of the death of forms. In the latter part of the Second Discourse, Sri Krishna discusses the question of this new quality of the mind which neither condemns nor justifies, which is caught neither in indulgence nor in denial. It is only with such quality of mind that Arjuna will be able to discharge his duties as a Warrior in the great battle of life which confronts him. The Lord tells him that running away from the battle is meaningless because there has to take place the destruction of forms for the emergence of new life. The destruction of forms must happen whether Arjuna likes it or not, and whether Arjuna participates in the discharge of his social obligations or not. The crux of the matter is: The bringing into existence a new quality of mind so that there is neither too much destruction nor too little. Destruction without cruelty, there must be; but there must be displayed also Destruction without any element of diffidence. The whole of the second discourse is concerned with this New Understanding of the Indestructibility of the Soul and of the Inevitability of the destruction of Forms. Arjuna must see this and be ready to discharge his social obligations without either being callous or calculating. This is the Sankhya Yoga of the Bhagavad Gita enabling Arjuna to move on without giving to his discontent an element of despondency.

The third facet of Yoga is revealed by the Bhagavad Gita in its Third Discourse under the title *Karma Yoga*. After Right Understanding indicated by *Sankhya Yoga* there must come Right Action. And it is this which is the subject matter of the third discourse. Arjuna is a little baffled because the Lord has described in the earlier discourse about the superiority of Knowledge or Understanding. If that be the case, then Arjuna asks as to why he is being pushed into action, and, that, too, of such a devastating nature as War. Now Understanding is not a way of escape from the requirements of action. It is a background for Right Action. Without it what takes place is only activity, and not action. Sri Krishna tells Arjuna that not even for one moment can man remain without performing action, for, to live is to act. But the question is whether man is engaged in mere activity or is he performing action. It has to be remembered that the emergence of action does not require abstaining from activity. It is activity itself which must be transformed into action. When man abstains from activity, it is his body that is quiet, but the mind is ceaselessly engaged in that very activity. This is what mostly happens when man renounces activity and becomes outwardly a hermit. The Bhagavad Gita describes such renunciation as *Mithyachara* meaning rank hypocrisy. When action does not emanate from Right Understanding then it surely has an element of falseness in it. Here Right Understanding has not be confused with Right Attitude. An attitude is only a mental construct, a mere conceptual exercise. Right Understanding really means Right Perception. It is this which is the source of Right Action. Sri Krishna discusses in the Second Discourse a state of mind which is free from the opposites of indulgence and denial. It is in this state of mind that Right Perception is born. A mind caught in the play of the opposites has only a comparative view of things. But a comparative view can never be a direct view. In comparison the mind of man sees things indirectly. Right Perception is a direct perception, and it is this which is described as Right Understanding. When one is established in Right Understanding then there is no problem of the interval between thought and action. It is this interval which is the cause of hypocrisy or *Mithyachar*.

The Bhagavad Gita describes Right Action as Sacrifice or *Yagna*. An action becomes a sacrifice only when it is free from the opposites of denial and indulgence, of condemnation and justification. An action that emerges from Right Perception is indeed a sacrificial action. For an action to become a sacrifice there has to be a complete elimination of all motives. And the motive remains so long as the sense of "I" remains. It is only in this context that the following verse appearing in this discourse becomes meaningful :

> The righteous who eat the remains of sacrifice
> are freed from all sins; but the impious who dress
> food for their own sakes, they verily eat sin.

Here is given a clear indication about the motives of action. When action is freed from all motives then alone it becomes truly spiritual. But the elimination of motives is truly the state of Right Understanding where the mind is free from the play of the opposites. Not to cook food for oneself but to eat the remains of sacrifice can be understood only in the context of the elimination of all sense of "I". The first verse of the Isavasya Upanishad speaks exactly about enjoying what has been left, for, that indeed is the meaning of the phrase *Tena-tyaktena-bhunjitha*. Right Understanding is that state where the mind is free from all motives, good as well as bad. In the twenty-seventh verse of the Third Discourse we get an intimation of what is meant by a state of motivelessness. It says: "The individualised self, deluded by egoism, thinketh 'I am the doer'". Right Action or Yagna is that in which the individual ceases to be the doer. But the mind of man is unable to understand this, for, it argues that if the doer is not there then how can the action be done? This is a question which the mind cannot understand. It is because of this that Sri Krishna tells Arjuna that Buddhi is higher than the mind. He indicates to the disciple that it is only when there is movement from Mind to Super-Mind that the understanding of action without the actor comes. From Intellect to Intelligence -- that is the path suggested by Sri Krishna to Arjuna if the latter is to comprehend the mystery of Right Action where action is performed without the actor. But the question is what is the nature of Intelligence and how is the movement from Intellect to Intelligence initiated?

This question brings us to the Fourth Discourse where the Yoga of the Bhagavad Gita takes us deeper into the understanding of the great science of Yoga. This Discourse is known as *Gnana-Vibhaga-Yoga* meaning Yoga of Wisdom. It is the Yoga of discriminative knowledge. This discourse is also known as Renunciation of Action in Knowledge. The Sanskrit phrase is *Gnana-Karma-Sanyasa-Yoga*. How can Action be renounced in knowledge? It indicates that renunciation of action lies not in giving up activity; it consists in the non-possessive quality of the mind. *Aparigraha* or Non-possession does not mean the giving up of things; it signifies the giving up of a sense of possession. And this sense of possession is rooted in the mind. So long as the mind is engaged in the process of acquisition so long there is no *aparigraha*. The acquisitive mind revels in knowledge, and still more knowledge. It is a stranger to wisdom or intelligence. It is in the soil of the non-possessive mind that wisdom or intelligence is born. It is only such a mind that knows renunciation of action in knowledge.

The fourth discourse of the Gita deals with the problem of Action, Reaction and Inaction wherein this question of renunciation in knowledge is clearly indicated. *Vikarma*, *Karma* and *Akarma* are the three topics on which Sri Krishna instructs Arjuna. This whole discourse emphasises the fact that "he who seeth inaction in action, and action in inaction, he is wise among men". Thus the characteristic of wisdom is the co-existence of action and inaction, of *Karma* and *Akarma*. A co-existence implies the existence of two things at the same place and at the same time. Now this is something which the mind can never understand, for, space and time are the framework in which alone mind can think. And so co-existence is something which belongs not to the mind but to that which transcends the mind. It belongs to the sphere of Buddhi or Intelligence. Wisdom is the intimation of Buddhi or Intelligence in the field of the mind. It is not of the mind but dawns upon the mind.

The Bhagavad Gita, like all spiritual lore throughout the world, abounds in paradoxes. One of the great paradoxes of the Gita is Action in Inaction and Inaction in Action. All co-existences seem to the mind contradictory and therefore utterly meaningless. It can make a meaning out of co-existences only by putting an interval of time or space. Mind can understand the existence of two things one after the other. But existence of two things at the same time and at the same place seems to it devoid of validity. And so Arjuna raises his doubt about the co-existence of renunciation and action. How can they be together? It is this which constitutes the subject matter of the Fifth Discourse which is called the *Karma-Sanyasa-Yoga* which does not mean renunciation of action but Yoga dealing with renunciation in action. The Gita has never suggested renunciation of action; it has only indicated renunciation in action. Every action has fundamentally two constituents — one, its pattern, and the other, its motive. Now in this context, renunciation of action would mean giving up the patterns of action or in other words, the giving up of activity. But renunciation in action indicates the giving up of the motive.

the very source from where activity emanates. For the motives of action, the Gita uses the phrase *Karma-phala* meaning the fruit of that which one does. The fruit of action is embedded in action from the very beginning. The fruit of any action resides in its motive. The very motive of action contains its fruit. It is the motive which gives direction to action. And is not the direction indicative of the fruit that must be reaped? Sri Krishna tells Arjuna that refraining from activity has no meaning whatsoever — in fact, to refrain from action is itself another form of action. And so one can never live without performing an action. But what is demanded of a student of Yoga is the establishment of the ground of Motive-less-ness for any action that has to be performed. The result of action and the fruit of action are two completely different things. The result is incidental, while the fruit is something to be consciously striven for. Here the question must arise: If all motives are eliminated then what inducement can there be for action? But before one goes into that question one has to enquire as to whether a condition of motive-less-ness can ever be created, and if it can be, then what is the method that leads one to that state where renunciation and action co-exist?

It is this question which brings us to the Sixth Discourse of the Bhagavad Gita known as *Adhyatma Yoga*. It is also known as *Dhyana Yoga*. Now Dhyana is the state where the agitations of the mind have ceased. And that is indeed the Spiritual state referred to by the *Adhyatma Yoga*. It is only when the agitations of the mind cease that the flow of time also subsides. When this happens then the co-existence does not seem paradoxical. It is in the cessation of time that co-existence is seen as a fact. When the flow of time ceases then is one established in the Ground of the Timeless. This is the state of Inaction or *Akarma*. But it is not a passive state; on the contrary it is intensely dynamic. From the dynamic state of Inaction emerges true Action or *Karma*. Thus is one able to see Inaction in Action and Action in Inaction. But the question is: How to bring about the cessation of thought? How to free the mind from all its agitations? The cessation of mind's agitations is described by the Bhagavad Gita in the Sixth Discourse as follows :

> As a lamp in windless place flickereth
> not....

When the flame does not flicker, it is absolutely steady. The mind freed from agitations is a still mind. It is not the stillness of passivity, but of intense negativity. It is the stillness born of extraordinary sensitivity. It may be called the Deep Silence arising in a consciousness that is rendered supremely sensitive. This sensitivity is indicated by the Gita in its thirtieth verse of the Sixth Discourse wherein it stays :

> He who seeth me everywhere, and seeth
> everything in me....

The Creation and the Creator are not separated one from the other. In the entire creation, the Creator abides; and in the Creator, the whole creation, its past, present and future, abides. There is a co-existence of the Creator and the Creation. He who sees this has come to a sensitivity of consciousness. For him the Time and the Timeless exist together. If this sensitivity demands a complete cessation of the agitations of the mind, then the question is: How does one come to this stillness? Arjuna tells Sri Krishna :

> The mind is verily restless, O Krishna; it
> is impetuous, strong, difficult to bend; I
> deem it as hard to curb as the wind.

It is to this question of Arjuna that Sri Krishna replies and gives the famous formula by which the restless mind can know what peace and quiet are. This formula seems to be one of the cardinal approaches of Hindu Psychology, for, it appears in the Upanishads, and it is also found in the Yoga Sutras of Patanjali. The formula is *Abhyasa* and *Vairagya* which means Practice and Dispassion. Now Practice and Dispassion have to be together, not one after the other. There has to be a co-existence of *Abhyasa* and *Vairagya*. It looks as if Sri Krishna is only begging the question, moving round and round, for, in this formula he has only repeated the earlier idea of the co-existence of Action and Inaction. Practice indicates Action even as Dispassion signifies Inaction. And so once again Sri Krishna tells his disciple that in dissolving the paradox of Action and Inaction he will find a solution to the problem of the agitated mind. The secret of the Yoga of the Bhagavad Gita lies in resolving this paradox of Practice and Dispassion, of Action and Inaction. This discourse, as we have stated earlier, is known also as *Dhyana Yoga*. Perhaps the indication is that the above paradox can be resolved only in the state of meditation. It is in this state that one can comprehend the co-existence of *Abhyasa* and *Vairagya*, of Practice and Dispassion. But what is the Way of Meditation, and how does one tread it?

For this it necessary to understand clearly what is Knowledge and what is Wisdom, or to use the terminology of the Upanishads - What is *Apara Vidya* and what is *Para Vidya*. The Seventh Discourse of the Gita goes into this question, for, the discourse is known *Gnana-Vignana-Yoga*. This means Yoga of Knowledge and of Distinctive Knowledge. These two types of knowledge are lower and higher or *Apara* and *Para* Vidya. Unless one understands the nature of these two categories of knowledge one cannot comprehend the Way of Meditation where alone the Great Paradoxe can be resolved. Now the Way of Meditation demands a sense of deep inquiry. It is in moments of deep inquiry that one suddenly comes upon Wisdom. Wisdom is not an extension of knowledge. It dawns upon human consciousness only when the frontiers of knowledge end. It is hardly necessary to say that it is in deep inquiry that one comes to the frontiers of knowledge. In the Seventh Discourse of the Gita one is given a clear indication of the nature of this deep inquiry. It says that there are mainly four types of enquirers -- they are the *Arta, Jignasu, Artharthi* and *Gnani*, meaning those afflicted by suffering, those motivated by curiosity, those seeking personal profit and those who are the real seekers. Obviously the sense of deep inquiry arises only in one who is a real seeker, for, in the other three categories of inquiry there is a personal motive. The real seeker is he who is in a state of search but in whom all seeking has ended. What can one seek? Surely one seeks only that which one knows or may be a slight modification of what one already knows. All the activities of the mind are in the field of the known, and the known is the manifest. But manifest by itself makes no sense; the meaning to the manifest is given by the Unmanifest. He who can listen to the whisper of the Unmanifest in the manifest, he alone knows the Way of Meditation. To respond to the intimations of the Unmanifest in the manifest requires an extraordinary sensitivity of consciousness. The knowledge of the manifest is the *Apara Vidya* while the response to the intimations of the Unmanifest is the *Para Vidya*. The Unmanifest is not away from the Manifest; it is *in* it but not *of* it. In this context the following verse of the Gita appearing in the Seventh Discourse is very significant :

> Those devoid of reason think of Me, the Unmanifest as having manifestation, knowing not My supreme nature, imperishable, most excellent.

There is a co-existence of the Manifest and the Unmanifest. In fact it is due to this co-existence that the Manifest is given a quality of livingness. If the Unmanifest withdraws then the manifest is devoid of life. And so the livingness of anything is due to the intangible touch of the Unmanifest. To feel this intangible touch is to come to a remarkable sensitivity of consciousness. The Unmanifest is the seed of the Manifest. However, the mind caught in the play of the opposites, is unable to see the intangible presence of the Unmanifest in the manifest. In the Seventh Discourse the Gita says that it is the pairs of opposites which create delusion. It is the very nature of the mind to move between the opposites. But when this movement ceases then the mind is rendered mindless, and this is indeed the sensitivity which comes in the moment of meditation.

As we have stated above Meditation is the awareness of the Timeless in Time. It is in the Eighth Discourse that we get a further clarification of this inspiring idea. The eighth discourse is called the *Akshara-Brahma-Yoga*. In the Upanishads there is given a two-fold understanding of Brahman or the Ultimate Reality. This is: Brahman with Attributes and Brahman without Attributes. The Bhagavad Gita describes this as *Kshara* and *Akshra* meaning

Brahman in Time and Brahman beyond Time.

In this context the following verse appearing in the Eighth Discourse is very significant :

> That Unmanifested, Indestructible, It is
> called; It is named the Highest Path. They
> who reach It return not. That is My
> supreme abode.

In the earlier verse the Gita speaks of the Higher Unmanifest than the Unmanifest itself. One may say that the lower Unmanifest is the Invisible, while the higher unmanifest is the Transcendental. Sri Krishna says that it is this higher unmanifest or the Transcendental which is His true abode. The universe may be conceived of as existing in three categories — the Visible, the Invisible and the Unmanifest. Sri Krishna says that His supreme abode is the Unmanifest which indeed is Timeless as also Spaceless. Thus to meditate on the Lord would imply establishing a communion with the Unmanifest or the Timeless. The above verse says that such a person does not return. What does this mean? Obviously it means that he who establishes a communion with the Unmanifest is freed from the repetitive process of life. He alone knows what true creative living is. Our life is a constant repetitive drudgery. This is because we know only the Visible world, or at best have some intimation of the Invisible world. But we are utter strangers to the intangible presence of the Unmanifest in the midst of the manifest. The Unmanifest is not away from the Manifest; it is in it and yet not of it. The Unmanifest is intangibly present at all points of manifestation, for, without this intangible presence, the Manifest would die and wither away.

But a communion with the Unmanifest demands an experience of death — not physical but psychological death. It is in death alone that communion is possible. In the Eighth Discourse the Bhagavad Gita speaks of the "time" when death must occur. This however is not chronological time but psychological time. To interpret the following verse appearing in the Eighth Discourse in physical terms is to miss the very meaning that the verse seeks to convey. The verse says :

> Fire, light, day-time, bright fortnight. Six
> months of the northern declension of the sun — then
> going forth....

Here the Gita speaks of that psychological moment when alone death can be experienced. We have discussed the implications of the above verse at length in the text and so do not propose to explore its meaning further. The mind as free as the cloudless sky of Uttarayana, the northern declension and yet filled with the intensity of love as symbolised by the bright fortnight — it is this which verily is the state of death in the psychological sense of the term. It is a state where the Personal and the Impersonal co-exist. In this moment of death one knows of the intangible presence of the Unmanifest in the Manifest itself. The question remains: How does one come to such a state? It has to be noted that being impersonal often induces one to become indifferent, almost callous to others, but being personal leads one not infrequently to become greatly involved, almost entagled in the affairs of others. To be both personal and impersonal at the same time — this is the state where the intangible presence of the Unmanifest can be felt even in manifestation itself. Speaking about the purpose of Evolution, Sri Aurobindo says in his monumental epic SAVITRI that it is "to evoke a Person in the Impersonal Void". If person appears without the impersonal void then it is too personal; but if no person emerges in the impersonal void, then it is devoid of vitality and dynamism. To create a person in the impersonal void is indeed the Yoga of the Bhagavad Gita. The whole universe is surcharged with the presence of the Person, but He can be seen only in the ground of the Impersonal Void. The Void itself is the Plenum. The "ME" of the Bhagavad Gita is indeed the Person in the Impersonal Void. In the Ninth Discourse of the Gita we find the following significant verse which says :

> By Me, the Formless, all this world is
> pervaded; all beings have root in Me, I am
> not rooted in them.

In the next verse the Gita says: "The support of beings, yet not rooted in beings". The question is: How is one to commune with Him who is the support of all beings and yet is not rooted in them, one who sustains the Manifest and yet is supremely Unmanifest? In the Ninth Discourse, the Bhagavad Gita speaks of the Yoga of Kingly Science and Kingly Secret — *Raja-Vidya-Raja-Guhya-Yoga.* One may ask: What is this kingly secret? Surely it is the secret of discovering the Person in the Impersonal Void, of communing with the Unmanifest in manifestation itself, of knowing the ONE in the midst of the Many. But how is this to be done? The Gita tells us in this discourse that it is only the unwavering mind, the mind capable of experiencing a Totality of Attention, that can know this Royal Secret. The thirtieth verse in the Ninth Discourse says :

> Even if the most sinful worship Me with
> undivided attention, then he too must be
> accounted righteous for he hath rightly revolved.

The secret of spiritual life is indicated here as a state of undivided attention. In the state of Total Attention there comes into existence a complete transformation, a mutation, where even the most sinful comes to the sudden awakening of virtue. It is in Total Attention that one can commune with the Unmanifest. Any communication that emerges out of such Communion is supremely virtuous. This Total Attention is the Impersonal Void in which arrives the Person, Supreme and Transcendental. The question is: How to come to the experience of the Undivided Attention?

Before we examine this question it is necessary to understand the Nature of the Person that emerges in the Impersonal Void. This means we must clearly know the nature of the experience that is indicated by the arrival of the Person in the Impersonal Void. It is this problem which is discussed in the Tenth and Eleventh Discourses of the Bhagavad Gita. They speak of the *Vibhuti Yoga* and the *Viswa-darshan Yoga.* Very often the distinction between the Unmanifest and the Invisible is not clearly understood. Obviously they are not the same; in fact, there is a qualitative difference between the two. The Invisible exists in the field of manifestation although it is not cognised by the senses. Now the Bhagavad Gita speaks of the Unmanifest in the *Vibhuti Yoga*, and deals with the Invisible in the *Viswarupa-darshan Yoga*. Here one may ask: Is there any relationship between the Manifest and the Unmanifest? If so, what is the nexus that connects the two? One may say it is Intangibility which constitutes a nexus between the Manifest and the Unmanifest. In other words, the Unmanifest is intangibly present in the Manifest. The Purusha is intangibly present all the time in the Prakriti. It is about this intangible presence that Sri Krishna speaks in the Tenth Discourse of the Bhagavad Gita. How is one to come to this experience of the Intangible in the midst of the Tangible? Arjuna is troubled by this very question and so he places his difficulty before Sri Krishna in the following verse of the Tenth Discourse :

> How may I know Thee, O Yogi, by constant
> meditation? In what aspects art Thou to be
> thought of by me, O blessed Lord?

It is in reply to this question of Arjuna that Sri Krishna describes his *Vibhutis*, his splendours, in this world of manifestation. He says his vibhutis are innumerable and so it would be impossible to detail them exhaustively. He says that even if Arjuna were to know all the detailed descriptions of His vibhutis, this would be of no value at all for only with one Fragment of myself I remain in the universe which is pervaded by Me. Even though He pervades the Universe, He is at the same time above it. But in order to give to Arjuna some indication as to where He, the Unmanifest, can be found in Manifestation, Sri Krishna gives certain illustrations where the intangible presence of the Unmanifest can be known. Among other verses the following verse of the Tenth Discourse is significant :

> I am the gambling of the cheat, and the
> splendour of splendid things I; ..... and
> the truth of the truthful I.

Sri Krishna does not say that he is the cheat, He says that he is the gambling of the cheat. Now cheat is something tangible, but the gambling of the cheat is something intangible — it is a quality which one can perceive but cannot hold. Similarly He says that he is the splendour of the splendid things. Once again splendid things are tangible but not the splendour. In the above verse He says that He is the truth of the truthful. The truthful is the tangible, but truth of the truthful is something intensely intangible. This is something like what the Kenopanishad says when it speaks of the eye of the eye and the ear of the ear and the mind of the mind. The eye of the eye or the ear of the ear does not exist in some invisible realm. It is here and now as the very living quality of the manifested universe. It can be perceived by one who has the sensitivity of perception. But most often the student of spiritual lore is unable to make a distinction between the Unmanifest and the Invisible. The Invisible belongs to psychic or occult perception, but the Unmanifest is the experience of the man of mysticism — or the man of spiritual perception. The Occult and the Spiritual are not identical. The Intangible represents the Quality of things which can never be found by a quantitative approach, however precise and scientific it may be. The Unmanifest inheres the Manifest as the quality or the soul of things.

But Arjuna is desirous of seeing also the Universal Form of the Lord. While the *Vibhutis* deal with the Uniqueness of things, it is *Viswarupa* that reveals the Universality of things. The Tenth and Eleventh Discourses deal respectively with the subject of Uniqueness and Universality of the Godhead. For communing with the Unique one need not move in time or in space, for, it is here and now present at every point of manifestation. But for comprehending Universality there has to be movement in extension, either of time or of space or both. Universality is possible only by extended perception whether such extension is done through scientific instruments or through occult powers. This is made clear in the Tenth Discourse when Sri Krishna tells Arjuna that it would not be possible for him to see the Universal Form with the powers of perception that he has, he will have to be endowed with another perceptive instrument. The Lord imparts to His disciple this extended perception with which to look at the Universal Form. And what does Arjuna see? He sees a thousand mouths and a thousand eyes and a thousand heads. This quantitative description obviously implies an extension of perception, not an expansion of it. But at the end of this experience Arjuna is seized with terrible fear and makes a request to the Lord in the following two verses appearing in the Tenth Discourse :

> I have seen That which none had seen before,
> My heart is glad, yet faileth me for fear;
> Show me, O God, Thine other form again,
> Mercy O God of Gods, Home of all worlds,
> Diademed, mace and discus in Thy hand,
> Again I fain would see Thee as before :
> Put on again Thy four-armed shape, O Lord,
> O thousand-armed, of forms innumerate!

Arjuna did not have any fear while looking at the *Vibhutis* of the Lord, but His Universal Form evoked a terrible sense of fright. One may ask: Why? The experience of *Vibhutis* is the experience of that which is Timeless, but the *Viswa-rupa-darshan* is a vision of the Timeless entering the realm of Time. And in Time alone happen the processes of destruction. In the Eleventh Discourse while showing His Universal Form, the Lord says :

> Time am I, laying desolate the world
> Made manifest on earth to slay mankind.

It is Time that lays desolate the manifested world, for, Time is indeed the fore-runner of Death. It is in the flow of Time that Death arrives. The Universal Form seems particularly fearsome as it is shown to Arjuna because it appears in the background of the Great War of the Mahabharata. Occult powers function within the framework of Time. To a great Occultist future may be like an open book, but still future belongs to the Time-process. In the *Viswa-rupa-darshan*, Arjuna is given a pre-view of the Great War — what lies in future so far as the Kurukshetra war is concerned. While the *Vibhutis* belong to a Timeless state, the *Viswa-rupa* appertains the realm of Time. The Timeless and the Time, the Being and the Becoming, are the sublime subjects dealt with in the Tenth and the Eleventh Discourses. The Time, or, the process of Becoming, will cease to be fearsome if one is rooted in the state that is Timeless or the state of Being. The Becoming must seem meaningful only in the Ground of the Being. But the question is: How to be rooted in the state of Being from where all Becoming appears meaningful and significant? For this we must turn to the Twelfth Discourse.

In this Discourse we come to what the Bhagavad Gita describes as *Bhakti* Yoga or the Yoga of Devotion. In the Gita, Devotion is not just a middle term between *Gnana* and *Karma*, Knowledge and Action. While *Gnana* or Knowledge indicates freedom from reactions, *Karma* means in performance of Right Action. In the Gita, Karma is equated with Yoga and therefore it denotes True Action. While freedom from reaction is a negative condition, performance of right action is a positive state. What is the secret of this transformation from the negative to the positive? The secret lies in *Bhakti* or Devotion. It is the touchstone of *Bhakti* which brings about this miracle of transformation. *Bhakti* alone can transform knowledge into action. Ordinariiy the gulf between knowledge and action remains unbridgable because one is a stranger to the experience of *Bhakti* or Devotion. One may ask: Is *Bhakti* a negative state or is it a positive state? The truth of the matter is that it is neither. It is a state where the positive and the negative co-exist. It is in the simultaneous existence of the negative and the positive that the experience of *Bhakti* comes. The negative and the positive are the two opposites, and *Bhakti* arises in a state which simultaneously contains within itself the two opposites. *Bhakti* which limits itself to either *Saguna* — with attributes — or *Nirguna* — without attributes — is no *Bhakti* at all. True *Bhakti* contains the *Saguna* and *Nirguna* at the same time. This is made abundently clear in the following verse of the Twelfth Discourse of the Gita :

> He who wants nothing, is pure, skillful,
> unconcerned, untroubled, renouncing every
> undertaking, he, My devotee, is dear to me.
> He who neither loveth nor hateth, nor
> grieveth nor desireth, renouncing good and

evil, full of devotion, he is dear to Me.

Bhakti is a state of Transcendence where the two opposites are transcended, not just reconciled. The Gita says that the devotee is one who renounces all undertaking, in other words, he never begins anything. The phrase used is *Sarvarambha-parityagi*. This is a strange description of the *Bhakta*. What does it mean? It implies that there is no entity at all who can begin an undertaking. The culmination of the *Gnana Yoga*, the Path of Knowledge, lies in realzing that all knowledge acquired by the mind is indirect and therefore utterly inadequate. At the summit of the *Gnana Yoga*, all knowledge is negated. But the entity that negates all knowledge is still present, and this entity is the Knower. In the state of *Bhakti* the knower himself is negated. And so here the entity that engages itself in the knowing process is itself negated. There is no Knower, and therefore there is none that begins any undertaking. If the Knower does not exist then how can there be any existence of the Known. And so the whole process of knowing comes to an end. All knowing is indirect, and it is only when this indirect process ends that the prospect of direct realization opens out. *Bhakti* or Devotion is an experience of direct realization, but this can come about only when the duality of the experiencer and the experienced, of the observer and the observed, of the knower and the known, vanishes. *Bhakti* is a state of Void, not merely a state of Negation. The transformation of the Negative into the Positive arises only because of the Void. The life stream must pass on from the Negative to the Positive through this creative interval of the Void. It is this Void which bridges the gulf between Knowledge and Action, between Belief and Behaviour. In Twelfth Discourse, the *Bhakta* is described as *A-niketa* meaning Homeless. To be a devotee is to be rendered completely Homeless. It is not merely the negation of the contents of the Home but the Home itself. *Bhakti* is not inviting God to enter our home, it is entering the Home of God Himself. This state of Homeless-ness is indeed the state of Void. When both the patterns of reaction and the entity that reacts are negated then alone true action emerges, the action that never binds.

This subject of Knower and Knowledge is developed by the Gita in the Thirteenth Discourse which speaks of the *Kshetra* and the *Kshetragna*. This Discourse is termed *Kshetra-Kshetragna-Vibhaga Yoga* which means Yoga which distinguishes between the Field and the Knower of the Field. The *Kshetra* and the *Kshetragna* are the Known and the Knower. It is needless to say that Knowledge is only a relationship between the Knower and the Known. But are the Knower and the Known two separate existences? Do they exist separately by themselves? Surely there is no duality like the knower and the known. Truly speaking the Known is not different from the Knower, the observer is indeed the observed. The known is the extension or the projection of the knower. It is the Knower that brings the Known into existence. To regard the two as separate and distinct is to be caught in *Maya* or Illusion. It is therefore necessary to find out who is the knower, why does he bring the known into existence and how does he create the known. To comprehend the Who, the Why and the How with reference to the Knower is indeed to unravel the great mystery of life. In this connection the following verse of the Gita appearing in this Discourse is very significant :

> Whatever is born, immobile or mobile,
> know Thou, O best of Bharatas, that is
> born from a union between Kshetra and
> Kshetragna.

Thus all creation is the result of the knower-known or the observer-observed phenomena. What we call creation, whether mobile or immobile, is the product of this union between the experiencer and the experienced, between the observer and the observed. The Creator and the Creation are not two distinct things, for, creation has no intrinsic significance; it does not exist by itself. It has a dependent origination, not an intrinsic origination.... Creation exists because of the Creator; the observed exists because of the observer.

The question is: How has this difference between the Knower and the Known, between the Observer and the Observed, come into existence? Who has caused this dichotomy? By what process has this differentiation come into being? To understand this, it is the eye of Wisdom that is required. The following verse of the Gita gives us an indication of this. It says :

> They who perceive by the eye of Wisdom
> this difference between Kshetra and Kshetragna
> ----- they come to Supreme Understanding.

With the eye of Wisdom to know the difference between the Knower and the Known is to come to Supreme Understanding. But is there a difference between the two? It is the eye of Wisdom alone that can tell us that the difference is only apparent, that the seeming distinction has no validity at all. And it is this understanding which brings the liberation of the Spirit from the illusory snare of Matter. The Gita here speaks of *Bhuta-prakriti-moksham*. The Spirit is indeed eternally free, but it is caught in an illusion whereby It believes that liberation has yet to come. To know that the observer is the observed is to break through this veil of illusion. But this requires the opening of the Eye of Wisdom. The Fourteenth Discourse takes us to the examination of this subject of the opening of the Eye of Wisdom.

We have raised the question that if the knower and the known, the observer and the observed, are not different then from where does the difference arise and how does it arise. The answer to this question is vouchsafed to us in the Fourteenth Discourse which speaks of the *Guna-traya-vibhaga-yoga*, meaning the Yoga dealing with the Three Attributes and their distinctions. The subject of the Three Gunas or the Attributes is a unique contribution of Hindu Psychology to the world of thought. It speaks in clearest terms about the conditioning factors of human consciousness. Obviously it is the conditioned consciousness that creates an illusory distinction between the Knower and the Known, between the Observer and the Observed. The Eye of Wisdom opens only when the consciousness is freed from all conditioning factors. It is the conditioned consciousness, which acting as the observer brings into existence the observed. The Gita says in the Fourteenth

Discourse :

> When the seer perceiveth no agent other
> than the attributes, and knoweth THAT which is
> higher than the attributes, he entereth into
> MY nature.

To know that there is no other agent than the attributes or the *Gunas* is to break the illusion of the observer-observed phenomena. It is the *gunas* which by their functioning create the observed, and so the Gita instructs the spiritual aspirant to rise above the Three Gunas or the attributes. Here a pertinent question does arise, namely, that since all manifestation or action is possible only by the functioning of the Gunas, are not Gita's insistence on action and the rising above the Gunas contradictory? When *Sattva*, *Rajas* and *Tamas* operate, with the preponderence of one or the other, then alone action comes into existence. But if the Three Gunas are to be transcended, then what is the point of asking Arjuna to act? The Three Gunas may be translated, in terms of Sri Aurobindo, as Poise, Passion and Passivity — they are *Sattva*, *Rajas* and *Tamas* respectively. In the Fourteenth Discourse of the Gita it is said that it is he who renounces all undertakings that is truly *Gunateet* meaning above the three gunas. This really implies that when the three gunas are transcended then one comes to the state where action is without the actor. In all actions performed under the influence of the three gunas the actor is always present. In the functioning of the gunas it is the actor that operates. When the gunas are transcended then the actor vanishes. So long as the actor is present all actions are mere reactions. The transcending of the gunas is the state comparable to *Bhakti* which is an interval, a creative interval, between the negative and the positive. Here no actor, no thinker, no devotee can enter. From this state what emerges is Pure Action where the gunas do come into operation but without the corrupting presence of the actor and the thinker. If the Gunas do not operate then there is *pralaya*, a dissolution, where no manifestation can exist. The gunas have to be freed, from the presence of the actor then all manifestation is pure and unsullied. The last but one verse of this Discourse says that there can be no place for *Vyabhichar* or corruption in *Bhakti*. And the verse immediately says that such an incorruptible person, because he has gone beyond the three gunas, comes to the experience of the Eternal or the Timeless. The phrase used is *Gunan-samatitya*, meaning having crossed over the gunas. But the above verse declares that one who has crossed over the gunas enters the Eternal or the Timeless. *Bhakti* is indeed the experience of the Timeless where the gunas have been transcended. But the Timeless is the Unmanifest from where must arise a new manifestation in which there is action without the actor. And so the insistence on action and going beyond the gunas are not two contradictory statements. In fact action is possible only when the gunas are transcended — for, without this the so-called action is only a reaction.

In this context the Fifteenth Discourse becomes extremely significant. This Discourse describes what is called the *Purushottama Yoga*. In Hindu Philosophy there is a clear distinction made between God and Godhead. The former is Iswara while the latter is Brahman. One might say that Brahman-in-manifestation is Iswara. And so we have here the concept of Brahman in manifestation, and Brahman beyond manifestation - or as the Upanishads say, Brahman with attributes and Brahman without attributes. In this Discourse the Gita says :

> There are two Forces or Purusas in
> this world, the Kshara and the Akshara,
> the changeful and the changeless.

Here the Gita seems to indicate that there are two co-equal Forces, Spirit and Matter, the Immutable and the Mutable. For the Immutable or the changeless, the Gita gives the description of *Kutastha* meaning like one seated on a rock. If Spirit and Matter are co-equal then we are introduced to the cardinal doctrine of Sankhya. But does this duality explain the world phenomenon? The Bhagavad Gita is truly a book of Vedanta which stands for Non-dualism. This is evident from the following verse of the Fifteenth Discourse :

> The Highest Purusa verily is Another....
> Since I transcend the destructible, and am

> higher than the indestructible, therefore in
> the world and in Veda, I am proclaimed
> Purushottama or the Supreme Spirit.

Surely the mind of man cannot understand the nature of *Purushottama* for it functions only on the plane of duality. *Kshara* and *Akshara*, the Mutable and the Immutable, are the two opposites. What else can there be than either the changeless or the changeful? Apart from these two the mind cannot conceive of any third factor. But Gita posits the third factor of the *Purushottama*. What is the nature of the Supreme Spirit of the Gita? From the above verse it is clear that the *Purushottama* contains within Itself the mutable as well as the immutable. The changeful and the changeless exist simultaneously in the Supreme Spirit. Now for the mind, the co-existence of two opposites means only a Void. But strangely enough the Void is itself the Plenum for both the Mutable and Immutable, the *Kshara* and the *Akshara* have their abode in It. Sri Krishna says to Arjuna :

> He who undeluded knoweth Me thus as
> Purushottama, he all-knowing, worshippeth
> Me with his whole being, O Bharata.

According to the above verse true *Bhakti* or Devotion signifies workship with one's whole being. The term used by the Gita is *Sarvabhaven*. If the worship is not with one's whole being then it is fragmentary. But this worship with the whole being is possible only when the devotee knows the Lord as *Purushottama*, and not either as *Kshara* or as *Akshara*. True *Bhakti* is neither *Saguna* nor *Nirguna*, neither of the Form nor of the Formless — it is of THAT which is both Form and Formless at the same time, both *Saguna* and *Nirguna* at the same time, not one after the other. But surely the mind cannot comprehend this, for, it functions only on the plane of duality. *Bhakti* is a non-dual experience which does not demand the negation either of the Form or of the Formless. Worship offered from the plane of duality is bound to be fragmented. *Bhakti* with one's whole being — *Sarvabhaven* — is possible only when the plane of duality is transcended. The Bhagavad Gita again and again speaks of the non-dual state, whether in describing the *Sthitapragna* or the *Bhakta* or the *Yogi*. All its descriptions of the spiritual man either on the Path of Knowledge or of Devotion or of Action denote a non-dual state — the state that is *dwandwateet*. One may ask: How does one come to this non-dual state? For this one must understand how do the dual principles work in man and the universe. It is to this question that the Sixteenth Discourse turns as it discusses the problem of Good and Evil under the title *Daivasura-Sampad-vibhaga-Yoga* meaning the Yoga of division between the Divine and the Demoniacal.

There is a common belief that in the universe there are two distinct sets of powers or forces, one White and the other Dark, one Divine and the other Demoniacal, one Good and the other Evil. This is a completely mistaken notion of the *daiva-asura-sampad*, the forces of Light and Darkness. To conceive of distinct areas or planes as ruled either by gods or demons is to indulge in childish fancy. The universe in manifestation is just pure energy. This energy is neither good nor evil just as electricity is neither good nor evil. Energy is neutral, it is the medium through which it functions that imparts to it the qualities of goodness or badness. Thus the epithets of good and evil have no relevance with regard to energy that permeates the universe — they have relevance only with reference to the medium through which the energy passes or functions. Now so far as man is concerned this medium is his consciousness. We know that when a stick is put in water, it appears bent. It is a fact that the stick is not actually bent but it appears as bent because of the medium of water. Take the stick out of water, and it is completely straight. Similarly it is the medium of human consciousness that imparts to universal energy a quality that does not belong to it. In the Sixteenth Discourse the Gita describes in detail the divine and the demoniacal powers. If one examines the whole list, one finds that the description is not of something outer or objective, but something that is completely subjective, that is, something belonging to consciousness. It is interesting to note that the list of divine powers is headed by *Abhaya* or Fearlessness, and that of demoniacal powers is headed by *Dambha* or Hypocricy.

Fear arises when one tries to be other than oneself. And surely this is hypocricy. Usually one is afraid to be oneself, one puts on mask after mask to suit different occasions. We are terribly afraid of being found out, and so we cover ourselves up with all types of subterfuges. It is this which distorts one's consciousness so that it is no longer a pure medium. Similarly, Fearlessness or *Abhaya* truly means being oneself. It is fear that makes us appear what we are not. When we try to be other than what we are then this assumed "I" ness has to be vigorously guarded lest it be torn by some impact or the other. It is the desire to guard and protect which is at the root of fear. In this condition we want to make ourselves as invulnerable as possible. To be fearless is to be vulnerable, for, there is nothing to guard or to protect. In the process of trying to be other than what we are lies the whole movement of psychological becoming. There is a natural becoming which is completely different from psychological becoming. In the latter one is trying to become what one is not. In the Sixteenth Discourse, the Gita says :

> Triple is this gate of hell, destructive
> of the self — lust, hate and greed; therefore
> let man renounce these three.

The Sanskrit words for these three are *Kama*, *Krodha* and *Lobha*. *Kama* is Attachment and *Krodha* is Repulsion. These are the two opposites between which the mind continually moves. These are the dual principles which constitute the range of mind's activities. The question is: How to be free from them? For this the third term of the Gita in the above verse needs to be understood. The third term is *Lobha* or Greed. It is this greed which is the motivating factor inducing the movement of the mind between *Kama* and *Krodha*. So long as the motivating factor of Greed remains, one must continue to toss about between *Kama* and *Krodha*, between Attachment and Repulsion. It is greed which initiates psychological becoming, for, in greed there is a desire to be other than what one is. It is by greed that man strays away from *Swadharma* into *Paradharma*. And the instruments of *Lobha* are *Kama* and *Krodha*. When greed is eliminated then *Kama* and *Krodha* naturally disappear. There is Greed when one does not look at what is, but strives for what one would like to be. It is greed which brings distortion in the perceptive activities of consciousness. And thus initiates in one's psyche a conflict between good and evil. Greed regards *what is* as evil and therefore strives after *what should be* which it regards as good. And the instruments of conflict are *Kama* and *Krodha*, attachment and repulsion. But how is one to be free from Greed which brings into existence *Kama* and *Krodha*?

It is Lobha or Greed which indeed is the corrupting influence in man's psychological nature. And so obviously it is this Lobha which is the centre through which the *Asuri Sampad* or the Dark Powers function in man. It is Lobha which exposes the consciousness of man to its influence thus bringing into existence an inner conflict of good and evil. The consciousness that is freed from all centres of Lobha or Greed, whether material or so-called spiritual, alone is incorruptible. It is completely free and therefore above all influences, whether of the so-called good or of the so-called bad. It is to this that the Gita refers when it speaks of *Shubhashubh-parityagi*, meaning renouncing both good as well as evil. To be free from Lobha is to be free from all processes of psychological becoming. Needless to say, psychological becoming represents mind's desire to become something for the fulfilment of its unfulfilled desires. Becoming by itself does not imply any frustration, but when psychological becoming is super-imposed on the process of natural becoming then does inner conflict start. Man can expedite the movement of natural becoming, but he cannot superimpose upon it another movement which is the movement of psychological becoming. To do this is to be caught in the incessant inner struggle, the struggle which is called the conflict between the forces of Light and Darkness, between the Divine and Demoniacal. How is one to demolish the centre of Lobha or Greed if this centre is the begetter of one's psychological conflict?

It is obvious that psychological becoming comes into existence because there is no comprehension of one's own Being. The Becoming that emanetes from one's own Being is completely natural, but the Becoming that does not arise in the Ground of Being is devoid of natural-ness and therefore is utterly false and frustrating. The question must arise: How is one to know one's own Being so that all frustrating struggle of psychological becoming may cease? The breaking up of the centre of Lobha and the cessation of psychological becoming are not two different things. How to discover one's own Being — that is the fundamental question of spiritual life, and it is to this question that the Gita turns in the last two discourses.

The Seventeenth Discourse speaks of *Shraddha-vibhaga-traya-yoga*, meaning Yoga dealing with the problem of Faith. The implication of this Yoga is that one can discover one's own Being only in the moment of Faith. In the third verse of this discourse, the Gita says :

> ....The man consists of his faith, that
> which his faith is, he is even that.

The above verse seems to indicate that Faith is the man. After all man expresses himself in his behaviour. But the question is: From where does this behaviour emanate? What is the source of one's behaviour? If behaviour is Becoming then surely its source must be the Being. But if behaviour does not emanate from the Being then it is undoubtedly *mithyachar* or hypocricy. We saw earlier that in giving a list of *Asuri sampad* or the Dark Powers, the Gita puts in the very beginning *Dambha* or Hypocricy. And so behaviour which does not spring from one's being is nothing else than *Dambha* or hypocricy. Such behaviour is completely devoid of Faith, for, it has neither honesty nor sincerity. To act without Faith is to indulge in *mithyachar*. Thus the problem of one's Being is closely associated with the problem of Faith. And so the Gita discusses the all-important question of Faith in the Seventeenth Discourse. If one can discover one's own faith, or one's own source of behaviour, then one would know one's own Being. The path leading towards the discovery of one's own Being lies in inquiring into the source of one's own behaviour. What is it that induces one to act? — it is this question which is most fundamental to the discovery of one's own Being.

The Gita discusses this question by giving three categories which constitute the source of one's behaviour. They are *Tamasik*, *Rajasik* and *Sattwik*, meaning they arise either from the Ground of Passivity or Passion or Poise. Here Faith is used as implying the Ground or the Source of behaviour. It is because of this that the Gita, in this discourse, speaks of the three-fold *Shraddha* or Faith. They are the motivating factors of one's life. That which motivates is the faith, for, it is from there that one acts. The motivating factors may be due to Passivity or due to Passion or due to Harmony or Poise. The motivating factor is man's inner compulsion, for, without it he does not feel inclined to act. The word Faith or *Shraddha* is used in this discourse as the motivating factor inducing or compelling one to act. The activities or behaviour patterns of man described in this discourse are more illustrative than exhaustive. Even then the Gita gives a very wide range of behaviour patterns covering man's food-habits, his performance of religious worship, his austerities as also his giving of alms. In all this it is the underlying motive which constitutes the measuring rod with which to categorise the different patterns of action so as to know them as either *tamasik* or *rajasik* or *sattwik*. Faith being the motivating factor supplies the content to different patterns of action. And so while the patterns may differ, the indwelling content remains the same.

One may ask: What can be the nature of the *Tamasik* faith? Needless to say, the motivating factor is the driving power behind all actions. The driving power at the *Tamasik* level is indeed a habitual, or more still a superstitious faith. It is superstition that drives all actions of *tamasik* nature. It is obvious that superstition indicates a habitual frame of mind. And so the content of all *tamasik* actions is habit, whether physical or mental. The nature of the *Rajasik* faith is mental belief. It is with belief that the struggle begins to translate it into action, and *rajas* indicates a state of unending struggle. The struggle between Precept and Practice is indeed relentless, and behind this struggle the motivating factor is the belief which the mind of man has evolved for its psychological becoming. If mental belief is the faith of the *rajasik* nature, it is intellectual conviction which is the faith functioning at the *sattwik* level. There is a gulf of difference between Belief and Conviction. It is obvious that a conviction is a conclusion to which the mind has arrived, and so it has a greater force of faith than is seen in belief. It is this which beings the psychological struggle to a temporary end. Here one comes to a synthesis of psychological opposites. That is why *Sattwa* is described as Harmony or Poise. But a synthesis is not integration, and therefore it becomes a new thesis giving birth to its anti-thesis. And so we have three categories of faith — the faith sustained by Habit, the faith sustained by Belief, and the faith sustained by Conviction – they are respectively the *tamasik*, the *rajasik* and the *sattwik* categories of faith. These three categories of faith are the motivating factors governing patterns of action. The Gita says, whatever be the nature of action, whether *tamasik*, *rajasik* or *sattwik*, it should be impregnated by appropriate faith; otherwise the action performed is *Asat* or insincere. There must be sincerity at all levels. The sincerity at the *tamasik* level is faith in superstition, that at the *rajasik* level is faith in belief, and that at the *sattwik* level is faith in one's conviction.

But Faith in the true sense of the term is motiveless. One may say there is a lower faith and a higher faith. The former is with motive while the latter is bereft of all motives. Motives are the incentives to action, but a man of true faith needs no incentives. An action born of incentive or stimulation is a mere reaction. Faith is indeed the man, but the lower faith is indicative of one's acquired nature. It represents *Asmita* which is an I-sense born of false identification. But one cannot come to the understanding of one's true Being unless one knows the state of *asmita* and how it comes into existence. Obviously *Asmita* is born of Habit, Belief and Conviction. It is evident that Conviction is the final stage of *asmita* or the I-ness.

But conviction is not faith, or, if it is, it is lower faith. The true man of faith arrives at no conclusion, for, he is ever journeying into the realm of the Unknown. It is hardly necessary to point out that conviction arises out of the known. But true faith is born only when the known is completely negated, and therefore when one stands on the threshold of the Unknown. The Unknown contains the secret of one's true Being. But one can come to the understanding of the Being only when the whole nature born of *asmita* is broken up. For this, it is necessary to be aware of the three motivating factors of Habit, Belief and Conviction, because it is these factors that bring *asmita* into existence. In the very awareness of the fales, the real comes to view. When the false, being built through habit, belief and conviction, is seen then does one experience a breakthrough to the understanding of the true Being -- the Being which alone can become the natural ground for the Becoming of man. It is about the realization of the true Being of man that the last discourse of the Bhagavad Gita speaks under the title of *Sanyasa Yoga*

It seems a little strange that the Gita which has all along talked of Action should end with the note of *Sanyasa*. But this strangeness is only on the surface — there is no contradiction between the two. In fact, the last discourse comes as a coping stone for the whole edifice of Action which the Gita has built up in the course of its Seventeen Discourses. One of the meanings of *Sanyasa* is trust. It indicates that a true *sanyasi* is a trustee, not an owner. He acts in life as a trustee, holding everything as a trust, whether energy or time, whether talents or acquisitions. And the entire teaching of Sri Krishna enjoins Arjuna to become a *nimitta*, a mere instrument or a trustee. True action arises only when one ceases to be the actor and holds everything that has been given to one in trust, not regarding them as his own. That is the very core of *aparigraha*, meaning non-possessiveness. The Bhagavad Gita, in this discourse, speaks of the three constituents of Action. They are *Karanam*, *Karma* and *Karta* meaning the Instruments of Action, the Patterns of Action and the Actor. To keep the patterns and instruments of action in proper condition but not to use them as an actor is indeed the keynote of *Sanyasa*. To have the patterns and instruments of action in a state of disarray is to be steeped in *tamas* or indolence. To use them for one's own psychological becoming is to be caught in the entanglements of *rajas*. To use them for the purposes of so-called well-being of others is to work under the conditioning factors of *sattwa*. But to offer these patterns and instruments of action to the Great Unknown is to know the secret of *Sanyasa Yoga* which constitutes the theme of the Eighteenth Discourse. The sixteenth verse of this discourse says :

> ....he who, owing to untrained reason
> lookesth on himself as the actor, he of
> perverted intelligence, verily seeth not.

The phrase used in the above verse is *Akritbuddhitwat*, meaning with immature mind. He who regards himself as the actor is of immature mind. In an occult manual entitled *Light on the Path*, the spiritual aspirant is told: "Though thou fighest, be not thou the warrior". We find Arjuna in a state of confusion in the first discourse because he thought and believed he was going to be the warrior. The whole of the message of the Gita centres round one great idea, namely, to impress upon Arjuna that he was not going to be the actor in the Mahabharata War, he was asked only to supply the patterns and instruments of action. That is why Sri Krishna makes it clear to Arjuna that he need not think that because he refuses to fight, the Mahabharata War will not be fought. It is when the actor acts that action become utterly vitiated. It is the actor wanting to act which creates the conflict of two wills. The Bhagavad Gita ends with Arjuna's declaration: "Let Thy will be done". Why did Arjuna say this? Did he do so under compulsion? Obviously not, because Sri Krishna says to Arjuna in the Eighteenth Discourse that having heard what He had told him, Arjuna was free to act as he liked. However the Lord inquires of his disciple :

> Has this been heard by thee, O son of Pritha,
> with one pointed attention?

This inquiry indicates that if Arjuna had heard what the Lord had said with one pointed attention, then he was free to act. In listening with one pointed attention, the duality of the listener and that to which one listens vanishes. It is a state of pure listening, not broken up by that which is heard and by he who hears. The mind attains to freedom and maturity only in the state of Total Attention. And that is why Sri Krishna says to Arjuna that if he has listened with total attention then he is free to act. In Total Attention there is a clear perception of things; one sees that which is without any interference by the mind. And therefore what one sees is not what the mind has projected, but what actually exists. And surely to see what is without mind's projection is to discover the right starting point for action. In the Totality of Attention, there is a perception of the opposites at the same time, not one after the other. The mind sees the opposites one after the other, but to see them simultaneously is to come to pure intelligence. The Gita says :

> That which knoweth activity and abstinence,
> what ought to be done and what ought not to be
> done, fear and fearlessness, bondage and liberation,
> that reason is pure, O Partha.

When the two opposites are seen at the same time then the mind comes to a state of total negation or Void. The two opposites existing together would naturally cancel each other and therefore a void must come into being. But the Void of the Mind is the Plenum of the Spirit. It is in the Void of the Mind that the true Being of man is seen. It is from this Being that the natural Becoming emanates. Of this the Gita speaks when it says :

> Spontaneous action, O son of Kunti, though
> defective must not be abandoned. All under-
> takings indeed are clouded by defects as fire
> by smoke.

The Gita says that all undertakings, are clouded by defects. All beginnings are actions performed with effort; but the true action is effortless and therefore is never begun. It begins, it is never begun. To undertake something is to have an actor behind it; and where the actor is, action is never effortless. In all undertakings there is a motive. But the action that spontaneously and effortlessly emanates from the State of Being, which is the Void of the Mind, has no motive behind it. When this happens then the Becoming is just the natural expression of the Being.

What is the nature of the Being discovered in the Void of the Mind? Is it Individual or is it Universal? Who can say? Ask the dew-drop that slips into the sea? Has it disappeared in the universality of the vast sea? Or has the vast sea entered the dew-drop? The sea invites the dew-drop to merge its identity in its vastness. If the dew-drop clings to its identity then it remains just a tiny, utterly insignificant, dew-drop. But if it merges in the sea then the individual himself becomes the universal. In the following verse of the Gita we see the vast ocean inviting the dew-drop to merge its identity. Sri Krishna says :

> Abandoning all occupations, come into
> me alone for shelter; sorrow not, for I
> shall liberate thee from all bondage.

But the call of the Universal is heard only by the Being that has discovered its true Individuality in the Void of the Mind. It is never heard by the *asmita*, the I-consciousness, which exists in the fullness of the mind. The Being discovered in the Void of the Mind is one with the Universal. Then the Universal and the Individual are like the Lover and the Beloved. The Lover finds his fulfilment in the Beloved, and the Beloved finds her shelter in the Lover. How can there be the conflict of two wills? When the Beloved says to the Lover, "I shall do thy bidding", is there in it any compulsion imposed by an authority? If there is a compulsion, it is the compulsion of Love. When Arjuna discovers the Universal in the very heart of the Individual then does he declare "I will do Thy bidding"

Sanjaya who was giving an objective narration of the happenings on the battlefield to the blind king Dhritarashtra, says, at the end of the dialogue between Krishna and Arjuna, that he was firmly of opinion that wherever Krishna and Arjuna are together there can never be a defeat in the battle of life. When Arjuna is the instrument and Krishna the actor then is life's battle won; when the Universal acts through the instrument which the Individual is then is victory is assured even though the battle of life may be most fierce.

Thus in the Eighteen Discourses of the Bhagavad Gita we see one Yoga, the Integral Yoga, placed before us in all its various aspects. From *Vishada* Yoga to *Sanyasa* Yoga is Arjuna's journey undertaken by him in company with Sri Krishna. There is *Vishada* or despondency because man believes he is the actor, but when he realizes that there is the Master-Actor whose instrument he can become then all despondency vanishes. But for this the disciple must come to the state of *Sanyasa* which represents the Void of the Mind. Sri Krishna tells Arjuna to go to him with an unoccupied mind. This indicates the utter negativity of consciousness. In this negative consciousness takes place the birth of the Super-Mind, it is like the birth of Jesus through Virgin Mary. It is in the virgin consciousness of *Sanyasa* that.the vision of the Transecental is vouchsafed to man. And when such Vision comes, gone are sorrow and suffering, gone indeed are despondency and faint-heartedness. It is only the innocent, the virgin consciousness that can meet the challenge of life completely and adequately. When the response to the challenge of life is adequate then no problem is able to take root in one's mind. In the very appearance of the problem, the problem is dissolved, for, when the response to the challenge is adequate then there remains no residue, Thus is life freed from all the burden of the past. It is thus that man lives truly from moment to moment where each moment contains the richness of Eternity.

INDEX